Information Science and Technology

Information Science and Technology

Edited by Reuben Hammond

CLANRYE
INTERNATIONAL
www.clanryeinternational.com

Clanrye International,
750 Third Avenue, 9th Floor,
New York, NY 10017, USA

ISBN: 978-1-63240-605-7

Cataloging-in-Publication Data

Information science and technology / edited by Rueben Hammond.
    p. cm.
Includes bibliographical references and index.
ISBN 978-1-63240-605-7
1. Information science. 2. Information technology. 3. Information services.
4. Information resources. I. Hammond, Rueben.
Z665 .I64 2017
020--dc23

For information on all Clanrye International publications
visit our website at www.clanryeinternational.com

Printed in the United States of America.

Contents

Preface VII

Chapter 1   **h-index, h-type Indices, and the Role of Corrected Quality Ratio**................ 1
Muzammil Tahira, Arayti Bakri, Rose Alinda Alias, Ani Shabri

Chapter 2   **Preference and use of Electronic Information and Resources by Blind/Visually Impaired in NCR Libraries in India**..12
Shailendra Kumar, Gareema Sanaman

Chapter 3   **An Investigation of the Awareness and use of Open Access Initiative at the Federal Polytechnic, Offa, Kwara State, Nigeria**................................. 27
A.O. Issa, K.N. Igwe, B.R. Akangbe, M.B. Aliyu

Chapter 4   **Patterns of Citing Korean DOI Journals According to CrossRef's Cited-by Linking and a Local Journal Citation Database**............................38
Tae-Sul Seo, Eun-Gyeong Jung, Hwanmin Kim

Chapter 5   **Henry Fayol's 14 Principles of Management: Implications for Libraries and Information Centres**... 49
C. P. Uzuegbu, C. O. Nnadozie

Chapter 6   **Credibility Assessment of Online Information in Context**......................... 64
Soo Young Rieh

Chapter 7   **Age and Gender in Reddit Commenting and Success**.....................................76
S. Craig Finlay

Chapter 8   **Internal Structure of Information Packages in Digital Preservation**......................... 87
Seungmin Lee

Chapter 9   **Developing a Theory in Academic Research: A Review of Experts' Advice**... 101
Jacob Dankasa

Chapter 10   **Challenges and Opportunities of Knowledge Management in University Library**...112

Sk. Mamun Mostofa, Muhammad Mezbah-ul-Islam

Chapter 11   **Digital Libraries: Analysis of Delos Reference Model and 5S Theory**....................125
Abdulmumin Isah, Athulang Mutshewa, Batlang Comma Serema, Lekoko Kenosi

Chapter 12   **Normalization and Valuation of Research Evaluation Indicators in Different Scientific Fields**..135
Abdolreza Noroozi Chakoli, Roghayeh Ghazavi

Chapter 13   **Non-Governmental Organization (NGO) Libraries for The Visually Impaired in Nigeria: Alternative Format use and Perception of Information Services**..144
Niran Adetoro

Chapter 14   **Study of US/EU National Innovation Policies Based on Nanotechnology Development, and Implications for Korea**..154
Jung Sun Lim, Kwang Min Shin, Jin Seon Yoon, Seoung Hun Bae

Chapter 15   **Facebook: Hate it or Love it, But Can You Ignore it?**.......................................170
Shivani Arora, Daniel Okunbor

Chapter 16   **Principles for Helpful Sequence and Deduction of Knowledge Organization Systems**..179
A.Y. Asundi

Chapter 17   **Deriving the Properties of Object Types for Research Data Relation Model**..189
Suntae Kim

Chapter 18   **A Critical Study on Attitudes and Awareness of Institutional Repositories and Open Access Publishing**...198
S. Dhanavandan, M.Tamizhchelvan

Permissions

List of Contributors

Index

Preface

This book has been an outcome of determined endeavour from a group of educationists in the field. The primary objective was to involve a broad spectrum of professionals from diverse cultural background involved in the field for developing new researches. The book not only targets students but also scholars pursuing higher research for further enhancement of the theoretical and practical applications of the subject.

This book on information science discusses technology that is used to store, process and transmit information. This book explores all the important aspects of this field in the present day scenario. Information science is multi-disciplinary and has various allied fields and branches. Topics included in this book seek to add to the ongoing research in information science and technology. It includes some of the vital pieces of work being conducted across the world, on various topics related to information science and technology. It strives to provide a fair idea about this discipline and to help develop a better understanding of the latest advances within this field. Students, researchers, experts and all associated with information science and technology will benefit alike from this book.

It was an honour to edit such a profound book and also a challenging task to compile and examine all the relevant data for accuracy and originality. I wish to acknowledge the efforts of the contributors for submitting such brilliant and diverse chapters in the field and for endlessly working for the completion of the book. Last, but not the least; I thank my family for being a constant source of support in all my research endeavours.

Editor

h-index, h-type Indices, and the Role of Corrected Quality Ratio

Muzammil Tahira *

Department of Information Systems
Faculty of Computing
Universiti Teknologi Malaysia (UTM), Malaysia
E-mail: mufals@yahoo.com

Rose Alinda Alias

Department of Information Systems
Faculty of Computing
Universiti Teknologi Malaysia (UTM), Malaysia
E-mail: alinda@utm.my

Arayti Bakri

Department of Information Systems
Faculty of Computing
Universiti Teknologi Malaysia (UTM), Malaysia
E-mail: aryatib@utm.my

Ani Shabri

Department of Mathematical Sciences
Faculty of Science
Universiti Teknologi Malaysia (UTM), Malaysia
E-mail: ani@utm.my

ABSTRACT

This study examines the foremost concerns related to most noted research performance index. The most popular and widely acceptable h-index underestimates the highly visible scientist, the middle order group, due to citation distribution issues. The study addresses this issue and uses 'Corrected Quality Ratio' (CQ) to check the implicit underpinnings as evident in h-index. CQ helps to incorporate the aspects of a good research performance indicator. This simple revision performs more intimately and logically to gauge the broader research impact for all groups and highly visible scientists with less statistical error.

Keywords: Scientometric, Research Performance Evaluation, Corrected Quality Ratio, h-index, H', h-cpp, g-index, R-index, A-index, m-index, q^2-index

*Corresponding Author: Muzammil Tahira
Department of Information Systems
Faculty of Computing
Universiti Teknologi Malaysia (UTM), Malaysia
E-mail: mufals@yahoo.com

1. INTRODUCTION

Metrics/indices play a crucial role for peer-based, metrics-based, or hybrid research evaluation approaches. Selection and usage of indices to appraise quantity and impact of the productive core is a sensitive subject for Research Performance Evaluation (RPE). In evaluative scientometric studies, these parameters are measured by Activity Indicator (AI), Observed Impact Indicator (OII), journal related indices, and/or other newly introduced global indices (h and h-type indices). These indicators stand for the quantity, impact, influence, or quality of the scholarly communication. AI measures the quantity of the productivity core (publication) while OII stands for impact of productivity core (citation and its subsequent metrics).

Disciplinary perspectives, the use of indicators in different contexts, the arbitrary nature of indicators, and electronic publishing scenarios have turned the attention of scientometricians, policymakers, and researchers of other fields to modifying the existing indices and to discovering new metrics to gauge quantity and quality. Citation, its subsequent metrics, and the root indicator publications have a sound place in the decision-making process.

In 2005, Hirsch proposed h-index, which was immediately noticed by the scientometricians and warmly welcomed by all stakeholders. It is defined as: "A scientist has index h if h of his/her Np papers has at least h citations each and the other (Np − h) papers have no more than h citations each" (Hirsch, 2005, p. 16569). The said index aims to measure the impact of scholarly communication in terms of quality (citation) and productivity (publication) in an objective manner. It represents the most productive core of an author's output in terms of the most cited papers (Burrell, 2007). A continuous debate among scientometricians, policymakers, as well as researchers of other fields has made h-index one of the hottest topics in the history of scientometric research.

2. BACKGROUND OF THE STUDY

Rousseau (2006) introduced the term Hirsch core (h-core), which is a group of high-performance publications with respect to the scientist's career (Jin, et al., 2007). A good indicator should be intuitive and sensi-

tive to the number of uncited papers (Tol, 2009). Such an index should exceed from h-core papers (Vinkler, 2007) and "must assign a positive score to each new citation as it occurs" (Anderson, et al., 2008). Notwithstanding, h-index also suffers from several implicit disadvantages such as sensitivity to highly cited paper (Egghe, 2006a; Egghe, 2006b; Norris & Oppenheim, 2010), giving more weight to one or few highly cited publications (Glänzel, 2006; Egghe, 2006a; Costas & Bordons, 2007), lacking in sensitivity to performance change (Bihui, et al., 2007), disadvantaging earlier career work (Glanzel, 2006; Burrell, 2007), and being time dependent (Burrell, 2007). While highly cited papers may represent breakthrough results in computing h-index (Vinkler, 2007), this index is also criticized for its lack in accuracy and precision (Lehmann, et al., 2005).

Soon after h-index, several modification and improvements have been proposed. Due to its persuasive nature, the field dependence, self-citation, multi-authorship, and career length were also taken into account (Bornmann, et al., 2011; Norris & Oppenheim, 2009). It is important to note that most of the new indices focused on h-core only, while citation distribution in the head and tail cores remain ignored due to their formulaic limitations (Pathap, 2010; Bornmann, et al., 2011; Zahang, 2009; 2013). Fig. 1 shows the head, tail, and h-core. The publications and citations, which define h-index, are called h-core; whereas publications with citations more/less than h-core are defined as head and core, respectively.

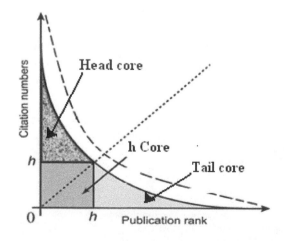

Fig. 1 h, head, and tail core (a modification of Harish's h-index figure)

The literature reveals that the h-index not only incorporates quantity and quality, but it is also simple, efficient, and has ease in use. It laurels over the other research evaluation metrics due to a blend of objectivity and subjectivity, and its scientific and persuasive nature. This index is insensitive to highly as well as zero cited articles and is robust (van Raan 2006; Cronin & Meho 2006; Imperial & Navarro 2007; Oppenheim 2007; Luz et.al., 2008; Bornmann, et al., 2008; Bouabid & Martin 2008; Lazaridis 2009, Norris and Oppenheim, 2010, Tahira, et al., 2013). These underpinnings have led to the introduction of numerous h-type indices, mostly focused on citation distribution issues. We refer to review studies by Norris and Oppenheim (2010) and Bornmann, et al., (2011). Though h-index has made its place for Research Performance Evaluation (RPE), yet there is a need to address its inherent reservations more intimately and logically.

3. METHODOLOGY

The actor CPP was considered as a multiplicative connection to the Corrected Quality Ratio (CQ) to incorporate the overall quality of production (Lindsey, 1978). The h_{G-H} model used it to link to publications (Schubert & Glänzel, 2007) and in p-index with citation as quantity indicator (Parthap, 2010). We are considering CPP actor to deal with the core issue of the citation distribution as evident in classic h-index. The aim is to address the implicit dimensions of original h-index.

Our proposed index uses 'Citation Per Publication' (CPP) as a balancing correction to improve the original h-index underpinnings related to citation distribution issues in the head and tail cores. It is expressed as a multiplicative connection between h and CPP with the geometric mean of these functions ($\sqrt[3]{h \times h \times CPP}$) (Fig. 1). We employed a geometric mean to compute different functions, which are multiplied together to produce a single "figure of merit" (Spizman & Weinstein, 2008).

Keeping in view the foundation issues of original h-index (see Table 1), we have designed three categories from the proposed h-type indices: modified h-indices, h-type indices dependent on h-core, and h-type indices independent of h-core. These categories are concerned with h-core, head, and tail citation distri-

butions. For the present study, we have considered at least one index from these categories. To avoid redundancy, a few indices which fall in these categories, like hw (Egghe & Rousseau, 2008) and v-index (Riikonen & Vihinen, 2008), are not considered. These selected indices along with the proposed h-cpp index are examined and evaluated to check their performance for evaluation purposes.

Two experiments are conducted at the author level. Jacso wrote a series of articles on pros and cons of popular online referenced enhanced databases e.g. Google scholar, Scopus, and Web of Science (WoS^{TM}) (Jacso, 2005a; 2005b; 2008a; 2008b; 2008c). He found WoS^{TM} appropriate for calculating h-index scores (Jacso, 2008c).

The study first refers to the case of the first 100 most productive Malaysian related engineers' data from WoS^{TM} over a ten year period (2001-2010). Our research term was 'Malaysia' and we limited to only those engineering categories from WoS^{TM} that have the word 'engineering' in common. The term 'Malaysian related engineers' is used for researchers who are affiliated to with11 selected Malaysian universities (> 50 publications) under nine WoS^{TM} engineering categories for document type articles and reviews only. The second data set used as the benchmark is the 100 most prolific economists dataset from Tol's study (Tol, 2009), with his permission.

4. EMINENCE OF SCIENTISTS

The eminence of scientists is manifested by their activity and impact indicators. Overall, much fluctuation is observed among scientists' positions when applying the original h, **H'**, and h-cpp indices. The CPP as a quality measure is criticized owing to its penalizing of high productivity (Hirsch, 2005; Tahira, et al., 2013). This fact is evident in Table 2. We discuss the positioning order of these authors by employing the four Cole and Cole (1973) criteria based on publication and citation behavior of author publishing.

A noteworthy fluctuation is observed in the positioning order of Malaysian related engineers by employing these indices (Beside these indices, there are various other potential indices. Such discrepancies in results lead to introducing new indices. All of these indices

Table 1. Salient Features of h-type Indices of Three Designed Categories

Focused Indices	Category	Definition	Advantages	Disadvantages
g-index	Modified	"The g-index is the highest number g of articles that together received g2 or more citations" (Egghe, 2006a, p. 8)	More weight to highly cited publication (HCP)	It is an integer, with long core, lack of thresholds, and lack of precision, ignoring citation distribution (Tol, 2009), and in particular cases fabricating articles with zero citations (Zhang, 2009)
q^2–Index	Modified	A composite index computed by the product of the h-index and median of the h-core citations (Cabrerizo et al., 2010)	This is a composite indicator, provide a balanced view of scientific production and solves the central tendency issues	Covers only the core of citation above the h-index
m-index	h-core dependent	"m-index is the median number of citations received by papers in the Hirsch core" (Bornmann et al, 2008)	Resolves the issue of central tendency	Based on h-core, ignores the citations above and below the core
A-index	h-core dependent	A-index is the average number of citations received by the articles in the h-core (Jin, 2006)	A simple variant	h-core dependent, "the better scientist is 'punished' for having a higher h-index as the A-index involves a division by h" (Jin et al., 2007 p. 857)
R-index	h-core dependent	R-index (Jin et al., 2007) is the square root of the total number of citations received by the articles in the h-core	Real number and is a modification of A-index	Insensitive to HCP, h-core dependent
e-index	h-core dependent	e-index (Zhang, 2009) is defined as to complement the h-index. It deals with the ignored excess citations, the excess citations received by all papers in the h-core (p. 1)	Complement to h-index, covers the excess citations, ignores by h-index, helpful for similar-h-index issue	More weight to HCP ignores the tail end
hg- index	h-core independent	hg, a composite index (Alonso et al., 2010), is the square root of the product of h and g indices	Incorporates the strengths of both indices	An integer, ignores the zero and less below the g-core citations as well as incorporating the weaknesses of both
H'-index	Deals with h-core, head and tail cores	It deals with the citation distribution function with head and tail ratio. It also incorporates the above mentioned e-index and formalizes as $h' = e.h/t$ (Zhang, 2013, p.2)	A real number which deals with the citation distribution issues and incorporates excess and tail h- citations	Not simple to calculate, insensitive to zero citation. Formulaic issue, if the denominator is zero (tail core is zero) the value goes infinite

either give some insight or add value in one or another way. Here, the question immediately arises, which index is the best to accomplish different dimensions of performance evaluation, with less reservation, or is there any possible improvement to handle the quantity and quality aspects of research evaluation?

Publication is a base and other measures such as activity, observed, expected, and relative impact indicators are developed from it. Publication is an indicator rather easy to handle and can be manipulated purposely. Eventually, these strategies have effect on impact in-

dices. Let us elaborate the case with four group analysis at author level.

To explore the effect of these strategies on publications and impact behavior, we applied Cole and Cole (1967; 1973) dichotomous cross classification criteria on our 100 most productive Malaysian related engineers' data. We used Coastas and Bordons' (2008) denomination of the groups as mentioned in Table 2. We categorized four groups employing the threshold strategy for P and CPP of their fifty percentiles. The median of the 'total number of documents' and 'citations per document rate' of this case was (P50=17) and (P50=4.6), respectively. Researchers are classified into four groups and are named as 'top producer,' 'big producer,' 'selective,' and 'silent' groups (as illustrated in Table 2).

5. DESCRIPTIVE ANALYSIS AND BOX PLOTS ILLUSTRATIONS OF FOUR GROUPS

Selective researchers' average Citation per Publication (CPP) as calculated from their group data is almost the same as for top producers (8.712 and 8.012) (See Table 3). On the other hand, big and low producer groups have the same average value of CPP (3.285 and 3.287). The four groups of Malaysian related engineers are compared for their performances via box plot illustrations (Fig. 2a-c). In accordance to h and g indices, the plots of the revised index demonstrate a better median for extreme upper and lower values.

6. SIGNIFICANCE IN THE DIFFERENCE BETWEEN TYPES OF SCIENTISTS

Raan empirically concluded that the h-index is not so good for discriminating among excellent and good peer rated chemistry groups. Costas and Bordons (2007) observed that highly visible scientists might be underestimated. The performance evaluation of traditional metrics (total publication and total citation) and h-index is observed to be similar in the case study at institutional level for two groups (RU and non-RU Malaysian universities) in engineering departmental data. We found that only CPP has an exception for RU and non-RU universities (Tahira, et al., 2013). On the other hand, at researcher level, Coastas and Bordons (2008) compared the h and g-indices for four group analysis. They argued that the g-index is slightly better in distinguishing author due to a longer core. Schreiber (2010) also made such observation.

In order to determine if the proposed revision creates any difference between types of scientists, we employed Mann-Whitney U on six variables as shown in Table 4. We hypothesized that these indices are good for discriminating at group level. The test statistics is examined by the Asymptotic Sig. (2-tailed) and Exact Sig. (2-tailed) and with their point of probability.

With reference to h and g indices, we can see no significant difference between big producers and selective researchers, whereas the h-cpp does discriminate among all groups including big producers and selective researchers. In Coastas and Bordons' (2008) case, similar findings were observed for these two groups of Natural Resource Scientists in relation to h and g indices. They argued that the g-index is slightly better because it is sensitive to selective scientists, and this group shows in average a higher g-index/h-index ratio and better positioning in g-index ranking.

Table 2. Typology of Malaysian Related Engineers

		Type I "Top researchers" P>17 CPP>4.6 Total No. of authors=19	Type II "Big producers" P>17 CPP<=4.6 Total No. of authors=24
No. of articles (P) P50=17	*High*		
	Low	Type III "Selective researchers" P<=17 CPP>4.6 Total No. of authors=30	Type IV "Low researchers" P<=17 CPP<=4.6 Total No. of authors=27
		High Citation Per Publication (CPP) P50=4.6	*Low*

Table 3. Descriptive Analysis

Groups	Indicators	Mean and SD	Median	Std. Dev.	Range (min-max)
Group1 (N=19)	TP	41.21	30	24.357	19-1138
	TC	380.47	237	312.152	90-1138
	CPP	8.712	8.3	2.967	4.711-16.492
Group 2 (N=24)	Tp	29.17	27	10.937	18-66
	TC	97.67	94.50	53.117	16-283
	CPP	3.2846	3.395	1.006	0.842-4.5
Group 3 (N=30)	TP	13.73	13.5	1.799	11-21.357
	TC	110.8	89	57.339	57-299
	CPP	8.043	6.630	4.012	4.615-21.357
Group 4 (N=27)	TP	14.22	14	2.063	11-17
	TC	46.3	45	14.18	23-72
	CPP	3.267	3.4	0.9026	1.588-4.6

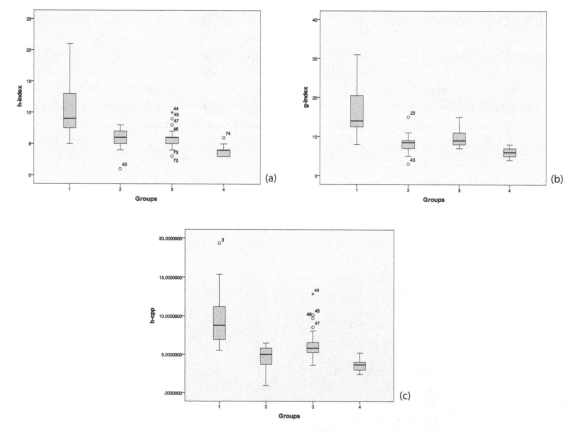

Fig. 2 (a-c). Box plot illustrations of h-index, g-index, and h-cpp

Table 4. Statistical Significance in Differences Between Types of Scientists (Mann-Whitney U)

Indices	Type of Researchers	Top Researchers		Big Producers		Selective Researchers	
		Asy. Sig.	Exact. Sig.	Asy. Sig.	Exact. Sig.	Asy. Sig.	Exact. Sig.
P	Big producers	NS	NS,	-	-	-	-
	Selective	0.000	P=.002	0.000	0.00	-	-
	researchers	0.000	0.000	0.000	0.000	NS	NS,
	Low researchers		0.000				P=.002
C	Big producers	0.000	0.000	-	-	-	-
	Selective	0.000	0.000	NS	NS.	-	-
	researchers	0.000	0.000	0.000	P=.003	0.000	0.000
	Low researchers		0.000		0.000		
CPP	Big producers	0.000	0.000	-	-	-	-
	Selective	NS	NS,	0.000	0.000	-	-
	researchers	0.000	P=.002	NS	NS, .004	0.00	0.000
	Low researchers		0.000				
h-index	Big producers	0.000	0.000	-	-	-	-
	Selective	0.000	0.000	NS	NS,	-	-
	researchers	0.000	0.000	0.000	P=.005	0.000	0.000
	Low researchers				0.000		
g-Index	Big producers	0.000	0.000	-	-	-	-
	Selective	0.000	0.000	NS	NS,	-	-
	researchers	0.000	0.000	0.000	P=.001	0.000	0.000
	Low researchers				0.000		
h-cpp	Big producers	0.000	0.000	-	-	-	-
	Selective	0.000	0.000	0.000	0.000	-	-
	researchers	0.000	0.000	0.000	0.000	0.000	0.000
	Low researchers						

Statistical significance when $p < 0.05$

7. VALIDATION OF REVISED INDEX

High correlation is observed in several studies among h-type indices. On the basis of correlation, it is not justified to differentiate and make a difference among the performance of different indices. For the evaluation of models in Table 1, we apply correlation analysis and three stage statistical techniques: Multiple regressions (R) with their Mean Square Error (MSE) and Mean Absolute Error (MAE). MSE and MAE can help out to differentiate the performance of these models better (Willmott & Matsuura, 2005).

At first, we evaluate the case of the 100 Malaysian related engineers and after that we re-examine a dataset of the 100 most prolific economists of in Tol's study for the same set of indices.

8. MALAYSIAN RELATED ENGINEERS CASE

A whole set of h-type indices are considered for the first case (Table 5); the results indicate that all indices show a high correlation with the traditional metrics, but this relation is stronger with the OII. Only H' shows no correlation with AI and A. H' and h-cpp have a high correlation with CPP (>0.8). A-index is h- core dependent, and the last two models address the head and tail citation distribution. On the other hand, g (a modified and a substitute of h-index) and R (h-core dependent) exhibit very good correlation (>0.7), while q^2 and hg as composite indices gives >0.7 and >0.2 values with CPP.

The proposed model (h-ccp) exhibits a high significant 'R' like other studied indices with the exception from g and R, while low values of MSE and MAE are observed for h-cpp compared to all competitors' indices (Table 6).

9. PROLIFIC ECONOMICS RESEARCHERS

In the second case (based on Tol's study), we could evaluate h, g, h-cpp, and hg models due to the non-availability of authors' all citation data. High order correlation of these indices with OII (C and CPP) is presented in Table 7. It is observed that among all indices, h-cpp shows a better correlation with CPP, whereas for C, the correlation is higher than h and less for g and hg indices.

All of the studied models (Table 8) have significantly high values of R (>0.9). Revised index depicts a slightly higher value of R than h and hg indices. However, h-cpp indicates low values of MSE and MAE for all cases. The revised index is intuitively reasonable and simple to compute. The new development provides a better model fit with less statistical errors.

Table 5. Results of Correlation Matrix

Indices	P	C	CPP	h-Index	h-cpp	g-index	A-index	R-index	m-Index	q-index	H'-index	hg-index
P	1	.820**	0.185	.797**	.629**	.757**	.445**	.708**	.493**	.728**	0.072	.785**
C	.820**	1	.600**	.926**	.893**	.943**	.720**	.929**	.710**	.915**	.422**	.816**
CPP	0.185	.600**	1	.608**	.813**	.722**	.842**	.792**	.707**	.721**	.881**	.283**

** Pearson Correlation is significant at the 0.01 level (2-tailed).
* Correlation is significant at the 0.05 level (2-tailed).

Table 6. Results of Regression Analysis

Results	h-index	h-cpp	g-index	A-index	R-index	m-Index	q-index	H'-index	hg-index
R	0.9400	0.9604	0.9729	0.8916	0.9842	0.7993	0.9505	0.8928	0.9758
MSE	0.6377	0.3580	0.8148	14.64	0.4475	11.244	4.3754	23.15	0.8525
MAE	0.8049	0.4744	0.8886	2.917	0.5267	2.591	0.9252	1.83	0.6908

Table 7. Results of Correlation Matrix

Indices	P	C	CPP	h-index	g-index	h-cpp index	hg-index
P	1	.501**	.228*	.591**	.525**	.443**	.562**
C	.501**	1	.908**	.888**	.954**	.914**	.934**
CCP	.228*	.908**	1	.802**	.895**	.912**	.862**

** Pearson Correlation is significant at the 0.01 level (2-tailed)
* Pearson Correlation is significant at the 0.05 level (2-tailed)

Table 8. Results of Regression Analysis

Results	h-index	h-cpp	g-index	hg-index
R	0.9125	0.9593	0.9644	0.9490
MSE	16.869	12.110	35.197	21.828
MAE	3.051	2.545	4.451	3.473

10. CONCLUDING REMARKS

The sole use of CPP as a quality measure is criticized owing to its penalizing of high productivity (Hirsch 2005, Tahira, et al., 2013). When this actor (CPP) is used with other metrics/indices as CQ, it characterizes the scientific output of researchers with aggregated values in a more balanced way as observed in cases of P-index (Parthap, 2009) and recent proposed development h-cpp. This incorporation holds h as representative of 'Quantity of the Productive Core' and CPP as 'Impact of the Productive Core. Previously the actor CPP was used with P and C to equate with the value of h-index' (Schubert & Glanzel, 2007; Parthap, 2010).

In order to tackle the implicit disadvantages of h-index, we have proposed a revision named *h-cpp* and empirically examined it for research performance evaluation. The incorporation of CPP as CQ with h-index makes it sensitive to hyper-cited articles, less below the index publications, zero citations, and similar h-index. CPP is a potential actor along with h-index to rectify inaccuracy and unfairness for broader impact. Reflection on h-type indices shows that another potential evaluative composite index is P-index. This composite index incorporates CPP as corrected quality ratio with an assumption that h^2 is nearly proportional to the 'C', and this index assigns more weight to total citations and aims to equate with h-index.

The beauty of the revised index is working closely with the h-index theory and inclusion of the implicit dimensions with a sort of normalization in dataset. Its value can be greater, equal, or less than the classic h-index. A single number cannot reflect all aspects (van Raan, 2005). Although this revision checks the h-index robustness as several other h-type indices: g, hg, q^2 etc., h-cpp as a composite indicator can be more informed, economical, and robust for RPE and incorporates the reservations of a good index for research. The fact that stands out as fundamental is the need to address the existing underpinnings logically to incorporate the reservations of a good index for research evaluation purpose in a single composite number. Another possibility is to bracket CPP with h-index in one set (representing both quantity and impact core) for evaluation purposes rather than use of CQ. We suggest more discussion and analysis at different aggregate levels with various composite indices to explore the dimensions of research activity.

ACKNOWLEDGEMENTS

One of the authors would like to thank Universiti Teknologi Malaysia and the Higher Education Commission of Pakistan for the award of the International Doctoral Fellowship (IDF) and Partial Support Grant.

REFERENCES

Alonso, S., Cabrerizo, F. J., Herrera-Viedma, E., & Herrera, F. (2010). hg-index: A new index to characterize the scientific output of researchers based on the h- and g- indices. *Scientometrics, 82*(2), 391-400.

Anderson, T. R., Hankin, R. K. S., & Killworth, P. D. (2008). Beyond the Durfee square: Enhancing the h-index to score total publication output. *Scientometrics, 76*, 577-588.

Bihui, J., LiMing, L., Rousseau, R., & Egghe, L. (2007). The R- and AR-indices: Complementing the h-index. *Chinese Science Bulletin, 52*(6), 855-963.

Bornmann, L., Mutz, R., Hug, S. E., & Daniel, H.D. (2011) A multilevel meta-analysis of studies reporting correlations between the h index and 37 different h index variants. *Journal of Informetrics, 5*(3), 346-359.

Bornmann, L., Wallon, G., & Ledin, A. (2008). Is the h index related to (standard) bibliometric measures and to the assessments by peers? An investigation of the h index by using molecular life sciences data. *Research Evaluation, 17*(2), 149–156.

Bouabid, H., & Martin, B. (2009). Evaluation of Moroccan research using a bibliometric-based approach: Investigation of the validity of the h-index. *Scientometrics, 78*(2), 203-217.

Burrell, Q. L. (2007). On the h-index, the size of the Hirsch core and Jin's A-index. *Journal of Informetrics, 1*, 170–177.

Cabrerizo, F.J., Alonso, S., Herrera-Viedma, E., & Herrera, F. (2009). q^2-Index: Quantitative and qualitative evaluation based on the number and impact of papers in the Hirsch Core. *Journal of Informetrics, 4*(1), 23-28.

Costas, R., & Bordons, M. (2007). The h-index: Advantages, limitations and its relation with other bibliometric indicators at the micro level. *Journal of Informetrics, 1*, 193-203.

Cronin, B., & Meho, L. (2006). Using the h-index to rank influential information scientists. *Journal of the American Society for Information Science and Technology, 57*(9), 1275-1278.

Egghe, L. (2006a). An improvement of the h-index: The g-index. *ISSI Newsletter, 2*(1), 8-9.

Egghe, L. (2006b). Theory and practice of the g-index. *Scientometrics, 69*(1), 131-152.

Egghe, L., & Rousseau, R. (2008). An h-index weighted by citation impact. *Information Processing & Management, 44*(2), 770–780.

Egghe, L. (2012). Remarks on the paper of A. De Visscher, "What does the g-index really measure?" *Journal of the American Society for Information Science and Technology, 63*(10), 2118-2121.

Glänzel, W. (2006). On the opportunities and limitations of the h-index. *Science Focus, 1*(1), 10-11.

Hirsch, J. E. (2005). An index to quantify an individual's scientific research output. *Proceedings of the National Academy of Sciences, 102*(46), 16569-72.

Imperial, J., & Navarro, A. (2007). Usefulness of Hirsch's h-index to evaluate scientific research in Spain. *Scientometrics, 71*(2), 271–282.

Jin, B. H., Liang, L. M., Rousseau, R., & Egghe, L. (2007). The R- and AR-indices: Complementing the h-index. *Chinese Science Bulletin, 52*(6), 855-863.

Jin, B. H. (2006). h-Index: An evaluation indicator proposed by scientist. *Science Focus, 1*(1), 8-9.

Lazaridis, L. (2010). Ranking university departments using the mean h-index. *Scientometrics, 82*(2), 11-16.

Lehmann, S. A. D., Jackson, & Lautrup, B. (2008). A quantitative analysis of indicators of scientific performance. *Scientometrics 76*(2), 369-390.

Lindsey, D. (1978). The corrected quality ratio: A composite index of scientific contribution to knowledge. *Social Studies of Science, 8*(3), 349-354.

Luz, M. P. et. al. (2008). Institutional H-Index: The performance of a new metric in the evaluation of Brazilian Psychiatric Post-graduation Programs. *Scientometrics, 77*(2), 361-368.

Mehta, C. R., & Pate, N. R. (2011). IBM SPSS Exact Tests. IBM.P.236. Retrieved on September, 30, 2013, from http://admin-apps.webofknowledge.com/jcr/jcr?pointofentry= home&sid= 4bowr-74js6miuqyl3av.

Moed, H. F. (2008). UK research assessment exercise:

Informed judgments on research quality or quantity? *Scientometrics, 74*(1), 153-161.

Norris, M., & Oppenheim, C. (2010). The h-index: A broad review of a new bibliometric indicator. *Journal of Documentation, 66*(5), 681-705.

Oppenheim, C. (2007). Using the h-index to rank influential British researchers in information science and librarianship. *Journal of the American Society for Information Science and Technology, 58*(2), 297-301.

Parthap, G. (2010). The 100 most prolific economists using the p-index. *Scientometrics, 84*(1), 167–172.

Riikonen, P., & Vihinen, M. (2008) National research contributions: A case study on Finnish biomedical research. *Scientometrics, 77*(2), 207-222.

Rousseau, R. (2006). New developments related to the Hirsch index. Industrial Sciences and Technology, Belgium. Retrieved from http://eprints.rclis.org/6376/.

Cole, S., & Cole, J.R. (1973). *Social stratification in science.* Chicago: University Press.

Schreiber, M. (2010). Revisiting the g-index: The average number of citations in the g-core. *Journal of the American Society for Information Science and Technology, 61*(1), 169-174.

Schreiber, M. (2010). Twenty Hirsch index variants and other indicators giving more or less preference to highly cited papers. Retrieved on October 31, 2013, from arxiv.org/pdf/1005.5227

Schreiber, M. (2013). Do we need the g-index? Retrieved on October 27, 2013, from http://arxiv.org/ftp/arxiv/papers/1301/1301.4028.pdf

Schubert, A., & Glänzel, W. (2007). A systematic analysis of Hirsch-type indices for journals. *Journal of Informetrics, 1*, 179-184.

Spizman, L., & Weinstein. M. A. (2008). A note on utilizing the geometric mean: When, why and how the forensic economist should employ the geometric mean. *Journal of Legal Economics, 15*(1), 43-55.

Tahira, M., Alias, R. A., & Bakri, A. (2013). Scientometric assessment of engineering in Malaysian universities. *Scientometrics, 96*(3), 865–879.

Tol, R. S. J. (2009). The h-index and its alternatives: An application to the 100 most prolific economists. *Scientometrics, 80*(2), 319–326.

Willmott, C. J., & Matsuura, K. (2005). Advantages of the Mean Absolute Error (MAE) over the Root

Mean Square Error (RMSE) in assessing average model performance. *Climate Research, 30,* 79–82.

van Raan, A. F. J. (2005). Fatal attraction: Conceptual and methodological problems in the ranking of universities by bibliometric methods. *Scientometrics, 62*(1), 133-143.

van Raan, A. F. J. (2006). Comparison of the Hirsch-index with standard bibliometric indicators and with peer judgment for 147 chemistry research groups. *Scientometrics, 67*(3), 491-502.

Vinkler, P. (2007). Eminence of scientists in the light of the h-index and other scientometric indicators. *Journal of Information Science, 33,* 481-491.

Zhang, C. T. (2009). The e-index, complementing the h-index for Excess Citations. *PLOS ONE 4*(5), e5429.

Zhang, C.T. (2013). The h' Index, effectively improving the h-index based on the citation distribution. *PLOS ONE, 8*(4), e59912.

2

Preference and Use of Electronic Information and Resources by Blind/Visually Impaired in NCR Libraries in India

Shailendra Kumar*

Department of Library & Information Science
University of Delhi, India
E-mail: shail3@yahoo.com

Gareema Sanaman

Department of Library & Information Science
University of Delhi, India
E-mail: gareema.sanaman@gmail.com

ABSTRACT

This paper aims to determine the preference and use of electronic information and resources by blind/visually impaired users in the leading National Capital Region (NCR) libraries of India. Survey methodology has been used as the basic research tool for data collection with the help of questionnaires. The 125 in total users surveyed in all the five libraries were selected randomly on the basis of willingness of the users with experience of working in digital environments to participate in the survey. The survey results were tabulated and analyzed with descriptive statistics methods using Excel software and 'Stata version 11.' The findings reveal that ICT have a positive impact in the lives of people with disabilities as it helps them to work independently and increases the level of confidence among them. The Internet is the most preferred medium of access to information among the majority of blind/visually impaired users. The 'Complexity of content available on the net' is found as the major challenge faced during Internet use by blind users of NCR libraries. 'Audio books on CDs/DVDs and DAISY books' are the most preferred electronic resources among the majority of blind/visually impaired users. This study will help the library professionals and organizations/institutions serving people with disabilities to develop effective library services for blind/visually impaired users in the digital environment on the basis of findings on information usage behavior in the study.

Keywords: Blind/vision impaired, Electronic Resources, Internet, Information Resources, NCR Libraries

*Corresponding Author:** Shailendra Kumar
Associate professor
Department of Library & Information Science
University of Delhi, India
E-mail: shail3@yahoo.com

1. INTRODUCTION

Information is a key currency in today's society with ICT as its primary means of delivery. To bridge the gap between the information rich and information poor is essential by ensuring that no one is denied access to these services due to any disability or lack of equipment that exists, in order to broach such difficulties at the point of access to ICT services (Cahill and Cornish, 2003, p.193). As the information needs of people with disabilities are similar to those of able-bodied people (Koulikourdi, 2008), libraries can act as the common platform to minimize the gap of ability and disability by ensuring an effective library service to all its patrons (Kishore, 1999). Information technology has progressed rapidly but the socially disadvantaged such as the disabled are marginalized from the benefits of information services. Today the biggest problem faced by the disabled is insufficient access to digital information services provided by libraries. Thus, the assessment of the usability of information by the disabled should be carried out to have a profound understanding of the information needs and information use behavior of the disabled to advance library information services for users with disabilities (Kwak and Bae, 2009). In this regard, the preference and use of the electronic information and resources by blind/vision impaired users to assess their specific information needs along with the impact of ICT tools/applications are the pertinent issues to this study. Thus, the present study consists of the following objectives:

1) To study the preferred source of information among blind/vision impaired users;
2) To identify the preferred Internet services/applications by blind/vision impaired users;
3) To find the influence of ICT tools/applications in the lives of People with Disabilities;
4) To explore the challenges faced by blind/vision impaired users during the use/access of the Internet;
5) To know the purpose of accessing and using e-resources among blind/vision impaired users; and
6) To determine the types of electronic resources preferred in support of work.

2. SCOPE AND METHODOLOGY

The scope of the present study possesses certain limitations as the study is limited to the National Capital Region (NCR) only and the survey population in each library is taken on the basis of availability of users during the time of the survey. The total number of 25 (=100%) users in each of the five libraries was selected as survey respondents on the basis of willingness to participate in the survey with the experience of working in digital environments. The total number of users surveyed is based on random selection and categorised as Faculty members, Research scholars, Graduates, Post-graduates, and High school and Intermediate students enrolled in various academic and vocational training courses in different institutions in the National Capital Region, Delhi (India). The National Capital Region in India refers to the metropolitan area which encircles the entirety of Delhi and adjoining urban areas. According to the National Capital Region Planning Board (NCRPB) Act of 1985, there are in total 15 districts in the three neighboring states of Haryana, Uttar Pradesh, and Rajasthan along with the National Capital Territory of Delhi that constitutes the National Capital Region (NCR) of India (NCRPB, 2010).

The data is collected through survey methods with the help of questionnaires along with the personal assistance provided to the users as and when required by them due to the different degree of impairment/disability suffered by the users (i.e. mild, moderate, severe, or complete). The accessibility and availability issues regarding the information were discussed with the experts, teachers, and disabled individuals and the questions proposed by them were included in the questionnaires prepared for the final research study. Interviews with the users with disabilities were also done to get conceptual clarity about the various issues related to disability and barriers faced by them during access of information in the digital environment. The total number of 125 questionnaires were distributed among the users i.e. 25 (=100%) in each library, out of which 80% (i.e. 20) responses are received from ADRC and HKU each, 72% (i.e. 18) each from BL and RNBT-BL, and 60% (i.e. 15) from DDCL respectively.

The survey results show that a very few faculty members (i.e. 8%) from BL, University of Delhi took part in the survey among all the libraries. The total number of Graduates (35) constitutes the major category of the users responding in the survey, i.e. 80% from ADRC, 48% from DDCL, and 12% from RNBT-BL, followed by the Post Graduates (21), constituting 40%, 32%, and 12% from HKU, BL, and DDCL respectively. Only 18 Research Scholars participated in the survey, i.e. 10(40%) from HKU and 8(32%) from BL while only 15 (i.e. 60%) High School/Intermediates from RNBTBL responded to the questionnaire.

The total five academic and special libraries were selected for the following study of blind/vision impaired people which includes:

* Amba Dalmia Resource Centre (ADRC), Miranda House
* Durgabai Deshmukh College Library (DDCL), Blind Relief Association
* Braille Library (BL), University of Delhi
* Hellen Keller Unit (HKU), Jawaharlal Nehru University
* Ram Nath Batra Talking Book Library (RNBTBL), National Association of the Blind

The data collection has been analyzed with descriptive statistics methods using Excel software and 'Stata version 11,' and presented in the form of Tables and Graphs for the goal of a clear understanding of the survey results.

3. LITERATURE REVIEW

The library profession has long championed providing services and materials to all its patrons equally, which is one of the fundamental beliefs inherent in the profession (Riley, 2002, p.179). People with disabilities are one the most important segments of society which are greatly affected by and benefit from the new technologies of the electronic age. In India, members of the National Knowledge Commission (NKC) have asked librarians 'to identify the constraints, problems and challenges to recommend changes so that necessary steps can be taken to mobilize and upgrade the existing

library and information systems and services.' Hence, libraries can provide the leadership role to show their expertise and initiate new innovative means to develop and provide specialized services to these special groups who do not have access to normal services, as it is the democratic and constitutional right of differently-abled users (Roy and Bandyopadhyay, 2009, p.629). In the evolving information-based society, providing digital information services to people with disabilities has become an issue of major concern for the libraries. Today if libraries focus on offline content such as Braille books for the blind it is nothing but an anachronism (Kwak and Bae, 2009). People with disabilities are part of every demographic group imaginable. Thus, regardless of library type or location, people with disabilities represent an identifiable component of the constituency a library serves (Chalfen and Farb, 1996). As librarianship is an enabling profession, librarians need to think beyond their personal discomfort and try to provide the same level of service to this category of population as they provide to mentally capable persons (Cohen, 2006, p.62-63). The rapid growth of the Internet and its applications over traditional means of communication in terms of flexibility, speed, and reach makes it an obvious route for the dissemination of information among people with disabilities.

In a recent study, Sugano et al. (2010) states that the best resource for facilitating direct access to digital information for blind users can be 'eBraille,' a web-based translation program which easily converts Japanese text into braille documents. Moreover, it is a free system for creating braille text files for anyone who has access to a web browser. When eBraille translation accuracy was evaluated, it was found that it is equivalent to or better than the other standalone braille translation programs and it achieved the goal of being applicable for practical use.

The demand for access to the Internet by people with disabilities is steadily increasing and now it has become a human rights issue. There are several factors which inhibit the use of ICTs by people with disabilities, depending on the type of disability an individual has (Dobransky and Hargittai, 2006). Much like people with physical disabilities have inhibited keyboard use, visual impairment inhibits screen use and learning disabilities prevent large numbers of users from participating in the benefits of the Internet and its rich resources (Cullen, 2001). Beverley, Bath, and Barber (2007) identified several factors that may affect a visually impaired person's information behavior with the help of two existing models of information behavior. Human resources and information technologies are identified as major challenges to the future of information access for people with disabilities. People with disabilities are already affected by disparities in education and income, and therefore further marginalization of their communication and information access creates a greater barrier to access to critical information needs and effective participation in a community (Baker, Hanson, and Myhill, 2009). The development of the Internet has made possible unprecedented access to information but evidence shows that people with disabilities lag behind the rest of the population in Internet use. This lower level of internet use among those with disabilities is mainly due to the fact that they have to incur the extra costs of adaptive technology for accessing the Internet (Vincente and Lopez, 2010). Another significant factor which prevents Internet use by many disabled people is the lack of ICT skills and support for them (Cullen, 2003, p.250). Huang and Russell (2006, p.162) state, "People with disability are only half as likely to have access to the internet as those without a disability." To overcome these problems, users need to receive adequate training and educational opportunities that can enhance their use of the computer and the Internet with the help of a few vital skills like evaluating search engines, choosing alternate keywords, and initiating their own searches to achieve optimal results in their quest for information (Russell and Huang, 2009).

Horwath (2002) evaluated the accessibility of four Web-based proprietary databases by blind or visually impaired who were comfortable in using the World Wide Web. Not a single database clearly emerged as completely accessible on all levels, but the Encyclopaedia Britannica Online and EBSCOhost MasterFile Elite were found to be the most accessible among the databases. The largest factor affecting ease of use and accessibility was the design of the resources themselves.

Craven and Booth (2006) present the methods and findings of two research projects that explored user behavior and usability issues relating to the use of Web-based resources by people with disabilities. Both studies provided evidence of the problems faced by disabled users when using Web-based resources. The study also revealed information about the types of features preferred by users and how they overcome navigational problems, and what types of features enhanced a user's experience. Further, both studies confirmed the importance of involving users in accessibility and usability assessments and including their feedback for the design of electronic resources.

In a more recent study, Dermody and Majekodunmi (2011) studied the impact of library databases on students with print disabilities who use screen reading technologies to navigate online resources. Users performed online searches to complete a series of tasks in three different online databases and rated Expanded Academic ASAP and Sociological Abstracts as difficult while using their screen reader to read the full text articles. The articles in PDFs were inaccessible as the PDFs were image based and were not tagged for screen readers. The amount of links on the results page in all three databases also posed a barrier and interfered with the screen readers.

In a study of website accessibility for the disabled, a sample of 33 academic library web sites were examined to study how many websites offered access to text-only versions of the databases and emphasized this access for visually impaired users. The study focused on how well academic library websites guide visually impaired people in the use of the eight larger databases including EBSCO, JSTOR, Ovid, and Proquest using two screen reading programs, JAWS (version 7.0) and WindowEyes (version 5.5). Results showed that only 5 of 33 libraries mentioned database accessibility in any way on their websites (Power and LeBeau, 2009).

The information world is rapidly changing. There is a shift in technology from analog to digital, which has resulted in a change in the availability of information resources in a variety of formats to the users. Earlier mainly printed material like books and magazines constitutes the core collection of the library but today technological advances have produced information packed in an assortment of formats, resulting in products like online databases, CD-ROMs, multimedia kits, and DVDs (Salinas, 2003). Similarly, for people with disabilities, Braille, large print, and analog tapes are no longer the only possible formats as libraries are adding digital formats for disabled people to read text and listen to audio books. Therefore, due to the emergence of such changes in collection development with the proliferation of formats and products, libraries are challenged to plan their services with all the possible formats in mind (Epp, 2006) to derive solutions to bridge the digital divide to continue to work on the mission of providing equal access regardless of format.

The advent of the World Wide Web (WWW) and its resources has caused a dramatic evolution in academic libraries (Byerley and Chambers, 2002, p.169). Today access to electronic resources and services has been enhanced through Web-based interfaces in libraries. Library websites have evolved into information gateways providing access to various library services and resources including electronic databases, library catalogs, research tools, and the Internet (Yu, 2002, p.406). The applications of computer technology, particularly the Internet, have a strong impact on the environment of libraries. The Web provides the main channel for the dissemination of a variety of educational resources like official Web pages with administrative information, various course materials, online tutorials, and Web-mediated distance education programs. Libraries are most affected due to the digital revolution, with a great responsibility to store, organize, and provide access to the wide variety of electronic information (Schmetzke, 2001, p.35-36). Thus the main challenge for technology librarians is to be proactive in staying updated and abreast of technological advances in order to provide Web based information and services to patrons of all kinds (Vandenbark, 2010, p.28). Moreover, it is not feasible for librarians to test the accessibility of every online product they are considering for purchase, and therefore librarians must be at least aware of accessibility issues and should demand assurance from database vendors that their products are accessible (Byerley and Chambers, 2002).

Today disabled users depend very much on the web for most of their information needs and requirements. Therefore the impact of web-based resources needs to be evaluated through user-focused studies based on the user's preferences and the information seeking behavior of the user in an academic and research environment for completing their tasks successfully. In this regard, many earlier studies have been conducted to study the information needs and preference of blind/vision impaired persons for sources of information (Balini, 2000; Williamson, 1998). Also, within the last few years, similar studies have been conducted on the use and access of electronic resources by Scientists (Kumar and Singh, 2011) and Faculties and Research scholars (Madhusudhan, 2010; Tahir, Mahmood, and Shafique, 2010), but no such study on the preference and use of e-resources by blind/vision impaired users in the National Capital Region libraries of India has been conducted so far.

4. FINDINGS AND DISCUSSION

4.1. Referred Sources for Locating/Accessing Information

The use and preference of information sources differs from user to user on the basis of their needs, convenience, and availability of the information sources for them. It can be noted from Table 1 that the first source of information is 'Internet' among the majority of users in HKU (36%), BL (32%), and RNBTBL (24%) respectively. The 'College Library' is found as another important source for locating/accessing information among the majority of users in ADRC (i.e. 36%) and DDCL (i.e.28%). Also, the 'University Central/Braille Library' in HKU with 36% and 'Teacher' in RNBTBL with 24% are found to be equally important to 'Internet' as a source of information.

The above results (Table 1) clearly show that 'Internet' is the most popular source of information among the maximum number of blind/vision impaired users in all the libraries due to its easy availability (i.e. 24/7) and accessibility (i.e. with the help of assistive technology) for them.

4.2. Use of Internet Facilities by Users

The Internet enables access to vast amounts of information to be independently retrieved by users at anytime from anywhere in the world. Visually impaired users can benefit themselves with several online services and facilities like chat, email, online banking, and online reservations. According to the survey results

Table 1. Preferred First Source of Information for Users

Source of Information	Name of the Library				
	ADRC	DDCL	BL	HKU	RNBTBL
University Central/Braille Library	5(20%)	-	1(4%)	9(36%)	-
Department Library	-	-	1(4%)	-	-
College Library	9(36%)	7(28%)	3(12%)	-	-
School Library	-	-	-	-	4(16%)
Internet	4(16%)	5(20%)	8(32%)	9(36%)	6(24%)
Teacher	2(8%)	1(4%)	5(20%)	2(8%)	6(24%)
Other (i.e. colleague, seniors, etc.)	-	2(8%)	-	-	2(8%)

Note: n=25 (i.e. equal to 100%), Representative population from each Library

(Table 2), 13 (52%) respondents each in ADRC and HKU and 7 (28%) in RNBTBL use the Internet 'Everyday' at their respective libraries whereas 9 (36%) and 7 (28%) users in BL and DDCL respectively use the Internet 'Occasionally' only when the need arises for them.

When an individual with a disability uses the Internet, other users do not know that the person has a disability. Hence, Grimaldi and Goette (1999) examined the role of the Internet and its usage on the level of perceived independence among people with physical disabilities. It was found that an increase in the number of Internet services used had a positive influence on the perceived level of independence among

Table 2. Frequency of Use of Internet at the Institution/Library

Frequency	Name of the Library				
	ADRC	DDCL	BL	HKU	RNBTBL
Everyday	13(52%)	-	2(8%)	13(52%)	7(28%)
Once a week	-	2(8%)	1(4%)	-	1(4%)
Twice a week	2(8%)	-	1(4%)	3(12%)	3(12%)
Occasionally (when need arises)	4(16%)	7(28%)	9(36%)	4(16%)	5(20%)
Never	1(4%)	6(24%)	5(20%)	-	2(8%)

Note: n=25 (i.e. equal to 100%), Representative population from each Library

Various Reasons for Using the Internet					
It provides access to current up-to-date information	9(36%)	7(28%)	6(24%)	4(16%)	7(28%)
It provides easier access to information	4(16%)	1(4%)	4(16%)	6(24%)	5(20%)
It provides faster access to information	3(12%)	2(8%)	5(20%)	4(16%)	3(12%)
It provides access to a wider range of information	8(32%)	4(16%)	5(20%)	9(36%)	3(12%)
All of the above	1(4%)	3(12%)	3(12%)	6(24%)	4(16%)

Note: n=25, where percent exceeds 100% as users were allowed multiple responses

individuals with physical disabilities. Also, the study revealed that usage of the World Wide Web and Telnet mainly benefits independence among users. Similarly, the present survey findings (Table 2) indicate that the majority of users, i.e. 36% in ADRC, 28% each in DDCL and RNBTBL, and 24% in BL, access the Internet as 'it provides access to current up-to-date information' for them related to their academic or research work. In HKU, a majority of users (i.e. 36%) states that they access the Internet because 'it provides access to a wider range of information' related to their academic or research work, which allows them to avoid moving around to other libraries in search of information (i.e. it reduces their mobility problem to other places). The results reveal that the majority of users in all the libraries access the Internet as it provides access to 'current up-to-date and wider range of information' for them.

4.3. First Approaches to Browsing the Internet for Information Access

The approach to browsing the Internet for informa-

tion among vision impaired users depends on their awareness/knowledge about the source of information, availability, and easy accessibility of the resource, the user's requirements, and suitability of the user in finding the information. The study findings reveal that a majority of users in all the libraries, i.e. 18 (72%) in ADRC, 14 (56%) in RNBTBL, 13 (52%) in HKU, 10 (40%) in DDCL, and 8 (32%) in BL, prefer to search /access the information through 'Search Engines' as they find them easy to use. The second approach to browsing the Internet for information access among 7 (28%) users in BL, 5 (20%) in HKU, 4 (16%) each in DDCL and RNBTBL, and 2 (8%) in ADRC is through 'Specific Websites.'

Figure 1 clearly shows that 'Google' is the most preferred search engine among the majority of users in all the libraries. 20 (80%) respondents each in ADRC and HKU, 18 (72%) in BL, 16 (64%) in RNBTBL, and 12 (48%) in DDCL prefer to use only Google to browse for any kind of information from the Internet and find it more comfortable and easy to use than any other search engine.

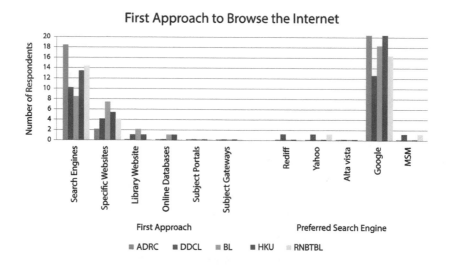

Note: n=25 (i.e. equal to 100%), Representative population from each Library

Fig. 1 User's First Approaches in Browsing the Internet

4.4. Preferred Format for Reading Electronic Content

Individuals with disabilities not only require infrastructure and assistive technology facilities but also resources in accessible formats on the basis of the degree of impairment suffered by them. The survey results (Figure 2) show that the most preferred format among blind/vision impaired users is the 'Doc' format which is completely compatible with the screen readers available today and allows users to make changes and the required modifications in the data accordingly.

The results indicate that the highest (i.e. 15; 60%) number of users preferring the 'Doc' format are from ADRC and RNBTBL each, 9 (36%) are from BL and HKU each, and 7 (28%) from DDCL. The majority of users preferring 'Doc' format are completely or 100% blind. The next preferred format is 'DAISY,' which helps users to read digital document with the help of the DAISY player, which is an easily portable device. DAISY is the Digital Accessible Information System standard that was developed by an international consortium of libraries for the blind beginning in 1996 (Auld, 2005). It can be noted (Figure 2) that 5(20%) users each from BL and DDCL, 4 (16%) from ADRC, and 1 (4%) user each from HKU and RNBTBL prefer to use the 'DAISY' format for reading documents.

4.5. Preferred Internet Services/Applications by Blind/Visually Impaired Users

The Internet provides access to a variety of services and applications for users, and therefore respondents were asked to rank any three of the following Internet services/applications on the basis of their preference of use for their personal or academic purposes. As indicated below (Table 3), the highest number of users in all the libraries, i.e. 40% in RNBTBL, 36% each in ADRC, DDCL, and HKU, and 32% in BL ranked 'E-mail' as their first choice (I) on the basis of their preference of use and familiarity with the concept of Email. 'Internet browsing' was ranked second (II) by the second highest number of users in all the libraries, i.e. 44% in ADRC, 40% in RNBTBL, 32% each in DDCL and HKU, and 24% in BL respectively. Lastly, 'Downloading informative material from the Internet' was found to be the third (III) preference among 32% of users in RNBTBL and 24% of users each in DDCL, BL, and HKU while in ADRC, 28% users ranked Email as their third choice.

The high rate of involvement in 'E-mail, Internet browsing and Downloading informative material' indicates that all categories of blind/vision impaired users (i.e. Faculty members, Research scholars, Post graduates/Graduates, and high school/Intermediates)

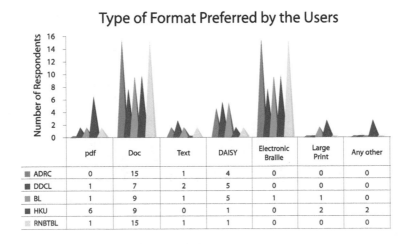

Type of Format Preferred by the Users

	pdf	Doc	Text	DAISY	Electronic Braille	Large Print	Any other
■ ADRC	0	15	1	4	0	0	0
■ DDCL	1	7	2	5	0	0	0
■ BL	1	9	1	5	1	1	0
■ HKU	6	9	0	1	0	2	2
RNBTBL	1	15	1	1	0	0	0

Note: n=25 (i.e. equal to 100%), Representative population from each Library

Fig. 2 Type of Format Preferred to Read Electronic Content

Table 3. ICT-based Internet Services/Applications Accessed/Utilized by Users

Internet Services/Applications		Name of the Library				
Services	Rank Order	ADRC	DDCL	BL	HKU	RNBTBL
E-mail	1	9(36%)	9(36%)	8(32%)	9(36%)	10(40%)
	2	-	4(16%)	5(20%)	6(24%)	3(12%)
	3	7(28%)	2(8%)	2(8%)	2(8%)	4(12%)
Internet Browsing	1	3(12%)	2(8%)	1(4%)	3(12%)	3(12%)
	2	11(44%)	8(32%)	6(24%)	8(32%)	10(40%)
	3	3(12%)	-	3(12%)	3(12%)	3(12%)
Real-time chat	1	-	-	-	-	1(4%)
	2	1(4%)	-	1(4%)	-	-
	3	3(12%)	-	1(4%)	-	1(4%)
Database Searching	1	-	1(4%)	6(24%)	2(8%)	-
	2	-	-	1(4%)	3(12%)	-
	3	-	1(4%)	1(4%)	4(16%)	-
E-Journal Access	1	-	-	1(4%)	3(12%)	-
	2	-	-	-	-	-
	3	-	-	2(8%)	5(20%)	-
Downloading informative material	1	5(20%)	3(12%)	1(4%)	1(4%)	2(8%)
	2	7(28%)	2(8%)	3(12%)	3(12%)	4(16%)
	3	5(20%)	6(24%)	6(24%)	6(24%)	8(32%)
For an online course	1	-	-	-	-	-
	2	-	-	-	-	-
	3	1(4%)	-	-	-	-
Newsgroups/mailing lists/Listserv	1	-	-	-	-	-
	2	-	-	1(4%)	-	-
	3	-	-	1(4%)	-	-
Bulletin Board	1	-	-	-	-	-
	2	-	-	-	-	-
	3	-	2(8%)	1(4%)	-	-
Downloading academic/learning content provided online	1	3(12%)	-	1(4%)	2(8%)	2(8%)
	2	1(4%)	1(4%)	1(4%)	-	1(4%)
	3	1(4%)	4(16%)	1(4%)	-	2(8%)

Note: n=25, where percent exceeds 100% as users were allowed multiple responses

surveyed in the NCR libraries of India are aware of the basic communication and information aspects of the Internet. The Internet acts as the current, easier, and faster mode of communication providing access to a variety of online information resources to users to fulfill their academic and research related needs.

4.6. Impact of ICT Tools/Applications in the Lives of People with Disabilities

ICT along with assistive technology creates an adaptive environment for people with disabilities to perform various information related tasks easily. In an ICT based study for access to information services for disabled people, Myhill (2002) found that providing access to information for all users, irrespective of their physical disabilities, is a requirement for all libraries and ICT can be used to assist in this. The study describes a range of projects and services that have been developed by Gateshead libraries using ICT to provide a gateway to the wealth of information available in digital formats. Similarly, through this study it is found that a majority of respondents, i.e. 44% in ADRC and 40% each in DDCL and HKU, state that 'ICT provides various opportunities to engage them in all aspects of life including teaching and learning.' For the majority of users, i.e. 32% each in BL and RNBT-

BL, 'ICT helps them in communication with others via Internet applications like chat, email, online discussion groups etc.'

In addition, Table 4 clearly indicates that a majority of users in ADRC and HKU, i.e. 8 (32%) and 7(28%) in BL, believe that 'ICT has the potential for reducing the discrimination in the society.' Thus, it is found that ICT plays a major role in the lives of people with disabilities and has a positive impact on their level of independence which increases the level of confidence among them to perform various day-to-day activities.

4.7. Challenges Faced during Use/Access of the Internet

Even though the Internet provides access to a large amount of resources and facilities to blind/vision impaired users, there are various barriers faced by users during access of the Internet. The study findings (Figure 3) show that 'Complexity of the content available on the Net' is the major barrier faced during Internet use by a maximum users in ADRC (11; 44%), RNBTBL (10; 40%), and HKU (9; 36%). The 'Lack of sufficient ICT and Infrastructure facilities' in the library is found as the next major barrier faced in BL (12; 48%) and DDCL (6; 24%).

The 'Complexity of the content available on the Net' is the common barrier reported by a majority of users

Table 4. Impact of ICT Tools/Applications on the Level of Independence of Users

Role of ICT tools/applications	Name of the Library				
	ADRC	DDCL	BL	HKU	RNBTBL
ICT has the potential for reducing discrimination in society	8(32%)	3(12%)	7(28%)	8(32%)	5(20%)
ICT helps to receive specialized training to perform various information-related tasks with ease	4(16%)	7(28%)	3(12%)	4(16%)	6(24%)
ICT offers a range of specialized software and hardware solutions for communication, storage, and access of information	2(8%)	2(8%)	2(8%)	7(28%)	2(8%)
ICT provides various opportunities to engage people with disabilities in all aspects of life including teaching and learning	11(44%)	10(40%)	5(20%)	10(40%)	5(20%)
ICT helps in communication with others via Internet applications like chat, email, online discussion groups etc. with the help of Assistive Technology	7(28%)	3(12%)	8(32%)	6(24%)	8(32%)

Note: n=25, where percent exceeds 100% as users were allowed multiple responses

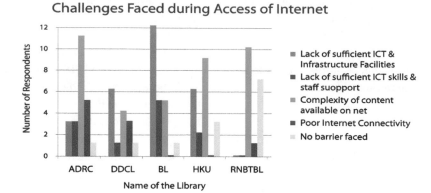

Note: n=25, where percent exceeds 100% as users were allowed multiple responses

Fig. 3 Barriers Faced by Users during Internet Access

in all the libraries. This includes the issue of screen design, the use of font size, color, the use of patterns in screen backgrounds that make the text difficult to read, large amount of hyperlinks, and an excess of graphics. Guidelines for accessible design and accessibility checkers are freely available on the Internet, but designers are more concerned with the 'look' of the page to sighted people than accessibility to a minority of users (Oppenheim and Selby, 1999, p.335-43).

4.8. Types of Electronic Resources Preferred by Users

One of the core values of librarianship is to ensure access to the collections that libraries builds to all users, including people with disabilities (Salinas, 2003, p.132). Awareness about the preferences of blind/vision impaired users towards these resources can play an important role in framing collection development policies in libraries for them. Libraries can work towards balancing resources with user needs which can further facilitate and enhance the use of resources among users with disabilities. The survey findings (Table 5) clearly state that Audio books on CDs/DVDs are the first (I) preferred resource among a maximum number of users in ADRC, DDCL and RNBTBL, i.e. 64%, 44%, and 36% respectively. The DAISY books are found as the most preferred resource among 48% of users each in BL and HKU. In ADRC (40%) and DDCL (28%), Audio books on Cassettes/Tapes are the second (II) preferred electronic

resources among vision impaired users, followed by Electronic Text in BL (24%) and HKU (40%) and DAISY books in RNBTBL (20%) respectively.

The responses from all the libraries show that 'Audio books on CDs/DVDs' are the most preferred electronic resources among Graduates (i.e. in ADRC and DDCL) and High school and Intermediate students (i.e. in RNBTBL), followed by 'DAISY books' among the majority of Post Graduates and Research Scholars (i.e. in BL and HKU) respectively as these are easily accessible to them with the help of assistive technology. Also, 'Internet' is found as the commonly preferred electronic resource among the users in all the libraries.

4.9. Purpose of Access/Use of the Electronic Resources by Users

Internet resources are accessed/used for different purposes by different categories of users on the basis of their academic/personal needs and requirements. The study findings (Figure 4) shows that the major purpose for which Internet resources are accessed/used is 'Study and Updates' among 12; 48% of users in BL, followed by 11; 44% users each in DDCL and RNBTBL. In ADRC, the majority (14; 56%) of users (i.e. Graduates) access/use the Internet resources for 'Project and Academic assignments' allotted to them followed by 13; 52% of users accessing the Internet resources for study and updates; whereas, in HKU a maximum of Research scholars (11; 44%) access/use

Table 5. Types of Electronic Resources mostly used by Users

Electronic Resources	Name of the Library				
	ADRC	DDCL	BL	HKU	RNBTBL
Audio books on CDs/DVDs	16(64%)	11(44%)	3(12%)	-	9(36%)
Audio books on Cassettes/Tapes	10(40%)	7(28%)	2(8%)	1(4%)	1(4%)
DAISY books (i.e. DTBs)	1(4%)	2(8%)	12(48%)	12(48%)	5(20%)
Electronic Text	4(16%)	5(20%)	6(24%)	10(40%)	2(8%)
Internet	9(36%)	6(24%)	5(20%)	9(36%)	3(12%)
Digitized Catalog (online)	-	-	2(8%)	4(16%)	-
Electronic Indexes	-	-	-	-	-
Databases of DTBs (Digital Talking Books)	-	-	-	-	-
Web-Braille System	-	-	-	-	-
Online Reference Works	-	-	1(4%)	1(4%)	-
Library Website	-	-	-	1(4%)	-

Note: n=25, where percent exceeds 100% as users were allowed multiple responses.

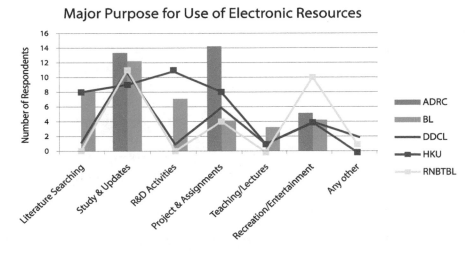

Note: n=25, where percent exceeds 100% as users were allowed multiple responses

Fig. 4 Purpose for which Electronic Resources are Used

the Internet resources for 'Research and Development' activities followed by 9; 36% of users who are interested in downloading and using the Internet resources for their study and updates.

The overall results indicate that 'Study and Updates'

is the most common purpose among the majority of users (i.e. Faculty members, Research scholars, Post graduates/Graduates and High school/Intermediates) in all the libraries for which Internet resources are mostly accessed or used by them.

4.10. Availing of Membership of More than One Institution/Library

There are various reasons due to which blind/vision impaired users visit other libraries for the access/use of information resources apart from their parent library. It can be determined from the data represented above (Table 6) that a majority of users in ADRC, BL, and DDCL are members of other libraries also. The major reason for taking membership in other libraries by the majority of users in ADRC (44%) and BL (40%) is 'Lack of sufficient e-resources,' compared to 'Lack of proper infrastructure and facilities' in DDCL (20%). The 'lack of resources in accessible format' is found as the common reason for availing of membership in other libraries by the users of BL (40%), ADRC (20%), DDCL (16%), HKU (12%), and RNBTBL (8%) respectively.

Moreover, the majority of users in RNBTBL (60%) and HKU (48%) prefer to use their Institution/ University library only due to the sufficient number of resources and facilities available for them in the libraries. In BL and RNBTBL, few users avail of memberships for the Braille wing of the Delhi Public Library to gain knowledge on Current affairs, Biographies, or Historical background to prepare themselves for various competitive examinations and personality development.

5. CONCLUSION AND SUGGESTIONS

It can be concluded that ICT plays an important role in the lives of people with disabilities as it helps them to work independently and increases the level of confidence among them. The Internet is the preferred source for locating accessing information among the majority of the blind/vision impaired due to its easy availability (i.e. 24/7) and accessibility (i.e. with the help of Assistive Technology) for them. 'E-mail, Internet browsing and downloading informative material' comprise the preferred Internet services/applications among the users, which indicates that people with disabilities are well aware of the advanced technologies available today. The electronic resources mainly preferred by users in leading National Capital Region libraries include the 'Audio books on CDs /DVDs and DAISY' books. Blind/visually impaired patrons face various barriers during Internet access but the 'Complexity of content available on net' is found as the major barrier faced by them, followed by 'Lack of sufficient ICT and Infrastructure facilities' at the institution/library. The findings demonstrate that the majority of blind/visually impaired users avail of the information services of more than one institution /library to fulfill their information needs and requirements. The various findings suggest that blind/visually

Table 6. Availing of Services of More than one Institution/Library

Member of other Library	Reasons	Name of the Library				
		ADRC	DDCL	BL	HKU	RNBTBL
Yes	Lack of sufficient e-resources	11(44%)	2(8%)	10(40%)	5(20%)	-
	Lack of resources in accessible format	5(20%)	4(16%)	10(40%)	3(12%)	2(8%)
	Lack of proper infrastructure and facilities	-	5(20%)	8(32%)	-	-
	Lack of staff support and guidance	-	-	1(4%)	-	-
	Other	-	-	2(8%)	-	1(4%)
No		8(32%)	4(16%)	2(8%)	12(48%)	15(60%)

Note: n=25, where percent exceeds 100% as users were allowed multiple responses.

impaired people in NCR libraries are utilizing the benefits of advanced ICTs such as Internet and Email to access and use the electronic resources for 'Study and updates' to keep themselves aware of the recent advancements taking place in their subject areas.

Access to web applications is becoming an important issue for people with disabilities; therefore libraries should emphasize on the accessible web design for the disabled to access and use the various online resources and services. "Advances in technology and use of the web have provided more choices in the delivery and access to information and resources" in libraries (Craven and Booth, 2006, p.179). Today libraries and their users rely heavily on electronic resources and databases for their information needs and requirements, and therefore it is essential that these resources be made accessible to users with disabilities along with other materials. Library web sites are the digital front door to library services as they reflect the priority libraries give to their services (Power and LeBeau, 2009, p.55-56). Therefore libraries should develop a webpage/website describing the services and facilities available for blind/vision impaired users in that particular library. In this regard, Vandenbark (2010, p.26) focuses mainly on three types of Web-based resources that can be offered by a library to its user community, which are access to the Internet, access to subscription databases, and a library's own webpage/website which needs to be accessible to people with disabilities as well. Also, there are various barriers faced by the blind/vision impaired in comparison to users with other types of disabilities during interaction with the Web, which need to taken into consideration by content developers of the Web to provide necessary solutions for them. There are several standards developed for 'Web Accessibility' by the W3C (World Wide Web Consortium), especially for people with disabilities, which can be followed before Web designing. As the libraries' primary task is to meet the information needs of all users, librarians should aim to bridge the current information gap concerning accessibility of the various electronic resources so that people with disabilities may navigate the online environment on equal terms with those without any disability (Schmetzke, 2002).

REFERENCES

Baker, P. M. A., Hanson, J. & Myhill, W. N. (2009). The promise of municipal WiFi and failed policies of inclusion: The disability divide. *Information Polity: The International Journal of Government & Democracy in the Information Age, 14*(1/2), 47-59.

Balini, B. (2000). A Needs Assessment of CNIB Library Services. University of Alberta, (April,12): 25.

Beverley, C. A., Bath, P. A. & Barber, R. (2007). Can two established information models explain the information behavior of visually impaired people seeking health and social care information? *Journal of Documentation, 63*(1), 9-32.

Byerley, S. L. & Chambers, M. B. (2002). Accessibility and usability of Web-based library databases for non-visual users. *Library Hi Tech, 20*(2), 169-178.

Cahill, K. & Cornish, S. (2003). Assistive technology for users in the Royal Borough of Kensington and Chelsea public libraries in the UK. Program: *Electronic Library and Information Systems, 37*(3), 190-193.

Chalfen, D. H. & Farb, S. E. (1996). Universal access and the ADA: A disability access design specifications for the new UCLA library online information system. *Library Hi Tech, 14*(1), 51-56.

Cohen, S. (2006). Enabling libraries: How to serve people with disabilities. *Tennessee Libraries, 56*(2), 62-73.

Craven, J. & Booth, H. (2006). Putting awareness into practice: Practical steps for conducting usability tests. *Library Review, 55*(3), 179-194.

Cullen, R. (2001). Addressing the digital divide. *67th IFLA Council and General Conference*, August 16-25 (pp.1-14). Retrieved from http://www.eric.ed.gov/PDFS/ED459714.pdf

Cullen, R. (2003). The digital divide: A global and national call to action. *The Electronic Library, 21*(3), 247-257.

Dermody, K. & Majekodunmi, N. (2011). Online databases and the research experience for university students with print disabilities. *Library Hi Tech, 29*(1), 149-160.

Dobransky, K. & Hargittai, E. (2006). The disability divide in Internet access and use. *Information, Communication & Society, 9*(3), 313-334.

Epp, M. A. (2006). Closing the 95 percent gap: Library resource sharing for people with print disabilities. *Library Trends, 54*(3), Winter, 411-429.

Grimaldi, C. & Goette, T. (1999). The Internet and the independence of individuals with disabilities. *Internet Research: Electronic Networking Applications and Policy, 9*(4), 272-280.

Horwath, J. (2002). Evaluating opportunities for expanded information access: A study of the accessibility of four online databases. *Library Hi Tech, 20*(2), 199-206.

Huang, J. & Russell, S. (2006). The digital divide and academic achievement. *The Electronic Library, 24*(2), 160-173.

Kishore, R. (1999). Voice of India's disabled: Demanding equality in library services. *65th IFLA Council and General Conference*, Bangkok, August 20-28 (pp.1-7). Retrieved from http://archive.ifla.org/IV/ifla65/papers/044-132e.htm.

Koulikourdi, A. (2008). Library services for people with disabilities in Greece. *Library Review, 57*(2), 138-148.

Kumar, S. and Singh, M. (2011). Access and use of electronic information resources by scientists of National Physical Laboratory in India: A case study. *Singapore Journal of Library and Information Management, 40*, 33-49.

Kwak, S. J. & Bae, K. J. (2009). Ubiquitous library usability test for the improvement of information access for the blind. *The Electronic Library, 27*(4), 623-639.

Madhusudhan, M. (2010). Use of electronic resources by research scholars of Kurukshetra University. *The Electronic Library, 28*(4), 492-506.

Myhill, C. E. (2002). ICT for access to information services for disabled people: An overview of projects and services at Gateshead libraries services. *Program, 36*(3), 176-181.

National Capital Region Planning Board (2010). *Rationale.* NCRPB. Retrieved from http://ncrpb.nic.in/rationale.php.

Oppenheim, C. & Selby, K. (1999). Access to information on the World Wide Web for blind and visually impaired people. *Aslib Proceedings, 51*(10), 335-345.

Power, R. & LeBeau, C. (2009). How well do academic library web sites address the needs of database users with visual disabilities? *The Reference Librarian, 50*, 55-72.

Riley, C. A. (2002). Libraries, aggregator databases, screen readers and clients with disabilities. *Library Hi Tech, 20*(2), 179-187.

Roy, P. C. & Bandyopadhyay, R. (2009). Designing barrier free services for visually challenged persons in the academic libraries in India. *Proceedings of the International Conference on Academic Libraries*, Delhi, October 5-8 (pp. 626-629). Retrieved from http://crl.du.ac.in/ical09/papers/index_files/ical-105_241_602_1_RV.pdf.

Russell, S. E. & Huang, J. (2009). Libraries' role in equalizing access to information. *Library Management, 30*(1/2), 69-76.

Salinas, R. (2003). Addressing the digital divide through collection development. *Collection Development, 22*(3), 131-136.

Schmetzke, A. (2001). Web accessibility at University libraries and library schools. *Library Hi Tech, 19*(1), 35-49.

Schmetzke, A. (2002). Accessibility of web- based information resources for people with disabilities. *Library Hi Tech, 20*(2), 135-136.

Sugano, A. et al. (2010). eBraille: a web-based translation program for Japanese text to Braille. *Internet Research, 20*(5), 582-592.

Tahir, M., Mahmood, K., and Shafique, F. (2010). Use of electronic information resources and facilities by humanities scholars. *The Electronic Library, 28*(1), 122-136.

Vandenbark, R.T. (2010). Tending a wild garden: Library web design for persons with disabilities. *Information Technology and Libraries, 29*(1), 23-29.

Vincente, M. R. & Lopez, A. J. (2010). A multidimensional analysis of the disability digital divide: some evidence for internet use. *The Information Society, 26*, 48-64.

Williamson, K. (1998). Discovered by chance: the role of incidental information acquisition in an ecological model of information use. *Library and Information Science Research, 20*(1), 23-40.

Yu, H. (2002). Web accessibility and the law: Recommendations for implementation. *Library Hi Tech, 20*(4), 406-419.

3

An Investigation of the Awareness and Use of Open Access Initiative at the Federal Polytechnic, Offa, Kwara State, Nigeria

A.O. Issa *

Department of Library and Information Science
University of Ilorin, Nigeria
Email: lanrewajuwahab@gmail.com

K.N. Igwe

Department of Library and Information Science
Akanu Ibiam Federal Polytechnic Unwana, Nigeria
Email: knigwe@yahoo.com

B.R. Akangbe

The Polytechnic Library
Kwara State Polytechnic Ilorin, Nigeria
Email: akangbebisi@yahoo.com

M.B. Aliyu

Department of Library and Information Science
Federal Polytechnic Offa, Nigeria
Email: mulikataliyu@yahoo.com

ABSTRACT

This study investigated the information environment of lecturers in Federal Polytechnic, Offa,Kwara State, Nigeria, in relation to their information seeking behavior, extent of use of the polytechnic library, perceptions of the resources and services of the library, level of awareness and extent of use of the open access model of scholarly communications, as well as the challenges of accessing and using information resources. It adopted the survey research method, using a questionnaire for data collection, while the descriptive statistics method was used to analyse the data, using tabular presentation and simple percentages. From a population of 280 lecturers for the study, a purposive sample of 164 was drawn. The findings showed that the lecturers' information needs are focused on online use; they hardly use the polytechnic library due to their perceptions of the resources and services of the

*Corresponding Author: A.O. Issa
Senior Lecturer
Department of Library and Information Science
University of Ilorin, Nigeria
Email: lanrewajuwahab@gmail.com

library. They are, to a greater extent, aware of open access initiatives, but do not publish in open access outlets, while various challenges affect their access and use of information resources for teaching and research. A recommendation was made, among others, that the polytechnic management should pay more critical attention to the library especially in the areas of adequate, current and comprehensive collections on all the programmes of the institution, as well as the provision of wireless internet services on the campus through a public-private partnership arrangement.

Keywords: Information Environment, Open Access, Lecturers, Federal Polytechnic Offa

1. INTRODUCTION

The concept of information environments has to do with factors associated with, and surrounding access to, as well as use of information resources by different categories of individuals in society. These factors include information needs, information seeking behavior, sources of information and challenges of accessing information and its resources. According to Mooko and Aina (2007), investigation in the context of information environments includes not only the information needs, but also the information seek-

ing behaviors, access to information and sources of information, used for meeting the information needs of users, which could either be heterogeneous, such as with rural inhabitants and artisans, or homogenous, as with students, professionals, policy makers, researchers, and lecturers. Uhegbu (2007) posits that understanding a user's information environment will help to place the information provider in a better stead to appreciate the psychology of a user in relation to his or her information seeking behavior. Diagrammatically, he represents the information environment of users as follows:

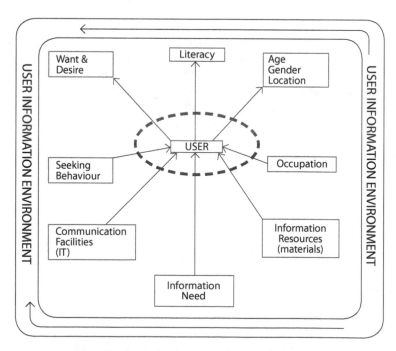

Fig. 1 Information Environment of Users (Uhegbu, 2007)

The Federal Polytechnic, Offa, Kwara State, Nigeria, is among the federal government-owned polytechnics in Nigeria. Established in 1992, it has five faculties namely: Applied Sciences and Technology, Communication and Information Technology, Business and Management Studies, Engineering Technology, and Environmental Studies, with twenty academic departments offering courses leading to the award of both National Diploma (ND) and Higher National Diploma (HND) certificates. In addition, there is a Faculty of General Studies, which is responsible for teaching students compulsory general studies courses such as citizenship education, communication skills, and use of the English language.

A study on the information environments will investigate issues surrounding the pattern of information seeking behavior, use, and contributions to the growth of knowledge in society. Information environments of lecturers, in this case, are limited to their information seeking behavior, perceptions of the resources and services of their major information sources, and the level of awareness and extent of use of open access (OA) initiatives for scholarly activities. Some investigations have taken place on the information environment of lecturers and users in various tertiary institutions in Nigeria such as universities, polytechnics and colleges of education (Adekunmisi, 2005; Igbeka & Atinmo, 2002; Odusanya & Amusan, 2003; Oyediran - Tidings, 2004; Nnadozie & Nnadozie, 2008), but are yet to be carried out in Federal Polytechnic Offa.

Whereas studies have been conducted on the information environments of professionals in their various fields and disciplines, especially those of lecturers in the universities in Nigeria, the polytechnic system has not been able to attract such research attention; and has thus suffered some form of neglect in this regard. Yet, a developing nation like Nigeria cannot truly develop technologically without a robust polytechnic system, which can only be by having in place a vibrant academic workforce among other vital ingredients. Their awareness and adoption of OAI are also key to sound academic callings. These concerns bring to the fore the issue of the state of the polytechnic library, which should be the predominant source of information for lecturers in such an environment. However, the literature is rather scanty on studies concerning the information seeking behaviors of polytechnic lecturers, the extent of their library use, their perceptions of the library resources and services, as well as their disposition to OA initiatives, a contemporary method of

scholarly communication geared towards challenging serials crises. Hence, the justification for this study, which sought to investigate the awareness and use of open access initiative at the Federal Polytechnic, Offa, Kwara State, Nigeria. Specifically, the study sets out to provide answers to the following research questions, namely:

i. What are the information seeking behaviors of lecturers at the Federal Polytechnic, Offa?

ii. How often do they seek information materials and services in the library?

iii. What are their perceptions of the resources and services offered by the library?

iv. What is the level of awareness and extent of use of Open Access Initiatives for scholarly activities among them?

v. What challenges do they face in information seeking and utilization for teaching and research?

2. REVIEW OF RELATED LITERATURE

The study of information environments as it relates to information needs and gathering behavior dates back to 1948, when Bernal and others presented a paper on scientific information at the 1948 Royal Society Conference (Tahir & Mahmood, 2008). Since then, a considerable body of literature has been produced dealing with information needs and information-seeking behavior of both individuals and groups in a variety of contexts (Anwar, Al-Ansari, & Abdullah, 2004). Also, studies have investigated the information-seeking behavior of library users in different information environments, subject interests, occupations, and geographical locations. Information needs and information-seeking behavior of academics have also been a popular area of research for information scientists for decades (Majid & Kassim, 2000). In Pakistan, for example, Tahir and Mahmood (2008) discovered that the purposes of information seeking by lecturers are for teaching and lecture preparation, guidance to students, and in support of research.

The Open Access (OA) model of scholarly communication is still in its infancy in Nigeria, as scholars, researchers, and lecturers are yet to fully adopt it. A study by Christian (2008) shows that over 73% of respondents in academic and research institutions in Nigeria is completely unaware and unfamiliar with the OA initiatives, let alone its adoption, usage and implementation. In their study, Utulu and Bolarinwa (2009) revealed that there was no significant use of OA resources among the academics studied. Similarly, studies by Ivwighreghweta and Onoriode (2012a, b, c) revealed that a good percentage of the lecturers surveyed at the University of Benin and Western Delta University, Oghara, as well as postgraduate students of the University of Ibadan, lack knowledge of OA journals. Identified major constraints to the adoption and use of OA initiatives were, among others, the unavailability of Internet facilities and lack of Internet search skills. Meanwhile, according to Gbaje (2010), efforts have been made via workshops in 2008 and 2009 at the Ahmadu Bello University, Zaria, to popularize the OA new model for scholarly communication in Nigeria. This was done in collaboration with Electronic Information for Libraries Network (www.elf. net). However, the impact is yet to be seen on the part of scholars publishing their findings in OA outlets.

In Nigeria, studies have also been carried out on the information environment of lecturers. Such information environments are job-related, specifically to teaching, research, and publications; and they vary according to lecturers' areas of specializations. Nnadozie and Nnadozie (2008) found out that lecturers' information needs are mainly in the area of teaching and research materials; and that the challenges encountered in information search include inadequacy of current and relevant information resources in the library, lack of ICT, incompetent staff, and shortage of reading spaces in the library.

3. HISTORICAL DEVELOPMENT OF OPEN ACCESS INITIATIVES

The open access initiatives (OAI) have had a history that is linked with the advent of the Internet, owing to its endless possibilities for information handling, including processing and distribution. The Internet has come to liberalize the publishing environment, by providing the tools to free scholars and authors from the unwanted and unwarranted access restrictions to information imposed by publishers, aforetime. The ultimate goal of the OA initiatives is the creation of an open knowledge society, where knowledge is seen as a common human heritage, which should be of benefit to all by being freely accessible and available. There is no doubt that the OA initiatives came at a time when libraries worldwide, especially those in developing countries, are undergoing difficult times occasioned by the increasing library budgetary cuts and soaring costs of subscriptions, thereby incapacitating their performance.

Specifically, the first free scientific online archive for physicists, called arXiv.org, and launched in 1991 by Paul Ginsparg, turned out to be forerunner of OA today. The initial fear that the attempt would affect journal subscriptions in Physics negatively was unfounded, after all, despite the fact that the articles are freely available on arXiv.org, usually before publication. Although the American Scientists Open Access Forum was launched in 1998, it was only in 2001 that the OA movement for the Life Sciences actually accelerated. That year, about 34,000 scholars all around the world, signed "An Open Letter to Scientific Publishers", which called for "the establishment of an online public library to provide the full contents of the published record of research and scholarly discourse in medicine and the life sciences in a freely accessible, fully searchable, interlinked form". The result was the establishment of the Public Library of Science, and its transformation into an open access publisher with a number of OA Journals.

However, the credit for the launching of the first global OA initiative went to the Budapest Open Access Initiative (2002) where the attendees signed an agreement to preferentially publish their findings in OA journals. This agreement still subsists and can be signed up to online today. There was also the 2003 Berlin Declaration on Open Access to Knowledge in the Sciences and Humanities, published after a conference, the ninth of which came up in 2011 in Washington, DC. The Scholarly Publishing and Academic Resources Coalition, an international alliance of academic and research libraries working to 'correct imbalances in the scholarly publishing system', also represents the OA movement.

The European counterpart called SPARCEUROPE also exists to promote OA at European universities and institutions, while NEBELAC is the platform used for collaboration between Europe and Latin-American Caribbean countries. The EU Commission for the Digital Agenda has also launched the OPENAire initiative in Europe, whereby scientists receiving European research grants are required to put their results in freely accessible repositories. The green road to OA has now been adopted by universities and institutions worldwide. Many of them have either made commitments to OA, or are in the process of reviewing their policies and procedures. The renowned Harvard and Princeton universities have also joined this group (Olijhoek, 2011).

Open Access journals, known as the "Gold Road" to open access, are peer-reviewed journals that are made available free of charge to the public through the Internet in open access publishing, where the end user is not charged to access journal articles. The initiative operates on such funding strategies as direct author fees, institutional membership to sponsor all or part of author fees, funding agency payments of author fees, grants to open access publishers, and institutional subsidies to offset the costs of publication (Ivwighreghweta & Onoriode, 2012). Studies in this area have highlighted the benefits of OA journals as including free access to information, and increased research impact (measured by citations/downloads) of open access articles versus non-open articles (Antelman, 2004), a possible solution to the so-called "serial crisis" or "journal affordability problem". Okoye and Ejikeme (2010) also identified the benefits of using open access journals as including the provision of increased citation to published scholarly work; free publishing of articles by authors, increasing the impact of researchers' work; online free of charge access to articles; provision of free online access to the literature necessary for one's research; helping in career development; and providing high quality scholarly work.

4. METHODOLOGY

This study adopted the survey design method with structured questionnaire as the tool for data collection. The population of academic staff in the polytechnic is 280 as of the 2011/2012 academic session (Academic Staff Union of Polytechnics, 2012). A sample size of 164 was chosen through the application of the formular of Yaro Yamane (1969) as found in Uhegbu (2009), thus:

$$n = \frac{N}{1+N(e)^2}$$

Where: n=the required sample; N=the total population; 1=constant; e=the level of significance or tolerable error, i.e. $(0.05)^2$

The structured questionnaire has part A, which is on the demographic data of respondents and part B, which

deals with the study objectives, with some aspects with a modified four-point Likert scale. Of the 280 academic staff of the polytechnic at the time of the study, 116 belong to the category of the newly recruited, the majority of who are in the lower cadre and so unsuited for the purposes of this study. Thus, the study's population came down to 164 completed. The justification of the study sample (164) from the population (280) was evidently representative considering the position of Edem (2005), referring to Krejcie and Morgan's sampling formula, which suggested that "a sample size of 384 will be sufficient for a population of 100,000; 370 for 10,000 and 248 for 700". Also, Ali and Denga (1989), while accepting that there is no universal rule for determining the appropriateness of sample sizes, stated that a sample should be about 15-30% of the population. Thus, the sample size of 164 or 58.57% of the population is considered adequate for the study.

5. THE FINDINGS

Out of the 164 copies of the questionnaire administered, 161 copies, representing 98.00% were properly completed, returned and found usable for the data analysis. Table 1 shows the demographic characteristics of respondents.

Table 1 shows that 74% of the respondents are males, as against 26% females; implying that there are more male lecturers in the institution than their female counterparts. The majority of the respondents fall in the age brackets of 41-50 (41.00%); followed by 51-60 (22.4%) and then 30-40 (21.1%). Those below 30 years of age constitute an insignificant 11.80% while those above 60 years had the least response rate of 3.7%. The implications of this finding is that the bulk of the academic staff in this polytechnic is still in their youthful and vibrant stage, which is a positive attribute for good teaching and research, being the hallmark of any higher institution.

Similarly, 27.10% of respondents had between 11-15 years of cognate experience and another 23.0% with experience of between 6-10 years, while those between 16-20 years constitute only 18.00%. Expectedly, those with between 21-25 years of experience had 11.80% while those with over 26 years had only 3.7%. These responses showed that the respondents are largely experienced and therefore likely to be matured on the job. This indicated

Table 1. Demographic Characteristics of Respondents

Demographic Characteristics of Respondents	Frequency	Percentage
Gender		
Male	119	74.0
Female	42	26.0
Total	161	100
Age Bracket		
Below 30	19	11.8
30 – 40	34	21.1
41 – 50	66	41.0
51 – 60	36	22.4
61 – above	6	3.7
Total	161	100
Years of Experience		
1 – 5	26	16.4
6 – 10	37	23.0
11 – 15	44	27.1
16 – 20	29	18.0
21 – 25	19	11.8
26 – above	6	3.7
Total	161	100
Status of Lecturers		
Assistant Lecturers and Lecturers III	34	21.1
Lecturers II and I	43	26.7
Senior Lecturers	36	22.4
Principal Lecturers	31	19.2
Chief Lecturers	17	10.6
Total	161	100
Distribution of Respondents by Faculty		
Applied Sciences and Technology	39	24.5
Business and Management Studies	28	17.4
Communication and Information Technology	20	12.6
Engineering Technology	32	19.9
Environmental Studies	24	14.9
General Studies	17	10.7
Total	161	100
Highest Academic Qualifications of Respondents		
HND and B. Sc.	39	24.2
Masters	115	71.4
Ph.D.	7	4.4
Total	161	100

that there is a very good spread regarding varying years of cognate working experience, which is a fundamental requirement for a vibrant academic institution.

However, the equation slightly changed when it came down to the ranks of the respondents, which tilted more towards Lecturers II and I with 26.7% followed by Senior Lecturers (22.40%), while Assistant Lecturers and Lecturers III had 21.1%. The top echelon of the institution's teaching staff, namely: Principal Lecturer (19.2%) and Chief Lecturers (10.6%) turned in the least number of responses; indicating that the institution's pyramidal structure of academic staffing is top-light and thus bottom-heavy. Though seemingly disadvantageous, this situation has been taken care of adequately by the good spread in the cognate years of experience possessed by the respondents, as revealed earlier on.

As for the distribution of respondents according to the various faculties in the institution, the Faculty of Applied Sciences contributed the highest number (24.5%), followed by the Faculty of Engineering Studies (19.9%) and then the Faculty of Business Studies (17.4%). The Faculties of Environmental Studies (14.9%), Communication and Information Technology (12.6%), and General Studies (10.7%) contributed the least responses in that order. Significantly, 71.4% of the respondents possess a Master's degree as their highest qualification 24.2% are with HND/BSc. and 4.4% are with Ph.D. These are in addition to a good percentage of them who are already on their PhD and Master's programmes.

Taking for granted that the respondents' information needs would naturally revolve around their primary duties and responsibilities of teaching, research, and community service, their information seeking behavior were sought, which led to the responses in the table below.

Given the variety of options to choose from, a majority engages in online information searching in cyber cafes (72.0%) or use their own modem to connect to the Internet (60.2%). However, as opposed to discussing with colleagues or consulting experts (23.6%), or sending people to do the search for them (11.1%), it is interesting to find that a significant 53.4% of others make visitations to the Polytechnic Library when searching for needed information. This indicates that the institution's library was considered relevant, to some extent, in spite of the attraction, which the Internet has come to represent for information users nowadays.

In contrast with the findings in Table 2, the data presented in Table 3 indicate that a majority claimed that they do not visit the library (38.6%) followed by those who only visit the library "occasionally" (30.5%). Thus, only 26% visit the library "often" while a 4.9% remainder indicated that they visit the library "very often" and "always".

The library's accommodations were not spacious enough as 34.2% and 27.3% disagreed and strongly disagreed, respectively. Worse still, was the conducive environment of the library for academic activities on which a majority 36.6% and 32.3% strongly disagreed, respectively. Progression along this line was recorded for the responses against the comfort of the library's chairs and tables where 37.2% and 33.6% strongly disagreed and agreed respectively. Even more so were their responses on the currency and quality of the library materials, to which 40.4% and 31.7% strongly disagreed and disagreed, respectively.

As for the cordiality of library staff in rendering necessary assistance to the users, a remarkable 52.2% strongly disagreed that the library staff possess this

Table 2. Information Seeking Behavior of Respondents

When in need of information, I:	Frequency	Percentage
Visit the polytechnic library for information	86	53.4
Visit the cyber café for online information search	116	72.0
Use my modem to link to the Internet	97	60.2
Discuss with colleagues and consult experts	38	23.6
Send people (assistants) to search for me	18	11.1

N=161

Table 3. Frequency of Respondents' Visits to the Polytechnic Library

I visit the Library:	Frequency	Percentage
Very often/always	8	4.9
Often	42	26.0
Sometimes/Occasionally	49	30.5
Never/Don't visit	62	38.6
Total	**161**	**100**

Table 4. Respondents' Perceptions of the Library's Resources and Services

In my opinion, the Polytechnic Library:	Strongly Agree (SA)	Agree (A)	Disagree (D)	Strongly Disagree (SD)	Total
has space enough to accommodate most users	26 (16.2%)	36 (22.3%)	44 (27.3%)	55 (34.2%)	161 (100%)
has a conducive environment for academic activities to thrive	20 (12.4%)	30 (18.7%)	52 (32.3%)	59 (36.6%)	161 (100%)
provides enough and comfortable reading chairs and tables	24 (14.9%)	23 (14.3%)	54 (33.6%)	60 (37.2%)	161 (100%)
stocks current, standard materials	17 (10.5%)	28 (17.4%)	51 (31.7%)	65 (40.4%)	161 (100%)
stocks materials in my area of specialization	21 (13.0%)	26 (16.2%)	47 (29.2%)	67 (41.6%)	161 (100%)
has friendly and cordial staff	31 (19.3%)	17 (10.5%)	29 (18.0%)	84 (52.2%)	161 (100%)
provides satisfactory services to the users	20 (12.5%)	22 (13.7%)	45 (27.9%)	74 (45.9%)	161 (100%)
provides satisfactory resources and services	12 (7.5%)	26 (16.1%)	71 (44.1%)	52 (32.3%)	161 (100%)

Table 5. Respondents' Awareness and Use of Open Access Initiatives for Scholarly Activities

Awareness and Use of OA Initiatives	Strongly Agree (SA)	Agree (A)	Disagree (D)	Strongly Disagree (SD)	Total
I am aware of OA initiatives and movements	36 (22.4%)	25 (15.5%)	43 (26.7%)	57 (35.4%)	161 (100%)
I am aware of many OA journals/resources on the internet	45 (28.0%)	59 (36.7%)	31 (19.3%)	26 (16.0%)	161 (100%)
I access and use OA resources in my teachings and research works	51 (31.6%)	44 (27.4%)	44 (27.4%)	22 (13.6%)	161 (100%)
I have excellent knowledge of citations and referencing of OA resources	21 (13.1%)	41 (25.4%)	47 (29.2%)	52 (32.3%)	161 (100%)
I have published my research works in OA journals	26 (16.1%)	22 (13.6%)	70 (43.5%)	43 (26.8%)	161 (100%)
Researchers should support the OA journals by publishing in them	98 (60.8%)	40 (24.8%)	10 (6.3%)	13 (8.1%)	161 (100%)

quality. Also, the services provided by the library were considered unsatisfactory as 45.9% and 27.9% strongly disagreed and agreed, respectively. It was therefore not surprising that 44.1% and 32.3% disagreed and strongly disagreed with the statement that the library's resources and services satisfied their needs.

On the respondents' level of awareness and extent of the use of OAI for scholarly activities, a majority 35.4% and 26.7% claimed lack of awareness of the initiatives and movements that started in 2002 for the free flow of knowledge and research findings for scholarly communication. However, 36.7% and 28.0%, respectively, claimed awareness of many OA journals. This may be due to the fact that respondents' familiarity with the Internet, overtime, would have exposed them to the existence of online OA resources, which also explains why 31.6% and 27.4% strongly agreed and agreed, respectively, to having had access to OA resources in their teaching and research works.

Regarding the respondents' possession of excellent knowledge of citations and referencing of OA resources, a majority 32.3% and 29.2%, respectively, claimed the lack of knowledge of these, which is a major setback for its use. It was, therefore, surprising that 43.5% and 26.8%, respectively, claimed to have published their research works, and papers in OA outlets, which seemed contradictory. In the end, a total of 85.6% respondents suggested the encouragement and support of OA initiatives in which researchers were enjoined to publish their works in furtherance of free flows of scholarly communication.

The major challenges affecting information access and utilization by the respondents, as contained in Table 6, and in order of significance are inadequate resources (74.5%), absence of Internet services (65.2%), and high cost of Internet subscription from major telecommunication companies (54.1%). This implies that the respondents' tendency for AO adoption through awareness and use would be greatly hampered by these factors.

6. DISCUSSION OF THE FINDINGS

The findings of this study showed that the information seeking behavior of the respondents are centered on the online environment. In other words, the lecturers prefer access to the Internet for online information resources. This is in contrast with the findings of Tahir and Mahmood (2008) where 77% of respondents prefer print-based information resources. However, these findings support those of Obuh (2009), which revealed that the attitudes of information users are focused on online use for desktop access to electronic information resources. That was why Ajala (2007) opined that information users resort, at a much greater cost, to cybercafés to satisfy their information needs, because they are aware of what the Internet provides. Thus, it can be inferred that for any library or information centre today to remain relevant and attractive to its users, it must provide access to, not only print-based collections, but also to online information resources.

The respondents' lack-luster attitudes towards library visits and use of its materials could be attributable to their negative perception of its resources and services, which they do not consider adequate to meet their needs. Indeed, the findings showed that the lecturers are not comfortable with the general resources and services provided by the library. This is closely related to the challenges affecting their access to information resources such as inadequate resources and absence of Internet access in the library. This supports the earlier findings of Nnadozie and Nnadozie (2008) that inadequacy of current and relevant information resources as well as lack of information and communication technologies hinder access and use of scholarly resources by academic staff of tertiary institutions in Nigeria.

The OA initiative for scholarly communication is, to a great extent, known to the lecturers; implying that

Table 6. Challenges affecting Respondents' Information Seeking and Utilization

Challenges	Frequency	Percentage
Inadequate information resources in the Polytechnic Library	120	74.5%
Absence of Internet services in the Library	105	65.2%
Cost of computer systems and Internet connectivity	46	28.5%
High cost of Internet subscription from telecommunication giants such as GLO,MTN,ETISALAT, and AIRTEL	87	54.1%
Poor computer skills and internet use skills	51	31.6%

N=161

they are familiar with contemporary trends in scholarly communication, with the claim that they access and use OA resources in their teaching and research works. This runs contrary to the findings of Christian (2008) and Utulu and Bolarinwa, but in line with that of Gbaje (2010). Meanwhile, the study also showed that although the lecturers are in support of OA initiatives support its continuation, they are not publishing their research works in OA journals and other OA outlets, thus contributing to weakening of the status of OA repositories in Africa (Ocholla, 2011). This may be attributed to concerns with copyright and plagiarism as noted by Gbaje (2010), not knowing that it is easy to detect plagiarism with online publications.

7. CONCLUSION AND RECOMMENDATIONS

From the study's findings, it is hereby concluded that lecturers at the Federal Polytechnic, Offa, have not fully imbibed the culture of adopting, using and publishing in OA platforms, in furtherance of the goal of their making research findings freely available the world over. This implies that this group of academics is yet to fully tap into the benefits of the OA initiatives. The study also revealed that the Polytechnic Library has not been in the fore-front of the OA crusade since it is yet to provide the e-platform for providing resources and services to its users, thereby discouraging, in turn, the use of the library by many of the lecturers. Thus, they hardly patronize the library due to their negative perception of its resources and services. Despite their awareness of the OA initiatives, they do not publish their works in OA outlets. Arising from the conclusions therefore, the study recommends that:

1. The polytechnic management should give adequate attention to the provision of current and adequate numbers of library resources for effective service provision to its users. This is with the view to positioning it as a 21st century learning resource centre for academic activities.

2. Specifically, the polytechnic library should be expanded to accommodate more users, while also providing ICTs and Internet services in the library for users, as well as engaging more active and service-driven librarians to re-engineer information services in the library.

3. Also, the polytechnic management should woo telecommunication service providers for the provision of wireless Internet services on campus. This could be done through public- private partnership between the polytechnic and service providers, whereby the method of operation that will be beneficial to the partners will be stipulated.

4. Seminars and workshops should be organized to sensitize lecturers on the essence of publishing in OA outlets. Information literacy programmes should also be organized at intervals for the lecturers so as to acquaint them with contemporary skills to function actively and optimally in the present knowledge-driven and OA society.

REFERENCES

Ajala, I.O. (2007). Internet awareness, accessibility and use by undergraduate and postgraduate students in Nigerian universities: a case study of Ladoke Akintola University of Technology, Ogbomosho, Nigeria. *The Information Technologist, 4*(2), 147-162.

Ali, C., & Denga, O. (1989). *Elements of Research Methodology.* Zaria: Gaskiya Publishing Ltd.

Anwar, M. A., Al-Ansari, H., & Abdullah, A. (2004). Information seeking behaviour of Kuwaiti journalists. *Libri, 54*(4), 228-236.

Adekunmisi, S. O. (2005). The information needs and information seeking behaviour of academic staff in the college of agricultural sciences, Olabisi Onabanjo University, Ayetoro, Ogun State. *Journal of Library and Information Science, 2*(1&2).

Christian, G.E. (2008). Issues and challenges to the development of open access institutional repositories in academic and research institutions in Nigeria. *A research paper prepared for International Development Research Centre, Ottawa, Canada.* Retrieved from http://idlbnc.idrc.ca/dspace/bitstream/10625/36986/1/127792.pdf

Edem, M. B. (2005). Library acquisitions of indigenous law textbooks and its utilization in selected federal universities as some factors influencing indigenous law textbooks publishing in Nigeria. Post Field Seminar. Department of Library, Archival and Information Studies, University of Ibadan.

March 15

Gbaje, E.S. (2010). Open access journal publishing in Ahmadu Bello University Zaria, Nigeria. *Paper presented at the 76ᵗʰ General Conference and Assembly of the International Federation of Library Associations and Institutions (IFLA)*, 10-15 August, 2010, Gothenburg, Sweden. Retrieved from www.ifla.org

Igbeka, J. U., & Atinmo, M. I. (2002). Information seeking behaviour and information utilization of agricultural engineers in Nigeria based on their different places of work. *Nigerian Libraries, 36*(1), 9-22.

Ivwighreghweta, O., & Onoriode, O. K. (2012a). Open access and scholarly publishing: Opportunities and challenges to Nigerian researchers. *Chinese Librarianship: an International Electronic Journal*, 33. Retrieved from http://www.iclc.us/cliej/cl33 IO.pdf

Ivwighreghweta, O., & Onoriode, O. K. (2012b). Awareness and use of open access journals by Lecturers at Western Delta University, Oghara, Nigeria. *Library Philosophy and Practice*: Retrieved from http://unllib.unl.edu/LPP

Ivwighreghweta, O., & Onoriode, O. K. (2012c). Awareness and use of open access journals by LIS Students at the University of Ibadan, Nigeria. *Library Philosophy and Practice*: Retrieved from http://unllib.unl.edu/LPP

Majid, S., & Kassim, G. M. (2000). Information-seeking behaviour of International Islamic University Malaysia Law Faculty Members. *Malaysian Journal of Library & Information Science, 5* (2), 1-17.

Nnadozie, C.O., & Nnadozie, C.D. (2008). The information needs of faculty members in a Nigerian private university: a self study. *Library Philosophy and Practice*. Retrieved from www.unllib.unl.edu/LPP/nnadozie_nnadozie

Mooko, N., & Aina, L.O. (2007). Information environment of artisans in Botswana. *Libri 57*, 27-33.

Obuh, A.O. (2009). Use of electronic resources by postgraduate students of the department of library and information science of Delta State University, Abraka, Nigeria. *Library Philosophy and Practice*. Retrieved from http://www.unllib.unl.edu/lpp/obuh.htm.

Ocholla, D.N. (2011). An overview of issues, challenges and opportunities of scholarly publishing in information studies in Africa. *African Journal of Library, Archival and Information Science, 21*(1), 1-16.

Odusanya, K. O., & Amusa, I. O. (2003). Information needs and information seeking habits of science lecturers at Olabisi Onabanjo University, Ago-Iwoye, Nigeria. *Journal of Library & Information Science, 1*(2), 50-55.

Olijhoek, T. (2011). *Open Access Week 2011: A Short History of Open Access*. Retrieved from http://www.openaccessweek.org/profiles/blogs/open-access-week-2011-a-short-history-of-open-access

Oyediran-Tidings, S.O. (2004). Information needs and seeking behaviour of library Users at Yaba College of Technology Lagos, Nigeria. *Lagos Journal of Library and Information Science, 2*(4), 77-88.

Tahir, M., & Mahmood, K. (2008). Information needs and information seeking behaviour of arts and humanities teachers: A survey of the University of Punjab, Lahore, Pakistan. *Library Philosophy and Practice*. Retrieved from www.unllib.unl.edu/LPP/tahir_mahmood

Uhegbu, A.N. (2007). *The information user: issues and themes*. 2ⁿᵈ ed. Okigwe, Nigeria: Whytem Publishers.

Uhegbu, A.N. (2009). *Research and statistical methods in library and information science*. Owerri, Nigeria: Barloz Publishers

Utulu, S.C.A., & Bolarinwa, O. (2009). Open access initiatives adoption by Nigerian academics. *Library Review, 58*(9), 660-669.

Patterns of Citing Korean DOI Journals According to CrossRef's Cited-by Linking and a Local Journal Citation Database

Tae-Sul Seo

Information Service Center,
Korea Institute of Science and
Technology Information,
Daejeon, Korea
E-mail: tsseo@kisti.re.kr

Eun-Gyeong Jung

Information Service Center,
Korea Institute of Science and
Technology Information,
Daejeon, Korea
E-mail: eunkog29@kisti.re.kr

Hwanmin Kim*

Information Service Center,
Korea Institute of Science and
Technology Information,
Daejeon, Korea
E-mail: mrkim@kisti.re.kr

ABSTRACT

Citing literature is a very important activity for scholars in writing articles. Many publishers and libraries build citation databases and provide citation reports on scholarly journals. Cited-by linking is a service representing what an article cites and how many times it cites a specific article within a journal database. Recently, information services based on DOIs (Digital Object Identifiers) have been increasing in number. CrossRef, a non-profit organization for the DOI registration agency, maintains the DOI system and provides the cited-by linking service. Recently, the number of Korean journals adopting DOI is also rapidly increasing. The Korea Institute of Science and Technology Information (KISTI) supports Korean learned societies in DOI related activities in collaboration with CrossRef. This study analyzes cited patterns of Korean DOI journal articles using CrossRef's cited-by linking data and a Korean journal citation database. This analysis has been performed in terms of publication country and the language of journals citing Korean journal articles. The results show that DOI, SCI(E) (Science Citation Index (Expanded)), and English journals are more likely to be cited internationally.

Keywords: Journal citation analysis, Korean journals, Reference linking, Digital Object Identifiers (DOIs), Publishing country, Publishing language

*Corresponding Author: Hwanmin Kim
Senior researcher
Information Service Center, Korea Institute of Science
and Technology Information, Daejeon, Korea
E-mail: mrkim@kisti.re.kr

1. INTRODUCTION

Many publishers and libraries build citation databases and provide citation analysis reports on scholarly journals. However, citation analysis depends on the size of citation databases determined by such variables as number of journals, preferential selection of citable journals, differential values to citations, and time duration. Citations also depend on wider accessibility and time of availability of the articles/journals to the researcher (Bharathi, 2011). Therefore, articles published through unknown journals are rarely cited.

Liu (1997) has reviewed literatures and categorized author citation practices into the following four major factors:

(1) *Physical accessibility*: If one is not aware of an article or cannot obtain it, it will not be read.

(2) *Cognitive accessibility*: If one faces difficulties in understanding an article, or cannot read the language in which it was published, identification of its content, quality, and significance will be unreliable.

(3) *Perceived quality*: If an article is considered to be of poor quality, it may be less likely to be cited.

(4) *Perceived significance*: If an article is not scientifically significant, it may be less likely to be cited, even though it is physically and cognitively accessible.

Meanwhile, the citation performance of Korean science in terms of the percentage of world share has been stagnant over twenty years while the Korean share of world publication output in the Science Citation Index has jumped from 40th in 1987 to 12th in 2007 (Kim, 2010). One of the reasons might be that most Korean journals are unknown to foreign researchers. Therefore, the Korean government has adopted policies to enhance Korean citation performance. One solution has been to increase the visibility of Korean science journals. However, many Korean journals are hardly known to foreign researchers and even to Koreans. These journals face difficulties in being cited except for citations by authors who not only are acquainted with Korean journals but also can understand articles written in Korean. Another possibility is that foreign authors can find Korean journal articles in the references of articles published in journals which are published in their own countries or are indexed on journal databases they use.

According to Liu's categorization, most Korean journals have weak points in physical and cognitive accessibilities; Korean journal articles are rarely read by foreign researchers because most of them are not included in famous journal indexes or databases and are published in Korean. This is so even when the quality or significance of the articles is high level.

CrossRef's DOI (Digital Object Identifier) system may provide Korean journals with an opportunity to increase citation rates through a reference linking service (Seo & Choi, 2011; Kim et al, 2012). CrossRef's cited-by linking service enables an author to know who is citing his or her article, to follow references, and to cite effectively by linking references of journal articles (Pentz, 2001). The number of DOI journals has been continuously increasing since November 1999 when CrossRef was established and is now even higher than those of Web of Science journals and SCOPUS journals. Therefore, Korean journals can have more opportunities to be cited by DOI journals worldwide. DOI became an ISO standard in 2012 (ISO, 2012).

KISTI, performing the function of a national scientific and technical information center, has been building Korean scientific and technical journal databases. As part of the internationalization of Korean journals KISTI has been participating in CrossRef since 2007 as a sponsoring member, which executes DOI works for Korean journal publishers or learned societies. DOIs of 76,472 journal articles in 191 journals published by 156 learned societies have been deposited by KISTI as of March 2012. In addition, KISTI has joined the CrossRef cited-by linking service, enabling authors to get a list of cited articles since 2009, and has applied it to scholarly information services at KISTI such as KoreaScience, which includes the landing (or response) pages of Korean DOI journal papers.

The number of Korean DOI journals, 191, is about 30% of the total of Korean scientific and technical journals registered with the National Research Foundation of Korea (NRF). The amount can be considered to be enough to estimate the effect of DOI business on Korean journals. Now it might be desirable to prepare materials for future business by analyzing how Korean DOI journals are cited.

The purpose of this study is to show the patterns of citing those Korean journal articles whose references are deposited in CrossRef using CrossRef's cited-by linking and a local citation database. It conducts the examinations of 1) how many articles cite Korean DOI journal articles in view of language written and country published; 2) comparison between CrossRef cited-by linking and the local citation database; and 3) comparison between SCI(E) and non-SCI(E).

2. PREVIOUS STUDIES

Citation analysis, a widely used method in bibliometrics, is the examination of the frequency and patterns of citations in scholarly literatures. Many researchers have conducted research for finding discernible patterns in citation such as preference of information type, information life cycle, collaborations among researchers, and demands for current information in academic fields or by researchers (Choi et al., 2011).

With regard to citing behavior, Bornmann and Daniel (2006) have reviewed studies on the citing behavior of scientists covering research published from the early 1960s up to mid-2005. They showed that the probability of being cited depends on non-scientific reasons such as time-dependent factors, field-dependent factors, journal-dependent factors, article-dependent factors, author/reader-dependent factors, availability of publication, and technical problems. Yue and Wilson (2004) developed an integrated conceptual model of journal evaluation from varying perspectives of citation analysis. They took into account in the model four external factors such as journal characteristics, journal accessibility, journal visibility, and journal internationality, together with journal citation impact. The model also includes non-scientific factors such as publication language of journals (Van Leeuwen et al., 2001) and author geographic location (Lancaster et al., 1990), which act as barriers for Korean journals in being cited internationally. However, as both studies predate DOI, neither takes it into account in journal-

dependent or journal accessibility factors.

There are some studies on citation patterns of Korean journals; several articles have conducted citation language analysis on Korean journals (Cho, 2010; Choi, 1996; Choi et al., 2011; Kim et al., 2011), while others include citation country analysis on Korean journals (Cho & Cho, 2005; Lancaster et al., 1990; Kim, 2002; Kim, 2003). However, all of the studies have conducted the citation patterns of Korean authors other than cited patterns of Korean journal articles. There are few studies which have conducted the patterns of citing Korean journal articles.

3. CITED-BY LINKING

CrossRef provides a reference linking service called 'cited-by linking.'[1] Reference linking is the general term for establishing links from one information object to another. Other systems, including Web of Science, SCOPUS, Google Scholar, and PubMed Central, have also been developed for reference linking services to provide citation information.

For enabling reference linking, each article has a unique identifier and URL (Uniform Resource Locator) (Lee & Lee, 2010). The publisher supplies metadata about each article to be stored in the databases (a reference database and a location database) as shown in Figure 1. Readers access the databases through the interactions shown in the figure. For each article, the reference database contains metadata corresponding to the information in a citation. Clients who wish to find the content associated with a reference send a query to the reference database. This database returns a list of identifiers for articles that match the query. A client sends an identifier to the location database, which returns one or more URLs. The client selects the URL to retrieve the object. This is known as "resolution" of the identifier. Although they fit within the parameters shown in Figure 1, most systems differ in detail. The NASA Astrophysics Data Service derives

---

[1] For more information on cited-by linking, visit http://www.crossref.org/citedby/index.html.

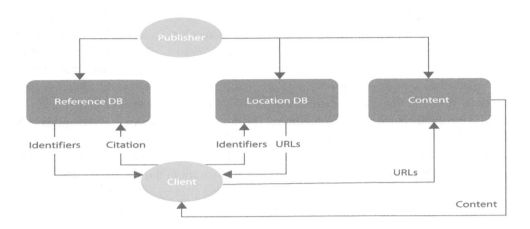

Fig. 1 Reference linking framework (Caplan & Arms, 1999)

references algorithmically, bypassing the reference database lookup. PubMed and the Web of Science combine the citation and location databases. PubMed's LinkOut experiment permits users to provide URLs in addition to those provided by publishers.

CrossRef uses the Handle System, which is capable of multiple resolutions[2] of DOI (Caplan & Arms, 1999). Publishers who wish to use the cited-by linking service of CrossRef are asked to deposit DOIs for references so that CrossRef can create reference linking. The process of cited-by linking for CrossRef members is as below:

1. Publisher A registers DOI 10.1234/X for article X with the following metadata: Journal= "Good Science", author="John Smith", volume="21", first page="100" year="2007"
2. Publisher B deposits metadata for article Y and assigns it DOI 10.5678/Y. The deposited references for article Y include the following:

```
<citation_list>
  <citation key="reference to article X">
```

```
    <author>Smith</author>
    <journal_title>Good Science</journal_title>
    <cYear>2007</cYear>
    <first_page>100</first_page>
    <volume>21</volume>
  </citation>
</citation_list>
```

3. The CrossRef system establishes a cited-by relationship between article X and Y
4. Publisher A later sends a query asking who 'cites' article X and is given the DOI for article Y and its metadata.

(source : http://help.crossref.org/#citedby_overview)

4. DATA SETS AND RESEARCH METHOD

Data sets from CrossRef and KISTI were used in this study rather than international citation databases such as Web of Science and SCOPUS.

First of all, the citation information from CrossRef has been regularly collected and processed according

---

[2] When there are several URLs to different copies of the article, the system is faced with selective resolution: the client may wish to select a specific version based on variations of content, different licensing arrangements, or network performance.

to the process as shown in Figure 2. CrossRef provides XML data containing cited-by relationships among DOIs as requested through a designated URL composed of a user ID, a password, and a DOI. Then, the XML data is parsed to create cited-by linking data which are to be stored in the analysis database. In order to conduct analysis related to SCI(E), language, and publication country, more data on journals, such as whether they are SCI(E) journal articles or not, what languages they are written in, and what countries they are published in, are also added to the analysis database.

nical journal articles together with a variety of information on articles such as bibliography, subject category, and citation relationship, while KJCR reports various indicators such as impact factor, immediacy index, ZIF, self-citing rate, and self-cited rates of journals in the form of tables and charts by which trends can be shown. Figure 3 shows the relationship of KSCD with KSCI and KJCR.

For comparison with KSCD, the scope of journals to be analyzed in this study was determined by the fact that the cited-by linking data of the journals are available from CrossRef in the same time the journals are

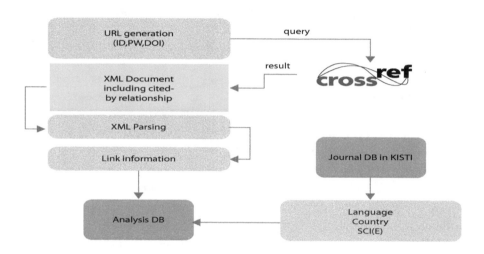

Fig. 2 Data processing flow for cited-by linking data

KISTI operates the Korea Science Citation Index (KSCI) and Korea Journal Citation Reports (KJCR) based on the Korea Science Citation Database (KSCD), which covers over seven million references from 376,700 journal articles published in 746 scientific and technical journals. KSCI is a portal site that provides searching and browsing of Korean scientific and tech-

included in KSCD. Consequently, a total of 53,147 articles from 68 journals published between 2002 and 2010 were selected and analyzed. 18 journals are indexed in Web of Science (8 journals) or SCOPUS (16 journals). 25 journals are published in English while others are in Korean.

For the analysis of publication countries, the number

Table 1. Data coverage of KSCD

Year	2002	2003	2004	2005	2006	2007	2008	2009	2010	2011	Total
No. journals	418	421	435	454	459	453	450	447	727	746	746
No. articles	30,040	32,392	33,918	34,584	35,100	34,251	35,721	36,818	51,071	52,805	376,700
No. references	501,271	543,948	592,121	597,158	644,418	660,001	699,593	726,580	1,054,121	1,115,590	7,134,801

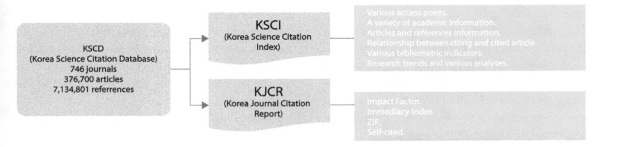

Fig. 3 Relationship of KSCD with KSCI and KJCR

of articles with the same publication country is counted. In this case, the publication country of an article means the country of the publisher who publishes the article. The analysis of publication language is also conducted through the same fashion of the analysis of publication country. The citation rates, used in comparisons between CrossRef and KJCR and between SCI(E) and non-SCI(E), are calculated based on KSCD including the references of the selected journal articles.

5. RESULTS AND DISCUSSION

5.1. Country and language

The most interesting pattern of citing Korean DOI journal articles must be how many foreign authors cite them. Publication country and publication language of journal articles citing Korean DOI journal articles can be indicators for that.

The total citation number reaches to 32,011 based on CrossRef's cited-by linking database. 74% of the total citation number was cited by articles of SCI(E) and SCOPUS journals. Figure 4 shows the distributions of publication countries of journal articles citing Korean DOI journal articles selected for this study. It shows that 44% (14,159) of the total citations came from Korean journal articles while the rest, 56% (17,852), came from foreign journal articles. In other words, Korean journal articles were cited by foreign journal articles about 12% more than Korean journal articles were (Kim et al., 2012). Among the foreign citation number, 46.4% are from the United Kingdom

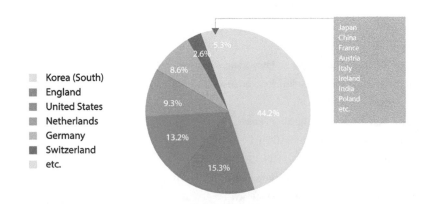

Fig. 4 Distribution ratios of publication countries of journal articles citing Korean DOI journal articles

(15.3%), United States (13.2%), Netherlands (9.3%), and Germany (8.6%), which have large international journal publishers.

The results show that quite a large number of foreign journal articles cite Korean journal articles even though some of the articles are written in Korean. Table 2 shows the top 20 foreign journals citing Korean DOI journal articles. The top journal is *ChemInform* published by Wiley & Sons, which cites over a thousand Korean DOI journal articles for nine years from 2002 to 2010. The results also show that six famous publishers publish the top 20 journals: Elsevier (10), Wiley (5), Royal Society of Chemistry (2), IOP (1), Taylor & Francis (1), and AIP (1).

There may be several motives for citing Korean journal articles. First of all, most citations of Korean DOI journal articles by foreign journal articles are probably contributed by SCI(E) and SCOPUS jour-nals. The remainder of citations might be from authors who are acquainted with Korean journals. Another possibility is that authors can refer to Korean journal articles in the reference lists of articles published in the journals which are published in their own countries or indexed on journal databases they use. However, more investigation is required to clarify the motives for cit-ing Korean journal articles.

Figure 5 shows the distributions of publication lan-guages of journal articles citing Korean DOI journal articles selected for this study. It shows that approxi-mately 70% of citations are from articles written in English whereas about 30% are from articles written in Korean. This shows that authors publishing their arti-cles in international journals written in English cite Korean DOI journal articles more than authors who are publishing in domestic journals written in Korean do.

Table 2. Top 20 foreign journals citing Korean journal articles (2002 - 2010)

Ranking	Journal name (Publisher)	Number of citing Korean DOI journal articles
1	ChemInform (Wiley)	1,195
2	Tetrahedron Letters (Elsevier)	554
3	Angewandte Chemie (Wiley)	186
4	Bioorganic & Medicinal Chemistry (Elsevier)	168
5	Chemistry - A European Journal (Wiley)	143
6	Tetrahedron (Elsevier)	134
7	Chemical Communications (Royal Society of Chemistry)	134
8	Journal of Molecular Structure (Elsevier)	126
9	European Journal of Organic Chemistry (Wiley)	121
10	Journal of Mass Spectrometry (Elsevier)	119
11	Food Chemistry (Elsevier)	111
12	Journal of Mathematical Analysis and Applications (Elsevier)	106
13	Biochemical and Biophysical Research Communications (Elsevier)	104
14	The Astrophysical Journal (IOP)	99
15	Synthetic Communications (Taylor & Francis)	98
16	The Journal of Chemical Physics (AIP)	98
17	Angewandte Chemie International Edition (Wiley)	93
18	Organic & Biomolecular Chemistry (Royal Society of Chemistry)	91
19	Applied Mathematics and Computation (Elsevier)	89
20	Journal of Chromatography A (Elsevier)	84

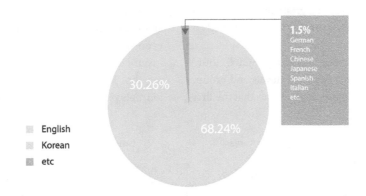

Fig. 5 Distribution ratios of publication languages of journal articles citing Korean DOI journal articles

5.2. Comparison with KJCR

One of the important aspects of citing Korean DOI journal articles may be the advantage of DOI journal articles compared with other journal articles without DOI. To show this, the citation pattern based on CrossRef cited-by linking is compared with that based on KJCR, even though some journals in KJCR may have DOIs.

Table 3 is a comparison between citations counted based on CrossRef's cited-by linking and KJCR. It shows that the total citation number from CrossRef's cited-by linking is lower than that from KJCR. It means that non-DOI journals have more impact than DOI journals in the scope of KJCR. However, as shown in Table 3, CrossRef's cited-by linking has an advantage over KJCR in the number of articles cited one or more times (other than citation number). This means that Korean DOI journal articles have more chances to be cited in international journal articles than journal articles without DOIs have, regardless of the citation rate. Therefore, the impact of DOI journals may also increase if the number of DOI journals increases in KJCR.

5.3. Korean vs. English

As Liu (1997) pointed out, publication language is an important factor when authors cite articles. The languages used in Korean journal articles are Korean and English. In this study which language is dominant and how the impact of journals with Korean and English as the publication language differs are examined.

When considering languages of articles deposited to CrossRef, articles written in Korean were cited more frequently by Korean journal articles (85%) than foreign journal articles (15%) were. Journal articles written in English, however, received more citations from foreign journal articles (80%) than Korean journal articles (20%) did, even those published by Korean learned societies, as shown in Figure 6. This shows that publication language is an important element for increasing international citation.

5.4. SCI(E) vs. non-SCI(E)

Finally, an interesting aspect of patterns of citing Korean journal articles is whether the journal being cited is indexed in a prestigious international database.

Table 3. Comparison between citation analysis results from CrossRef and KJCR

CrossRefs Cited-by		KJCR	
number of all citations received	number of articles cited one or more times	number of all citations received	number of articles cited one or more times
32,011	14,027	60,331	8,503

In this study the SCI(E) journal group and non-SCI(E) journal group in Korean journal articles deposited to CrossRef are compared.

As shown in Table 4, the first group, SCI(E) journals, has a higher citation rate than the second group, non-SCI(E) journals. A closer look reveals that the first

lication language and country analyses show that articles published by Korean journals are cited worldwide, even though the total citation number of 32,011 is insufficiently high for an international level considering that Korean authors can publish their articles in journals published in foreign countries or in other lan-

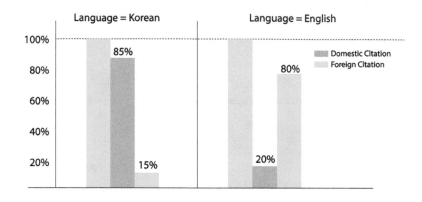

Fig. 6 Citation patterns with respect to publication language

group has a noticeably lower self-citation rate on average and a far higher citation rate from foreign journal articles and foreign SCI(E) journal articles than the second group has. The result shows that Korean SCI(E) journals are perceived as higher quality over non-SCI(E) journals, as generally expected.

One more interesting detail is that the citation rate from foreign journals of Korean SCI(E) journals is higher than that from SCI(E) journals, while the citation rate from foreign journals of non-SCI(E) journals is smaller than that from SCI(E) journals.

5.5. Summary

In this study how Korean journals are cited is investigated quantitatively in view of publication language, publication country, DOI, and SCI(E). First of all, pub-

guages. Regarding publication language, it is clear that articles published in English, which is widely accepted as an international language, have an advantage in receiving citations from international journal articles.

Comparison between Crossref's cited-by linking data and KJCR shows that KJCR has more citations than DOI journals do. This does not mean that Korean journal articles are cited more by articles in domestic journals than articles in DOI journals are, because citation numbers of DOI journal articles do not include other citations from articles in journals without DOIs, whereas those of KJCR includes all citations. On the contrary, the important conclusion derived in the comparison is that articles published in DOI journals have an advantage over articles published in journals without DOIs in their opportunities for citation.

Table 4. Comparison of citation rates between SCI(E) vs. non-SCI(E)

8 SCI(E) Journals				60 Non-SCI(E) Journals			
Citation rate	Self-citation rate	Citation rate from foreign journal articles	Citation rate from SCI(E) journal articles	Citation rate	Self-citation rate	Citation rate from foreign journal articles	Citation rate from SCI(E) journal articles
144%	14%	90%	87%	32%	51%	21%	24%

Finally, through comparison between SCI(E) and non-SCI(E), it is found that SCI(E) journals have more impact than non-SCI(E) journals do as generally known. Going into detail, eight SCI(E) journals among the Korean DOI journals have 4.5 times the impact of 60 non-SCI(E) journals.

6. CONCLUSION AND FUTURE WORK

In this study we obtained generic patterns of citing Korean DOI journals using CrossRef's cited-by linking and KJCR. The patterns are related with citation number and rate, and especially countries and languages of journals citing Korean DOI journals.

We can conclude the following:

1) Korean DOI journal articles are being cited by a considerable number of foreign journal articles.

2) Korean DOI journal articles are more likely to be cited in international journal articles than in journal articles without DOIs, regardless of the citation rate.

3) It is an effective strategy to change a journal's language to English in order to increase international citation of Korean journals.

Consequently, the purpose of this study has been achieved as discussed and concluded above. The results obtained in this study can be useful information for conducting DOI business and future research. But more detailed analysis is needed to obtain more concrete evidence for the effects of DOIs in international citation.

Additionally, we can conclude that the data set based on CrossRef's cited-by linking is useful in citation analysis. So it is desirable that more studies be conducted using CrossRef's data as research material incorporating Web of Science or SCOPUS data.

This study may also have limitations due to its narrow coverage of Korean DOI journals. Therefore, a further study with a much broader scope is desirable in the future in order to obtain more reasonable results and also to clarify the motives for citing Korean journal articles.

ACKNOWLEDGEMENTS

This research was performed as a part of the 2013 KISTI project, "S&T Content Construction and Service."

REFERENCES

Bharathi, D. Gnana. (2011). Methodology for the evaluation of scientific journals: aggregated citations of cited articles. *Scientometrics, 86*, 563-574.

Bornmann, L., & Daniel, H.-D. (2006). What do citation counts measure? A review of studies on citing behavior. *Journal of Documentation, 64*(1), 45-80.

Caplan, P., & Arms, W. (1999). Reference linking for journal articles. *D-Lib Magazine* (online), July/ August. Retrieved from: http://www.dlib.org/dlib/july99/07caplan.html

Cho, H.-Y. (2010). A comparative study on researchers' language preference for citing documents in different subject fields. *Journal of the Korean BIBLIA Society for Library and Information Science, 21*(1), 212-221.

Cho, H.-Y. & Cho, H.-S. (2005). A comparative study on the citing behavior of scholars in four major engineering fields. *Journal of Information Management, 36*(2), 1-24.

Choi, S.-H., Kim, B.-K., Kang, M.-Y., You, B.-J., Lee, J., & Park, J.-W. (2011). A study of citing patterns of Korean scientists on Korean journals. *Journal of the Korean Society for information Management, 28*(2), 97-115.

Choi, S.-Ki. (1996). Comparative study on citation analysis in the field of mechanical engineering in Korea and Japan. *Journal of the Korean Society for Information Management, 13*(2), 121-142.

International Organization for Standardization. (2012). ISO 26324:2012 Information and documentation -- Digital object identifier system.

Kim, B.-K., Choi, S.-H., Kim, S.-Y., & Seo, T.-S. (2012). Citation analysis of Korean journal articles based on Digital Object Identifiers. *Proceedings of the 8th International Conference on WIS* (pp. 395-399). Seoul: KISTI.

Kim, B.-K., Kang, M.-Y., Choi, S.-H., Kim, S.-Y., You,

B.-J., & Shin, J.-D. (2011). Citing behavior of Korean scientists on foreign *journals in KSCD. Journal of the Korean Society for information Management, 28*(2), 117-133.

Kim, H.-R. (2003). A study on the citation analysis of the information resources on science & technology. *Journal of the Korean Society for Information Management, 20*(4), 1-21.

Kim, K. (2002). The co-occurrence phenomenon of both Korean and Non-Korean literatures within the Korean References: An analysis on the citation motivations and references by social scientists. *Journal of KLISS, 36*(4), 21-47.

Kim, M.-J. (2010). Visibility of Korean science journals: an analysis between citation measures among international composition of editorial board and foreign authorship. *Scientometrics, 84*, 505-522.

Lancaster, F. W., Kim, S.-Y., & Diluvio, C. (1990). Does place of publication influence citation behavior? *Scientometrics, 19*(3-4), 239-244.

Lee, Y.-S., & Lee, S.-G. (2010). The Reference Identifier Matching System for Developing Reference Linking Service. *Journal of Information Management, 41*(3), 191-209.

Liu, Z. (1997). Citation theory in the framework of international flow of information: new evidence with translation analysis. *Journal of the American society for information science, 48*(1), 80-87.

Pentz, E. (2001). Brief communication: reference liking with CrossRef. *Interlending & Document Supply, 29*(1), 20-23.

Seo, T.-S., & Choi, H.-Y. (2011). Global dissemination of domestic scholarly journals using DOI and open access. *Journal of Information Management, 42*(4), 1-15.

Van Leeuwen, T. N., Moed, H. F., Tijssen, R. J. W., Visser, M. S., & Van Raan, A. F. J. (2001). Language biases in the coverage of the science citation index and its consequences for international comparisons of national research performance. *Scientometrics, 51*(1), 335-346.

Yue, W., & Wilson, C. S. (2004). Measuring the citation impact of research journals in clinical neurology: a structural equation modelling analysis. *Scientometrics, 60*(3), 317-332.

5

Henry Fayol's 14 Principles of Management: Implications for Libraries and Information Centres

C. P. Uzuegbu *

Department of Library and Information Science
Michael Okpara University of Agriculture
Nigeria
E-mail: chimezie.patrick.uzuegbu@gmail.com
       fortenews@yahoo.com

C. O. Nnadozie

Department of Library and Information Science
Michael Okpara University of Agriculture
Nigeria
E-mail: cnnadozie2000@yahoo.com
       chumannadozie2000@gmail.com

ABSTRACT

This paper focuses generally on the 'fourteen principles of management' by Henri Fayol. However, it specifically analyses their application to and implications for libraries and information centres. An extensive review of published works on management generally, and library management in particular, was conducted. This yielded vital insights on the original meaning and later modifications of these principles, as well as their application in the management of various organisations. Consequently, the strengths and weaknesses of these principles were examined to determine their suitability in libraries and information centres. Inferences, illustrations, and examples were drawn from both developed and developing countries which gives the paper a global perspective. Based on available literature, it was concluded that Fayol's principles of management are as relevant to libraries as they are in other organisations. The paper, therefore, recommends that in addition to modifying some aspects to make these principles more responsive to the peculiar needs of libraries, further research should be undertaken to expand the breadth of these principles and ascertain their impacts on the management of information organisations.

Keywords: : Library Management, Management Principles, Library and Information Centres, Henry Fayol

*Corresponding Author: C. P. Uzuegbu
Lecturer
Department of Library and Information Science
Michael Okpara University of Agriculture, Nigeria
E-mail: chimezie.patrick.uzuegbu@gmail.com
       fortenews@yahoo.com

1. INTRODUCTION

An organisation can be defined as a group of people who collectively undertake certain actions such as planning, arranging, coordination, structuring, administration, organizing, management, logistics, and the like, in order to achieve a pre-determined goal. An online business dictionary (www.businessdictionary.com) affirms that the word *organisation* is synonymous with words such as: firm, business, company, institution, establishment, corporation, etc. Hence, an organisation can be a business or a government department. In other words, organisations can be private or public; small, medium or large-scale; profit or non-profit oriented. They can also specialize in different endeavours such as manufacturing, repackaging, sales, services, and so on. Library and information centres, as distinct departments of government and non-government institutions, are prime examples of service providing organisations. They are public-service kind of institutions and are comprised of men and women of defined and related knowledge backgrounds, who collectively pursue a goal of providing information services to particular groups of people at different places and times.

In view of this, library and information centres are not completely different from other organisations. All organisations require management to succeed. Management as defined by several researchers and scholars can be summarized as the judicious use of *means* to accomplish an *end* (Stroh, Northcraft, & Neale, 2002). Right from the late eighteenth century to the early nineteenth century, the importance of management as a factor that determines organisational success has all along been buttressed (Robinson, 2005; Witzel, 2003). Several experiments were conducted by different people such as Frederick Taylor, Henri Fayol, Max Weber, Elton Mayo, Abraham Maslow, Douglas McGregor, among others. These theorists are today regarded as the forerunners of management scholarship. The results of their experiments and/or experiences at the earliest industries and companies in Europe and America led to the postulations of several management principles, also called theories or philosophies. However, popular among the several management principles postulated by the management forerunners is Henri Fayol's '14 principles of management' (Witzel, 2003).

The popularity and wide adoption of Henri Fayol's management principles led to his being nicknamed the *father of modern management* (Witzel, 2003; Wren, Bedeian, & Breeze, 2002). Henri Fayol was a French engineer who lived from 1841-1925. Early in life, at about 19 years of age, he followed after his father's engineering profession. He enrolled and graduated from a mining academy in 1860 and took up a mining engineering job in a French mining company. By 1888, Fayol became the director of the company which he later turned around to become the country's biggest industrial manufacturer for iron and steel with over 10,000 staff in 1900. Fayol directed the affairs of this mining company until 1918 (Fayol, 1930; Pugh & Hickson, 2007). As a sequel to his wealth of experience and series of research endeavours, in 1916 Henri Fayol published the '14 principles of management' which later appeared in his boo *Administration Industrielle et Générale* in 1917 (Faylol, 1917; 1930).

Management researchers over the years opine that the '14 principles of management' propounded by Fayol is what metamorphosed into present-day management and administration, especially after 1949 when his book was translated from French to English, as *General and Industrial Administration* (Rodrigues, 2001; Fayol, 1949; Wren, Bedeian, & Breeze, 2002). It is believed also that every organisation on the globe today is influenced by Fayol's principles of management given their applicability to burgeoning administrative formation without which there will be no organisation - as a group of people pursuing a collective goal. It is on this premise, therefore, that this paper is set to critically analyse the implications of Fayol's 14 principles of management as culled from his 1949 publication (Fayol, 1949) with a view to highlighting their implications to the administration of library and information centres.

2. HENRY FAYOL'S 14 PRINCIPLES

2.1. Principle 1: Division of Work

Henry Fayol's first principle for management states that staff perform better at work when they are assigned jobs according to their specialties. Hence, the division of work into smaller elements then becomes paramount. Therefore, specialisation is important as staff perform specific tasks not only at a single time but as a routine duty also. This is good to an extent. In library and information centres, there are such divisions of work. The Readers' Services Department of the library (variously called User Services, Customer Services, Public Services, etc.) also divides its vast jobs into departments and units. Not only has this point been substantiated by other writers, it has also been proved to be applicable to Technical Services Departments (Aguolu & Aguolu, 2002; Ifidon & Ifidon, 2007). Fayol, no doubt, was accurate in his division of work principle in the sense that all jobs cannot be done together by all staff at the same time. Besides, efficiency and effectiveness of work are better achieved if one staff member is doing one thing at a time and another doing a different thing, but all leading to the same collective goal, at the same time. By this, work output can be increased at the end of a given time, especially in a complex organisation where different kinds of outputs altogether count for the general productivity of the organisation. Similarly, taking the cataloguing room of a library for instance, this principle also mandates that as one or two persons catalogue the books, another puts call numbers on them and another registers the titles as part of putting them together and readying them to move to the circulation wing. Even at that same time, another person at the circulation department may be creating space for their recording, shelving, and so forth. This is division of work and at the end of a day's work, the amount of jobs executed for the day can be more meaningful than when every staff member is clustered for each of the job elements, one after another. By implication therefore, staff are assigned permanent duties and are made to report to that duty every day.

However, as observed in recent library practices, some proactive librarians act contrary to this as they, from time to time, reshuffle staff in a way that takes staff to fresh duties. Critically, the era of staff staying put in a particular office or duty-post is nowadays obsolete given the nature of contemporary society. This points to the fact that current management practices in libraries no longer support that method (Senge, 1990) and the reasons are clear. First, in the library and information science profession, the practice of specialisation in one area or aspect is not clearly defined in the first instance. For instance, this is evident in the professorial titles accorded to professors in the library and information science discipline. Many of them are not tied to any specific library and information science research area by their professorial title compared to what obtains in other science, engineering, and social science disciplines. Likewise, in the classroom, even at the research degree level, scholars' research will often be informative of their possible areas of specialisation. But in practice (working in any library and information centre) it is rarely demonstrated. This is one internal point against the staff of libraries staying put in a specific job element for a long time and, for others, all through their service time. After all, teaching and learning in library and information science is generalized in content and scope and thus tends to produce men and women who can take up any job design in the practice of librarianship. So, library managers who allow staff to remain on a given job schedule on the excuse of specialisation may be dwindling job efficiency.

Secondly, judging from observations of the twenty-first century management style, generalisation of job design is advocated contrary to specialisation. Studies conducted in service rendering organisations show how managers in Western countries design jobs to suit all staff (Rodrigues, 2001). Thus, no single job design in today's organisations requires core specialised staff to execute. Going by the evolution of machines, as we can also see in their introduction in library and information centres in the form of computers, automation, digitalization, and so forth, employment of staff is per their ability to use the machines to execute any job in the organisation. Yet, this does not mean that there is no division of work. There is still a division of work formulas but the modification is that staff are now managed to work in any division at any time because of the generalization of the work design. Take the OPAC system for example: there may not be a need to have staff job-tied to the cataloguing workroom because the OPAC system, as a typical job design platform, will allow any staff from any department to add and/or delete content on the library database. So, library and information centres managers should note the paradigm shift from division of work via specialisation to division of work via generalization.

2.2. Principle 2: Authority

This principle suggests the need for managers to have authority in order to command subordinates to perform jobs while being accountable for their actions. This is both formal and informal and is recommended for managers by Fayol. The formality is in the organisational expectations for the manager (his responsibilities), whereas the informality (the authority) can be linked to the manager's freedom to command, instruct, appoint, direct, and ensure that his or her responsibilities are performed successfully. Again, the two are like checks and balances on the manager: he must not abuse power (authority). He must use it in tandem with the corresponding responsibility. Thus, Fayol believed that since a manager must be responsible for his duties, he should as well have authority backing him up to accomplish his duties. This is correct and quite crucial to organisational success.

In library and information centres, such is the case also. The Librarian-in-Charge is responsible for the affairs of the library and has corresponding authority to oversee it. Likewise, his or her deputies, departmental heads, and unit officers are accorded the same in their respective capacities. This makes the work flow smoothly. But by implication, the respective subordinates such as the assistant librarians, library officers, and library assistants or others, as the case may be, become bottled up in the one-man idea cum direction of the librarian. Unfortunately, most departmental heads become so conceited with their status, responsibility, and authority that they do not find it necessary to sometimes intermingle and relate with their staff. As a result, an icy relationship develops with attendant negative consequences, especially industrial disharmony and unwillingness of parties to share knowledge (Ohadinma & Uwaoma, 2000). This may not be in the interests of the library given the saying that "two ideas are better than one" (http://idioms.thefreedictionary. com/).

More so, it is the junior staff members that interact with the practical jobs daily and are likely to regularly have something new in the field to teach the head. Obviously then, there is need for a managerial amendment on this principle. The emphasis should no longer be on power to command subordinates. Rather, it should be on encouragement of staff participation and motivation to take some initiatives. As the research by Blackburn and Rosen (1993) shows, award-winning organisations in the world apply participatory management and staff empowerment against the authority and responsibility principle. With this style, managers and their deputies act more as coordinators rather than dictators. Hence, library and information centres may not need the control-freak type of headship but preferably an orchestra-kind of leadership. Such leadership style will accommodate ideas, innovativeness, meaningful contributions, and freedom of expression from the junior staff, which research has shown to have positive contributions to the growth and success of an organisation (Blackburn & Rosen, 1993).

2.3. Principle 3: Discipline

This principle advocates for clearly-defined rules and regulations aimed at achieving good employee discipline and obedience. Fayol must have observed the natural human tendencies to lawlessness. He perceived the level of organisational disorder that may erupt if employees are not strictly guided by rules, norms, and regulations from management. This is true and has all along resulted in staff control in organisations. But in recent times, it has not been the best method to achieve long-term organisational order and goals. Management scholars have observed that peer group participation and other kinds of informal unions are now taking the control lead in organisations (Mintzberg, 1973). The individual differences amongst staff feared by Fayol, which no doubt led most organisations to break down because of a lack of formal and binding organisational rules or weak and poorly enforced codes of practice (Cavaleri & Obloj, 1993), are seemingly surmountable now through informal control systems. Workers unions and staff groups are getting stronger and stronger every day and have ethics guiding them. In organisations where they are allowed to thrive, management tends to have little or nothing to do towards staff control. As well, they can create resilient problems for managements who will not build a good working atmosphere with them. Yet, they have come to stay nowadays and become stronger every day rather than being suppressed by managements. Trade unionism by staff is, therefore, an element of the democratisation of industrial organisations and government establishments because it accommodates the opinions and interests of the worker in certain management decisions (Ohadinma & Uwaoma, 2000;

Iwueke & Oparaku, 2011). Thus, the use of staff groups or unions is an informal control system. It can help organisations to maintain discipline. One hidden advantage managements that adopt this system have is that they save cost and time *ab-initio* allotted to managerial discipline.

Likewise, in library and information centres, this informal system of discipline can be adopted. Librarians are to become less formal in discipline rather than trying to enforce institutional rules and regulations at all cost. Proactive librarians can have fewer headaches from staff rumours, gossip, and other forms of attack that usually emanate in the process of enforcing institutional rules and regulations. They can achieve this by trying the system of allowing staff to form group(s) in their libraries. For instance, a vibrant junior staff group or senior staff group in a library can go a long way to infuse cooperation, unity, trust, commitment, and order among its members to the benefit of the library as an organisation. As long as the top library management gives them the free hand to exist, they will set up rules that can unite the library organisation more than it can divide it. Anecdotal observation shows that libraries whose staff members are happy with the level of love shown them via visits, celebrating/mourning with them, and so forth are such that have groups or unions in their library. This point is supported by some reports in some management textbooks which clearly suggest that industrial unions help to sustain discipline among their members and sustain industrial harmony (Imaga, 2001; Iwueke & Oparaku, 2011; Ohadinma & Uwaoma, 2000). So, while some managers quickly conclude erroneously that unions exist to fight management and make unnecessary demands, library and information managers should note that such groups can help the system to achieve order and maintain discipline. This out-weighs or counter-balances the fears of their existence.

2.4. Principle 4: Unity of Command

This principle states that employees should receive orders from and report directly to one boss only. This means that workers are required to be accountable to one immediate boss or superior only. Orders-cum-directives emanate from one source and no two persons give instructions to an employee at the same time to avoid conflict. And, no employee takes instructions

from any other except from the one and only direct supervisor. This tends to be somehow vague. Fayol was not explicit to show if it means that only one person can give orders or whether two or more persons can give instructions/directives to employees but not at the same time. If the case is the former, this principle is rigid and needs modification, especially in consonance with current realities in many organisations.

Looking at the prevalent situations in most organisations nowadays where work is done in groups and teams, it simply suggests that each group will have a coordinator or supervisor that gives orders. And, this coordinator is not the sole or overall manager. Likewise, in some complex establishments, staff belonging to a given work team would likely take orders from various coordinators at a time. For instance, the head of a Finance Department can give instructions to staff relating to finance; the Electrical Department head can do the same to the staff also relating to power and vice-versa. Thus, in large and small organisations, it is not unusual for a staff member to receive instructions from superiors outside his/her immediate units/sections or departments (Nwachukwu, 1988). In a library, the officer in-charge of cataloguing can instruct the Porter not to allow visitors into the cataloguing workroom; the circulation head can at the same time tell the Porter to watch out for a particular library user at the exit point of the reading hall. These are two different orders from different departments. The Porter, by this, would not say that he cannot take orders from any of them save the Chief Librarian or that only one of them should instruct him and not the two. The Porter may not effectively watch out for the suspected user and at the same have his eyes on the cataloguing workroom wing. However, tact is required as he/she is not expected to flagrantly flout the directives of superiors. The point being stressed is that in modern libraries and information centres, it has become conventional for staff to take orders from multiple bosses even as the primary job is discharged (Agoulu & Aguolu, 2002; Ifidon, 1979).

2.5. Principle 5: Unity of Command

This principle proposes that there should be only one plan, one objective, and one head for each of the plans. Of course, organisations run on established objectives (Drucker, 1954). But, this should not be misinterpreted with departments and units who seemingly have their specific objectives. What Fayol meant is that an organisation will naturally have central objectives which need to be followed and as well departmental and unit goals which also need to be reached in order to meet the unified objective.

Library and information centres are established to collect and manage the universe of information sources and provide information services to their users. But also, there are other goals from departments and units, sometimes differing from each other. This is in line with the job specifications and peculiar work routines of each of the various sub-systems that make up the library (Edoka, 2000; Nnadozie, 2007). However, the activities of each department or unit are aimed at supporting the library's central objective of providing information services to users. And for each of the departments to attain its goals, they set and implement multiple plans (not one plan). So Henri Fayol's original proposal that one plan should be pursued by one head only is no longer tenable. For example, the Circulation Department of the library has to offer lending services and also register library users. Does it mean that it will have separate heads because of the different assignments involved? No; it is true that plans are different, and in this case, one is set for how to register users and the other strategizes how to lend out library materials to people and ensure that they return them, or be responsible for not returning them on time or at all. Yet, that does not call for a separation in the job in terms of headship. Rather, what library managers should insist on is that department goals and plans should be pursued in an orderly manner so that staff will not have to get a special head for each plan of group activity. This approach to management is already in place in most libraries in Africa where few hands are used to deliver multiple tasks due to shortages of staff (Ifidon, 1979 & 1985).

2.6. Principle 6: Subordination of Individual Interests to Organisation's Interests

The interests of the organisation supersede every other interest of staff, individuals, or groups. Imperatively, employees must sacrifice all their personal interests for the good of the organisation. In other words, organisations should not tolerate any staff that are not committed to the organisation's objectives and

order even if it is to the detriment of personal and family interests. This is one hard way of pursuing organisational or corporate success. It may have worked before now, but it is not ideal any longer due to a series of reasons. First, Mayor (1933) and McGregor (1960) have shown that employees can do better at work when they are valued and shown a reasonable sense of belonging. Second, organisations are compliant to the inconsistency of change. They change their objectives as situations warrant and need their staff to adapt fast to the changes. And, one of the fastest ways to get staff to adapt and comply with organisational changes is to invest in the staff. Thus, staff training and retraining, which is at most times cost-effective for management, is not only an investment in the staff for the organisation to reap but also a commitment to staff personal development. During such training sessions, staff enjoy several benefits such as job security, payment of salaries, full sponsorship, and other allowances that makes staff happy and motivated to put in their best when they return from the training programme.

The application of this principle should not be frustrated in library and information centres. Library managers and administrators must learn to make staff work happily. Happy staff will always put in all their best at work. Ways of keeping staff motivated to work happily include, from time to time, showing a commitment to staff both formally and informally. Formal commitments can come from sponsoring staff to further training, short development courses, seminars, and conferences. Some informal commitments include holiday support packages for staff, open and regular communication, and flexibility to staff personal requests. Library managers and administrators also use these formal and informal incentives to show their staff a sense of belonging, thereby making them more productive (Ifidon & Ifidon, 2007). For instance, a staff member permitted to leave office early to pick up her children from school will be glad and, more often than not, reciprocate by a commitment to work during the periods she will be at work. On the contrary, a member that is not permitted to attend to such personal needs and is regimented to the opening and closing hours of work at the library may sit back in his office all day achieving nothing. If a psychological test is conducted on this case, the result may likely show that the latter staff member achieved nothing in the office, not primarily because he wanted to pay back the manager by not working, but more because he was not able to concentrate at work and even when he tried he could not focus because of where his mind was; this is especially so if the family need for which the excuse is denied is crucial. Productive library administrators ensure that an environment is created for staff to have a sense of appreciation, especially when they have some personal needs. Staff with such a sense of appreciation or recognition tend to put in their best in the discharge of their work and pursuit of the library's corporate goals (Aguolu & Aguolu, 2002). Thus, while it was held before that staff should give up their interests for the organisation, now the reverse is the case. This means that organisations commit itself to the interest of the staff so that they can be more productive and committed to the objectives of the organisation.

2.7. Principle 7: Remuneration

Payment of staff salaries should be as deserved. The salary should be reasonable to both staff and management and neither party should be short-changed. The salary of every staff member must be justifiable. A supervisor should receive more pay than line staff. Thus, whosoever management appoints to be supervisor takes more than the subordinates by virtue of his or her responsibilities. It does not really matter whether a subordinate works harder and is more productive than the supervisor. As long as management does not promote the subordinate he continues to receive lesser pay to what his boss gets even as he works more than his boss. The above generally encapsulates Fayol's position on remuneration.

However, this approach to the administration of the reward system is gradually giving way in contemporary library management practice. There is a noticeable modification in the application of this principle as it is arbitrary in nature (Ohadinma & Uwaoma, 2000). It is quite agreed that it will be inappropriate for a subordinate to receive more pay than his boss. So, management researchers have complemented Fayol's notion with a new modifications arguing that this system of remuneration discourages hard work and productivity (Cascio, 1987). As a result, the "performance based pay system" recommended by Wallace and Fay (1988)

is what is used nowadays. This pay system supports the idea that organisations should design a performance scale with which staff should be evaluated. Imperatively, productive staff get promoted and take more salary than non-productive staff. In a way also, this was Taylor's (1911) idea that has just re-surfaced. Taylor's idea supports hard work and extra commitment from the staff. His notion was that the more output from an employee, the more pay he receives. So, with this modification, every staff member receives a salary based on his or her measured output.

In present day library and information centres, this productivity measurement scale is adopted. In fact, the performance-based pay system is almost the norm everywhere. The only problem with some libraries and other information-related organisations is that they do not publish and/or orientate their staff on the measurement scaling or promotion criteria. Staff need to understand the criteria and have free access to the document. More so, library managers should as a matter of morality be just in the productivity measurement. Most librarians discourage their hardworking staff or make them resign for another job as they usually envy some member's speed of productivity and promotion. Some library managers and their deputies are in the habit of comparing the number of years a hardworking and productive staff member has spent on the job with the many years some lazy and unproductive staff have given on the same job as a reason for why the former should not rise faster or even above the latter. This point has been raised in some library science textbooks where non-adherence to the principles of the performance-based reward system has been faulted (Aguolu & Aguolu, 2002; Edoka, 2000). Library managers should, therefore, avoid sentiments and award promotions to whoever has worked for them as many times as their hard work qualifies them. This is crucial if a library must retain the best staff and survive in a highly competitive information environment.

2.8. Principle 8: Centralisation

This principle suggests that decision-making should be centralised. This means that decision-making and dishing-out of orders should come from the top management (central) to the middle management, where the decisions are converted into strategies and are interpreted for the line staff who execute them (decentralisation). This is still working in many organisations. Library and information centres also apply this principle. For instance, it is conventional for the Librarian-in-Charge to hold meetings with deputies and/or departmental heads to initiate broad policy guidelines while the deputies and departmental heads take management decisions to their departments and units where they are finally executed and monitored (Ifidon & Ifidon, 2007). Nonetheless, management researchers have found another system which is working for many western organisations. Blackburn and Rosen (1993) observe that successful organisations in the United States of America (USA) apply a group decision making and implementation system. This means that units and departments make decisions and strategize their implementation based on their task, control focus, and job specifics.

Bringing this to the library may nevertheless not be so clear, especially in the beginning. But if it can be tried, it means that library departments will be empowered to meet weekly or monthly, and to make decisions as relating to their department, design their jobs, and draw their roster and schedule of duty. Later on, the decisions and plans of the department will be forwarded to the Librarian-in-Charge for immediate input and approval. Such a system of decision making allows for innovativeness and broad thinking among staff of all levels and also allows the Librarian to be less burdened with the library's daily complaints. As well, librarians can have time to attend the numerous institutions' meetings which they are statutory members of by reason of their position. However, it should be noted that the group decision making system cannot survive in bureaucracy—a system where mails are delayed for long. The Librarian must be committed to treating mail every day. In his absence, he should appoint someone to deputize him. This is because the work group decision-making system requires management to approve or make input to the group's decision before they can commence work. Take for instance where the Digital Library Department of a library has met and taken a decision to be closed to users for three days to enable them to embed an anti-pornography firewall on their server system in order to save it from unauthorized downloads that may crash the server. The decision mail reached the Librarian's desk and for many days it was yet to be treated. Although oral communication to the Librarian can be faster in this case, in a management system where records are necessary for actions, the Librarian's delay in treating the mail would not do any good to the group's decision. So, while the system is good, it requires promptness on actions from both management and staff. Thus, Fayol's 'principle of centralisation' is like a trickle-down decision flow, routing decisions from top to the bottom. But the work group decision system suggested therein is a bottom-up movement, which allows the staff to initiate ideas and job specific decisions for the organisation.

2.9. Principle 9: Scalar Chain

This principle is a product of the formal system of organisation. It is also known as the hierarchy principle. It asserts that communication in the organisation should be vertical only. It insists that a single uninterrupted chain of authority should exist in organisations. Horizontal communication is only allowed when the need arises and must be permitted by the manager. This vertical organisational and communication arrangement is the conventional practice in most library and information centres where orders and similar directives flow from the Librarian-in- Charge to the Deputy Librarians, to the Departmental Heads, and to the Unit or Sectional Heads, respectively (Edoka, 2000; Nnadozie, 2007). This is a four-layer hierarchy. It is neither twelve nor three layers, as Braham (1989) argues that a three-layer organisational hierarchy does better and faster than a twelve-layer hierarchy. Also, it has been shown in research that US-based organisations that practiced one-layer hierarchy systems recorded far better results than others that operated three-layer systems and above (Hinterhuber & Popp, 1992). Nowadays, a horizontal or flat management hierarchy system is advocated against the vertical order canvassed by Henri Fayol. The argument is that the former helps organisations to take decisions and implement them faster without unnecessary bottlenecks, contrary to what is observed in the later. Should this be applied in library and information centres, the implication is that the relatively vertical hierarchy order in most libraries should be displaced with the flat or horizontal hierarchy system. Figure 1 is a comparative illustration of a typical vertical organisational structure and the horizontal alternative being proposed.

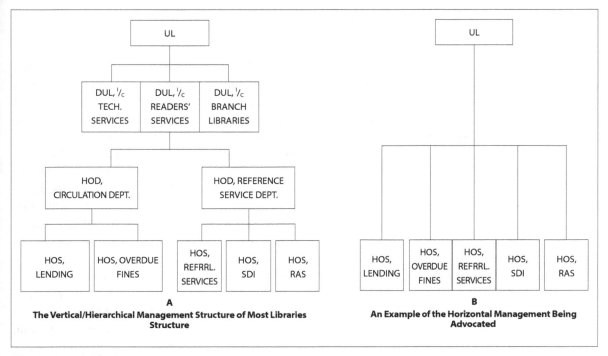

A
The Vertical/Hierarchical Management Structure of Most Libraries Structure

B
An Example of the Horizontal Management Being Advocated

KEY: UL = University Librarian
DUL = Deputy University Librarian
HOD = Head of Department
HOS = Head of Section
SDI = Selective Dissemination of Information
RAS = Readers' Advisory Services

Fig. 1 Scalar chain diagram illustrating Fayol's vertical order and the proposed horizontal order

Based on the above illustration, coupled with the new management findings that a horizontal organisational hierarchy allows for faster decision making and implementation than the vertical order system, library and information centres may have to operate a horizontal hierarchy system (Fig. 1 Diagram B) henceforth. The present system of having divisional heads, departmental heads, and in some cases, unit or sectional heads also (Fig. 1 Diagram A), may have to give way for a flat order where it will only be the Librarian-in-Charge and, most directly, the unit/sectional heads (as per specific job element or focus). However, this may not be welcomed by librarians in some institutions and countries where the deputy and departmental heads positions attract office allowances and other appurtenances. Yet, we must be realistic; such ladders on the management chart may not be helpful for library organisation in the nearest

future. But, this one thing can be done also: break down the vertical order (Diagram A) into a flat order (Diagram B), increase the Sections/Units based on job specifics and call them Departments (which is more conventional), and redistribute the office heads in the initial vertical order to head the departments. This way, the fear of losing office/headship allowances and other benefits is averted. The beauty of the horizontal organization being advocated lies in its adaptability to the peculiar needs of both small and large libraries (Ifidon & Ifidon, 2007). Besides, most library staff are at home with its flexibility bearing in mind that positions attained by promotion (such as Senior Librarian or Deputy Librarian positions), are not in any way to be affected in the horizontal system. Hence, Mr. A can be an Assistant Librarian by grade and heads a department while Ms. B can be a Deputy Librarian by grade, also heading a department.

Both of them report directly to the Librarian-in-Chief. Yet, the grade level and rank status of both is not the same and cannot be the same just on the grounds that both of them are departmental heads. Of course, there will be no problem with the remuneration system also as it is based on performance scale (grade level) and not on positional status (the headship privilege). The only thing that may be the same in this case is the headship allowance, if it is across the board for all staff grades. But, the normal annual salary (remuneration) due for each departmental head is purely determined according to grade levels and as such will vary among the heads.

2.10. Principle 10: Order

This is another formal organisational control system which has been interpreted in different ways. Some see it as the rule of giving every material its right position in the organisation and others think that it means assigning the right job to the right employee (Rodrigues, 2001). Whichever is the case, library and information centres must keep every information material in the right place and as well assign staff to jobs that suit them. A Library Assistant is not expected to handle the office and responsibilities of a Senior Librarian. This is because, among other things, their qualifications, job schedule, and remunerations are clearly different (Ifidon, 1985; Ifidon & Ifidon, 2007). However, buttressing more on the first suggested meaning of Henri Fayol's 'principle of order,' it is true that information resources in the library should be kept in the right place. Here, what makes a place right is the ease of access and use it avails the users. Let us take the location of offices for example. In a library complex of two or three floors, the office of Librarian has no convenience in being located at any of the offices at the upper floors. Visitors to the Librarian's office, who have nothing to do with the readings halls and other departments, have no business passing through or across them before they can access the Librarian's office. The Librarian's office should be located on the ground floor where visitors and users can access it easily. Likewise, the porter stand should be accessible to users immediately when they enter the library. This is the prevailing practice in the Nigerian university system in West Africa as most of the library briefs are in line with this proposal (Ifidon, 1985; Ifidon & Ifidon, 2007; Ononogbo, 2008). Users do not have to walk to one point to keep their bags and down to another point before they can enter the library.

In fact, if library and information centres must comply with this principle of order, it must be looked at from a more holistic point of view. For instance, taking a look at the present structure of offices and demarcations of most library buildings in Nigeria, the principle of order is practically compromised. This is in spite of the good suggestions in the available librarians' and architects' briefs for the construction of library buildings (Ifidon, 1985; Ifidon & Ifidon, 2007; Ononogbo, 2008). In a library that wants to infuse order right from the design of its work environment, the transparent partitioning system, as seen in Banks, is ideal for adoption. Nowadays, organisations operate the open office system. An open office is that in which there is little or no privacy as the only partition between offices could be just transparent glass walls. In some cases, dwarf walls or wooden boards are used. The major benefit of this arrangement is that it enhances transparency and ventilation (Idih, Njoku, & Idih, 2011). Staff can see themselves from their offices. The users can see them as well too.

The Readers' Services Departments of the library and their officers are the most likely to adopt this system of office sitting/demarcation. It allows the head of the department to see his staff and users also while they too see them. In this case, there will hardly be room for staff that do unethical things in the library such as sleeping, eating, and gossiping in the office. Likewise, users will be more cautious while in the library because staff from various offices can be watching them. In fact, the transparent partitioning of library staff offices will intuitively drive staff to work and not to relax or chat away during official hours. However, this transparent partitioning system should not be open to users in the case of Technical Departments. But within the technical departments, the offices should be transparent too so that staff can see themselves. These are some important elements of order which could be modified to suit the peculiar needs of libraries.

2.11. Principle 11: Equity

Another word for equity is fairness. Henri Fayol suggested that managers should be fair to their staff. But the fairness required, probably, is such that must make staff to comply with principle No. 6 - subordination of individual interests to organisational interests – which does not lead to desired productivity in organisations nowadays. As suggested earlier under principle No. 6 in this paper, the system of organisation that flourishes in today's society is such that accommodates staff and owns them up, as it were. Such organisations make staff feel at home, share a portion of profits with staff, communicate with staff, remain open to staff, share staff feelings, and identify with staff personal/family challenges. This is the type of organisation that succeeds these days. Managers of library and information centres can apply these strategies in their relationships with members of staff. Where they do, they will avoid all forms of partiality, treat all staff equally, deny no staff promotions, and encourage weak staff to shape up. More so, they advise staff regularly on how to grow on the job, mentor staff, avoid favouritism, build up an unbiased attitude, and disallow gossip. Staff of the library are rewarded or punished based strictly on their commitment, faithfulness, and productivity and not on either friendship or filial relationships (Ohadinma & Uwaoma, 2000). This means that openness to all and even- handedness are integral parts of the key to attaining equity in organisations. So, library managers should rather address issues relating to staff before them and not at their backs. In all, impartiality is the kernel of this principle. As a result, it must be upheld by library managers not only in the interests of the library as an organisation, but also for their own good since observation has shown that impartial managers are respected and appreciated by their staff.

2.12. Principle 12: Stability of Personnel Tenure

In this principle, Fayol expresses the need to recruit the right staff and train them on the job with a hope to retain them for long. The basis of this principle is the belief that such staff with a secured tenure will put back into the organisation the knowledge and experience which they may have garnered in the course of working for the organisation. This, however, is considered an old-fashioned way of approaching management. Contemporary management is suggesting the recruitment of staff that are already-made with experience and with the right qualifications. Some organisations have gone further to downsize staff recruited in the old system because of their unwillingness to adapt to new ways of performing jobs in the organisation. As a matter of fact, new generation organisations are not merely keen in recruiting men and women whom they will invest much

in from the start in order to get them working for the organisation. However, they are willing to spend on staff members that already have high success profiles and experience so that they can develop the organisation all the more. So, this is the era of recruiting the best qualified staff. The idea is that work can be very productive from the start and afterwards the staff can be trained to improve on what they already know how to do. This is one side of the principle and library and information centres managers should take note of it.

Another angle of Fayol's 'principle of stability of tenure' is that staff should be retained for as long as possible, sometimes up to retirement. But, this is not the order of the day in recent times, as mobility of labour is becoming the culture of many workers. For one, workers believe in having several opportunities—that new jobs can offer such things as better pay, job satisfaction, promotions, job security, societal recognition, and others. But this is not healthy for library and information centres. Brain drain is a factor that should be avoided. In fact, library and information centres should hold firm on Fayol's principle here. Staff should be developed via on the job training, seminars, conferences, mentoring, and further studies. Organisational culture is not always easy to transmit and retain (Shein, 1984) let alone a system to change workers often. The majority of the new workers coming are often from another organisation with a different culture. So, managers of library and information centres should retain Fayol's 'principle of stability of personnel tenure' but must avoid recruiting into the library men and women who will not be productive to the system until they are trained. An element of this is noticeable in the head-hunting and recruitment of subject-specialists by authorities of special libraries. Although this calibre of staff may be new when they report or resume, they have had previous exposure and experience in the public or private sectors (Nnadozie, 2007). When staff are recruited from other establishments, the direct and indirect costs involved in training staff upon employment should therefore be avoided. This, however, does not eliminate the need for on the job mentoring essential for both new and old staff.

2.13. Principle 13: Initiative

A good manager must be one who can be creative to initiate new ideas and also be able to implement them. Fayol was direct to managers at this point. He understood the importance of good ideas to the growth and success of organisations. But, on the contrary, he did not foresee the situation of today where staff are becoming the idea-banks of organisations. This has been observed in Western countries where group problem-solving systems are patronised against dependence on top level management as the problem-solving point (Magjuka, 1991 & 1992). Moreover, Mintzberg's study in his PhD research (Robinson, 2005) confirmed that managers of these days seem not to be very good in initiating and implementing ideas as they are often preoccupied with so many other related and unrelated commitments that, in the end, leave them running after "work current, specific, well-defined and non-routine" activities. So, it is advisable for managers to empower their staff and give them the level playing ground required to initiate and implement new ideas.

In library and information centres, the almost non-existence of new ideas among librarians (especially in developing countries) has made library organisation seem uncreative, stagnant, and old-fashioned. This is the reason why their library customers, especially adolescents and young adults, are resorting to the Internet, since there is nothing new in the library. Whereas the Internet and its accompanying technologies offer a lot of platforms for proactive librarians to work with and retain their customers, a good number of library staff and their managers are rather not systematic and reflective planners. It may be that staff are waiting for the Librarian for initiatives and the Librarians-in-Charge, as managers, are preoccupied with numerous other things. This should not continue if the library organisation hopes to avoid decline and liquidation (Ohadinma & Uwaoma, 2000). Administrators and managers of library and information centres therefore should imbue their subordinates with the confidence to create and develop new ideas, as well as to implement them. Rewards and encouragements should be there for creative and/or innovative staff members so that generation of ideas can become competitive to the glory of the management and for the good of the organisation as a collective body.

2.14. Principle 14: *Esprit de Corps*

This is a French phrase which means enthusiasm and devotion among a group of people. Fayol is of the view that organisations should enforce and also maintain high morale and unity among their staff. This is

imperative as the existence of an organisation is a result of the coming together of men and women under a collective interest. Thus, understanding, love for each other, unity, peace, and common determination is paramount to their success. The saying that *united we stand, divided we fall* is equally applicable in libraries and information centres. In the same manner, managers of library and information centres must ensure that the library organisation is characterized by staff unity and co-operation. This however does not mean that some staff members will not disagree or quarrel. It is natural with some human beings to quarrel once in a while. But library managers must be strategists in such cases to ensure that such misunderstandings amongst staff do not affect common goals of the library organisation.

3. CONCLUSION AND RECOMMENDATIONS

This paper has critically analysed the '14 principles of management' proposed by Henri Fayol (Fayol, 1949). Some of the principles have been redefined and re-interpreted in recent management research to become better and more effective to organisations in their application. Yet a few others have remained as Fayol postulated them and are still widely adopted in the management of today's organisations. Generally, all organisations are similar in some ways in the context of management as a practice. The issue of categorization of organisations, whether profit or non-profit, into manufacturing, marketing, sales, or services as products, does not demean the need for management in all types of organisation. A library and information centre is not different and therefore should also be treated as a business organisation. As a sequel to this, this paper has presented a modification or adaptation of each of Fayol's 14 principles meant to guide managers of library and information centres. The principles are borne out of discourse on Fayol's '14 principles of management.' The new modified principles are comparatively presented in Table 1.

This paper therefore recommends the application of these principles to library administration. More so, research surveys can be conducted on case study bases to show the level of application of Fayol's principles or similar principles in library and information centres. As a matter of fact, research into library management

Table 1. Fayol's 14 Principles and their Implication in Today's Library and Information Centres (LICs)

Principles	Fayol's Proposition	Its Implications for LIC Managers
1	Division of work by specialisation	The job schedule of staff should not be rigid or static. In addition to their core or primary duties, staff should be able to perform other tasks within the organisation.
2	Centralize the organisations of power	Power and authority in any organization should be decentralized without undermining corporate cohesion. This will encourage the creation of new ideas and the harnessing of staff creativity.
3	Formal system of control over staff	The various informal groups within the workplace should be strengthened. For instance, trade unions and other staff groups can be brought on board to exert some influence and control over their members.
4	Staff report to only one head	Staff can report to more than one head and still harmonize directives to work successfully
5	One plan and one head for each plan	Multiple plans from one or more heads at a time is possible in order to advance corporate objectives.
6	Organisation interests first even if at the detriment of staff	The interests and welfare of the staff should not be overlooked. It is only where staff are motivated that they work whole-heartedly for the organisation's interests.
7	Deserving pay system	The pay system should be structured in such a way that the remuneration for workers is strictly performance- based.
8	Top management led decision making system	Creativity should not be stifled. Staff should be emboldened to initiate and implement policies relevant to their areas of specialization.
9	Vertical hierarchy and communication	Horizontal organizational structure and communication should be encouraged to the best interests of the organization
10	Arrangement of staff and things as suitable to management	The overall interests of the customer should be taken into consideration. Arrangement of staff and things as convenient for customers (users)
11	Fairness to staff to make them work more	Fairness to staff to give them a sense of belonging. The resultant feeling of appreciation makes them work harder
12	Recruit, train staff and encourage them to remain	Recruit self-made and experienced staff but sponsor them to on-the-job training on regular basis.
13	Top management conceive and implement new ideas	As much as possible, staff should be empowered to conceive and implement new ideas for the overall benefit of the organization.
14	Ensure high moral and unity among staff	Efforts should be made to ensure high morale and unity of purpose across various cadres of staff

practices and methods should be encouraged. There are several management methods and approaches prevailing in contemporary society and only research can present a reliable picture of what the situation is in library and information centres. So, further research is not only needed to reveal management practices in library and information centres but also to identify contemporary management methods which can be adopted by library managers for the day-to-day administration of library organisation.

REFERENCES

Aguolu, C. C., & Aguolu, I. E. (2002). *Library and information management in Nigeria*. Maiduguri, Nigeria: Ed-Linform Services.

Blackburn, R., & Rosen, B. (1993). Total quality and human resources management: Lessons learned from Baldrige award winning companies. *The Academy of Management Executives, 7* (3), 49-66.

Braham, J. (1989, April). Money talks. *Industry Week, 17,* 23.

Cascio, W. F. (1987). Do good or poor performers leave? A meta-analysis of the relationship between performance and turnover. *The Academy of Management Journal, 30* (4), 744 - 762.

Cavaleri, S., & Obloj, K. (1993). *Management system: A global perspective*. Belmont, CA: Wadsworth.

Drucker, P. (1954). *The practice of management*. New York: Harper & Row.

Edoka, B. E. (2000). *Introduction to library science*. Onitsha, Nigeria: Palma Publishing & Links Coy.

Fayol, H. (1917). *Administration industrielle et générale; prévoyance, organisation, commandement, coordination, controle*. Paris: H. Dunod & E. Pinat.

Fayol, H. (1930). *Industrial and general administration* (J. A. Coubrough, Trans.). London: Sir Isaac Pitman & Sons.

Fayol, H. (1949). *General and industrial management* (C. Storrs, Trans.). London: Sir Isaac Pitman & Sons.

Hinterhuber, H. H., & Popp, W. (1992, January-February). Are you a strategist or just a manager? *Harvard Business Review*, 105-113.

Idih, E., Njoku, J., & Idih, C. (2011). *Business communication for office managers*. Owerri, Nigeria: Tropical Publishers.

Ifidon, S. E., & Ifidon, E. (2007). *New directions in African library management*. Ibadan, Nigeria: Spectrum Publishers.

Ifidon, S. E. (1979). Participatory management in libraries. *Bendel Library Journal, 2*(1), 1-10.

Ifidon, S. E. (1985). *Essentials of management for African university libraries*. Lagos, Nigeria: Libriservice.

Imaga, E. U. U. (2001). *Elements of management and culture in organizational behaviour*. Enugu, Nigeria: Rhyee Kerex Publishers.

Iwueke, O. C., & Oparaku, U. D. (2011). *Management*. Owerri: Classic Business Services.

Magjuka, R. F. (1991/1992). Survey: Self-managed teams achieve continuous improvement best. *National Productivity Review* (Spring), 203-211.

Mayo, E. (1933). The human problem of industrial civilization. Cambridge, MA: Harvard University Press.

McGregor, D. (1960). *The human side of enterprise*. New York: McGraw-Hill.

Mintzberg, H. (1973). *The nature of managerial work*. New York: Harper & Row.

Nnadozie, C. O. (2007). *Foundations of library practice*. Owerri, Nigeria: Springfield Publishers.

Nwachukwu, C. C. (1988). *Management: Theory and practice*. Ibadan, Nigeria: Africana-Feb Publishers.

Ohadinma, D. C., & Uwaoma, N. (2000). *Industrial personnel management*. Owerri, Nigeria: Rescue Publishers.

Ononogbo, R. U. (2008). Architect's brief for the design and construction of a university library building: A model draft. *Communicate: Journal of Library and Information Science, 10*(1), 67-77.

Pugh, D.S., & Hickson, D.J. (2007).*Great writers on organisations: The third omnibus edition*, 3rd rev. ed. Farnham, United Kingdom: Ashgate Publishing.

Rodrigues, C. A. (2001). Fayol's 14 principles of management then and now: A framework for managing today's organisations effectively. *Management Decision, 39* (10), 880-889.

Schein, E. H. (1984). Coming to a new awareness of organisational culture. *Sloan Management Re-*

views (Winter), 3-16.

Senge, P. (1990). *The fifth discipline*. New York: Doubleday.

Stroh, L. K., Northcraft, G. B., & Neale, M. A. (2002). *Organisational behavior: A management challenge*. Mahwah, NJ: Lawrence Erlbaum.

Taylor, F. W. (1911). *The principles of scientific management*. New York: Harper & Row.

Witzel, M. (2003). *Fifty key figures in management*. London: Routledge.

Wren, D. A., Bedeian, A. G., & Breeze, J. D. (2002). The foundations of Henri Fayol's administrative theory. *Management Decision, 40* (9), 906-918.

6

Credibility Assessment of Online Information in Context

Soo Young Rieh *

School of Information
University of Michigan, U.S.A.
E-mail: rieh@umich.edu

ABSTRACT

The purpose of this study is to examine to what extent the context in which people interact with online information affects people's credibility perceptions. In this study, credibility assessment is defined as perceptions of credibility relying on individuals' expertise and knowledge. Context has been characterized with respect to three aspects: Context as user goals and intentions, context as topicality of information, and context as information activities. The data were collected from two empirical studies. Study 1 was a diary study in which 333 residents in Michigan, U.S.A. submitted 2,471 diary entries to report their trust perceptions associated with ten different user goals and nine different intentions. Study 2 was a lab-based study in which 64 subjects participated in performing four search tasks in two different information activity conditions – information search or content creation. There are three major findings of this study: (1) Score-based trust perceptions provided limited views of people's credibility perceptions because respondents tended to score trust ratings consistently high across various user goals and intentions; (2) The topicality of information mattered more when study subjects assessed the credibility of user generated content (UGC) than with traditional media content (TMC); (3) Subjects of this study exerted more effort into making credibility judgments when they engaged in searching activities than in content creation. These findings indicate that credibility assessment can or should be seen as a process-oriented notion incorporating various information use contexts beyond simple rating-based evaluation. The theoretical contributions for information scientists and practical implications for web designers are also discussed.

Keywords: Credibility assessment, Credibility assessment effort, User-generated content, Information search, Content creation

*Corresponding Author: Soo Young Rieh
Associate Professor
School of Information
University of Michigan, U.S.A.
E-mail: rieh@umich.edu

1. INTRODUCTION

How to provide relevant information that fits into users' information needs has long been a core research question among information scientists and information professionals over several decades. Since the late 1990s when online information became prolific on the Internet, researchers and practitioners in information science have become interested in better understanding of people's assessment of information credibility, quality, and cognitive authority (e.g., Rieh, 2002), which were initially identified as primary user-centered relevance criteria in a variety of studies (e.g., Wang & Soergel, 1998). As the empirical findings of credibility research accumulated, several researchers began to recognize the importance of investigating people's credibility assessment as a research agenda in its own right beyond relevance criteria studies (Rieh, 2010; Rieh & Danielson, 2007).

The motivation for studying the credibility of online information is primarily drawn from dramatic changes in today's digital environments which allow people to create user-generated content easily using a variety of web publishing and social media tools. The credibility assessment of user-generated content available in various social media, such as blogs, microblogs (e.g., Twitter), Wikis (e.g., Wikipedia), social news sites, and social networking sites poses another layer of challenges for online users because people may not be able to rely on their primary criteria for credibility judgments – examining the characteristics of original sources (Rieh, 2002).

There are at least three important problems with current credibility research. First, there is a lack of consensus on definitions and notions of credibility. Therefore, each credibility study begins with different sets of assumptions and conceptualizations of credibility. Sometimes related concepts such as quality, authority, and reliability of information are used interchangeably without providing clear distinctions. What is more problematic is that credibility is conceptualized differently depending on the academic discipline. For instance, communication researchers, Human-Computer Interaction (HCI) researchers, and information science researchers have adopted distinct conceptual frameworks to conduct credibility research. Communication researchers (e.g., Johnson & Kaye, 1998) often use media-based frameworks to investigate the relative credibility perceptions of various media channels (i.e.,

online news, blogs, wikis, magazines, TV, etc.). HCI researchers, such as Fogg (2003), focus on evaluating website credibility, identifying specific elements which improve or hurt credibility perceptions. On the other hand, credibility research within information science tends to use the content-based credibility framework (e.g., Sundin & Francke, 2009). Despite the field-specific foundations of credibility research, there has been renewed attention to investigating the credibility of online information in various research communities as people increasingly select what information to use based on their judgments of information credibility.

The second problem is that the majority of previous credibility studies have investigated credibility assessment from the perspective of information consumers whose primary information activities are information seeking and reading. However, as people engage in many more diverse online information activities beyond seeking and reading in the Web 2.0 environment, they are not only information seekers or readers but also commentators, bloggers, user-generated content providers, raters, and voters in the online environment. The multiple roles that users play in today's digital environments have not been well incorporated into credibility studies.

The third problem is that most credibility research does not pay much attention to the contexts in which online information is used. Previous studies tend to treat credibility assessment as a binary evaluation question by asking study participants whether they can trust information by showing online content from web pages which contain particular features (Lim, 2013; Xu, 2013). Or, researchers often conducted surveys asking respondents about their general perception of online information from particular media or web sites (Flanagin & Metzger, 2010; Johnson & Kaye, 1998; Metzger, Flanagin, & Medders, 2010). These approaches have limitations as researchers often miss opportunities to understand the contexts associated with credibility assessment.

Putting these three problems together, this study claims that it is critical to examine what leads users to use online information in the first place and what it is that people try to achieve by using information. That is because people will eventually do something with the information they interact with. For instance, they will use information to create user-generated content, to learn something new, to make decisions, to solve problems, or to entertain themselves. Depending on the contexts in which they interact with information, their constructs of credibility, concern about credibility, effort put into credibility assessment, and strategies used for credibility judgments might be characterized distinctively.

This paper can be distinguished from previous research on credibility by emphasizing the importance of examining the contexts of people's information interaction. Saracevic (2010) formulated four axioms of context, and the first axiom seems to capture the approach to be taken in this paper clearly: "One cannot not have a context in information interaction." Saracevic states that every interaction between an information user and an information system is conducted within a context, also pointing out that context is an ill-defined term. Given the diversity of information activities, topics, user goals, and intentions, this study aims at offering a groundwork for drawing the attention of information science researchers in general and credibility researchers in particular for a better understanding of credibility assessment in contexts. Demonstrating the influence of contexts on credibility assessment has motivated this research.

This paper addresses three research questions:

Research Question 1: To what extent do people's goals and intentions when conducting online information activities influence their perception of trust?

Research Question 2: To what extent does the topic of information affect people's credibility perceptions of traditional media content (TMC) and user-generated content (UGC)?

Research Question 3: To what extent does the amount of effort that people invest in credibility assessment differ depending on the type of online activity (information search vs. content creation)?

2. RELATED WORK

2.1. Notion of Credibility

Credibility is a complex and multi-dimensional concept. Trustworthiness and expertise have long been known as the two key dimensions of credibility perception (Hovland, Janis, & Kelley, 1953). Most researchers agree that trustworthiness captures the perceived goodness or morality of the source, which is often phrased in terms of being truthful, fair, and unbiased (Fogg, 2003). Through numerous studies, additional related concepts

have been identified, including currency, fairness, accuracy, trustfulness, completeness, precision, objectivity, and informativeness (Arazy & Kopak, 2011; Rieh, 2010). Fogg (2003) defines credibility with respect to "believability." Fogg emphasizes that "it doesn't reside in an object, a person, or a piece of information" (p. 122), as credibility is a perceived quality. Rieh (2010) provides the definition of information credibility as "people's assessment of whether information is trustworthy based on their own expertise and knowledge" (p. 1338). In this definition, Rieh focuses on two important notions of credibility assessment: (1) it is people who ultimately make judgments of information credibility; (2) therefore, credibility assessment relies on subjective perceptions.

Hilligoss and Rieh (2008) have termed these multiple concepts "credibility constructs," illustrating that individual users conceptualize and define credibility in their own terms and according to their own beliefs and understandings. Rieh et al. (2010) adopted Hilligoss and Rieh's (2008) framework and tested eleven different credibility constructs using a diary survey method. They found that people evaluated the importance of credibility constructs differently depending on the type of information. When using user-generated content, traditional credibility constructs such as authoritativeness and expertise of the author were not considered to be important. On the other hand, trustworthiness, reliability, accuracy, and completeness were still considered to be important credibility constructs across different types of information objects such as traditional websites, social media, and multimedia content (Rieh et al., 2010).

2.2. Context in Information Behavior Research

Courtright (2007) provides a literature review on context in information behavior research. According to this study, in spite of growing emphasis on the concept of context, there is little agreement as to how context, as a frame of reference for information behavior, is established by users and how it operates with respect to information behavior research. Courtright has introduced typologies of context: Context as container, context as constructed meaning, socially constructed context, and relational context (embeddedness). Among these four typologies, this study will take the context as constructed meaning approach, which examines context from the point of view of an information actor. Courtright's definition of context with this person-in-context approach is that "information activities are reported in relation to contextual variables and influences, largely as perceived and constructed by the information actor" (p. 287).

Hilligoss and Rieh's (2008) unifying framework of credibility assessment includes context as a key factor influencing people's credibility assessment in terms of constructs, heuristics, and interaction. By guiding the selection of information or limiting the applicability of certain judgments, context "creates boundaries around the information seeking activity or the credibility judgment itself" (p. 1473). In their empirical study, context often emerged as an important factor when their study participants who were college students distinguished between class context and personal context or entertainment purposes and health context. Some contexts were closely related to individuals' goals and tasks and others were established as social contexts. The topic of the information seeking task could be also considered as one of the contextual factors. Hilligoss and Rieh's conceptualization of context provides a theoretical basis for this study in which context is investigated with respect to three different notions: (1) context as user goals and intentions; (2) context as topicality of information; and (3) context as information activities.

3. METHODS

The data were collected from two empirical studies which employed different data collection and analysis methods. The two studies allowed the researcher to capture people's perceptions of credibility assessment in both natural settings and lab settings.

3.1. Study 1: A Diary Study

Study 1 was a diary study which was designed to capture a variety of online information activities people engage in over time. Participants were recruited using a random sample of landline phone numbers belonging to residents in Michigan, U.S.A. 333 individuals agreed to participate in the diary study. Study participants received an email with a link to an online activity diary form five times a day over a period of three days. After removal of incomplete and inappropriate records, the data set included 2,471 diaries submitted by 333 respondents.

The diary survey asked respondents to report all online activities in which they had engaged during the preceding three hours when they received a new email. Two open-ended questions about what they were trying to accomplish by conducting the one activity they decided to report were asked, along with other rating questions about interest, confidence, and satisfaction regarding this activity. They were then asked to rate to what extent they trusted the information they chose to use for this activity. Respondents were also asked to indicate their ratings in terms of credibility constructs, heuristics, and interaction.

The first step in preparing this data for analysis was to code the responses to the two open-ended questions regarding participants' one activity and their reason for conducting this activity. Coding schemes for respondents' responses to these questions were developed iteratively using content analysis. Respondents' descriptions of what they were trying to accomplish in conducting their online activity were coded in terms of goals and intentions. Behavior codes were used to represent the specific action(s) that the respondents described taking. In this paper, analysis using goals and intentions from the diary entries will be reported with respect to their trust and other credibility-related responses.

3.2. Study 2: A Lab-Based Study

Study 2 was a lab-based study which was designed to make comparisons of credibility assessment processes across two different information activity types (information search vs. content creation), across two different content types (traditional media content vs. user generated content), and across four different topics (health, news, products, and travel). This method enabled the researcher to control the variability of the tasks, time allotted, physical settings, and the initial websites where the subjects began each search task. Subjects were recruited from the general local population in a small town located in a Midwestern state in the U.S.A. through random phone sampling. Data were collected from individual experimental sessions with 64 study subjects. These 64 subjects were randomly assigned to one of the two experimental conditions – information search activity or content creation activity. Every subject in either condition completed four different tasks – two of which involved interacting with user generated content (UGC) and two of which involved interacting with traditional media content (TMC) on the starting website.

Following Borlund's (2000) 'simulated work task situation' approach, 16 task scenarios were created in a way that simulates real life information needs. See Table 1 for sample scenarios. For information search tasks, subjects were asked to find information on an assigned topic and then copy-paste the URLs and portions of website content they found useful for the task into a Word document. For content creation tasks, subjects were asked to find information on an assigned topic and then write up a paragraph in a Word document. Subjects were given up to 10 minutes for each information search task and up to 20 minutes for each content creation task. Every subject had four tasks drawn from four topics: Health (getting a flu shot), news (international news in Japan), products (purchasing a new smartphone), and travel (a trip to Edinburgh, Scotland). The experiments were conducted one-on-one with each subject and lasted for 1.5 or 2 hours depending on the activity type (information search or content creation) to which the subject had been randomly assigned.

The data were collected from the post-task questionnaire and the background questionnaire. The post-task questionnaire asked subjects to respond to various questions about credibility of online information, search tasks given to them, perceived effort they exerted for making credibility judgments, and perceived outcome of their search performance and search experience. In the background questionnaire, subjects were asked to fill out questions about demographic information as well as their prior experiences with various types of online activities. In addition, exit interviews were also performed with each study subject to collect data about their understanding, perceptions, and credibility assessments of UGC in general. All interviews were audio-taped and then transcribed for data analysis purposes.

4. RESULTS

4.1. User Goals, Intentions, and Trust

Table 1. Task Scenario Example

Information Search context for health topic	Content creation context for health topic
A friend of yours has an appointment to get a flu shot tomorrow, but she has a cold. She is debating whether or not to keep her appointment. You would like to help her out by finding out what is generally recommended for people in her situation.	You run a forum in which people discuss various health issues. Someone has posted a question about whether or not they should get a flu shot if they currently have a cold. You would like to find out what is generally recommended in this situation and then post one paragraph in response to this person's post on your forum.

For each topic, two websites were selected and one of the two was assigned to the subject.
- Health
  - http://flu.gov (TMC)
  - www.healthexpertadvice.org/forum/ (UGC)
- News
  - www.cnn.com (TMC)
  - http://globalvoicesonline.org (UGC)
- Products
  - www.pcworld.com (TMC)
  - www.epinions.com (UGC)
- Travel
  - www.fodors.com (TMC)
  - www.tripadvisor.com (UGC)

Research Question 1: To what extent do people's goals and intentions when conducting online information activities influence their perception of trust?

The data for this research question was drawn from Study 1, a diary study. The user goal is the driving force that leads people to engage in information interaction (Xie, 2008). An intention is a sub-goal that a user intends to achieve during information interaction. Both goals and intentions were identified from an open-ended question in the diary: "What were you trying to accomplish in conducting this activity?" In the diary, we also asked respondents about trust with this question: "To what extent did you trust the information that you decided to select?" with a scale of 1 (not at all) to 7 (very much).

As presented in Table 2, respondents showed a higher level of trust for the information they decided to use in their everyday life. With a scale of 1 to 7, the highest average score of trust was 6.73 and the lowest average score was still higher than 6, scoring 6.09. Respondents trusted online information most when they engaged in information activities in order to sell a product online (M=6.73). When respondents selected information in the course of planning for the future (M=6.55) or performing a work-related task (M=6.48), they reported that they trusted the information more highly than they would for some other information activities. When their goal was to help other people (M=6.15) or to entertain themselves (M=6.09), their trust level toward the information selected was relatively lower.

While we identified nine different kinds of intentions, keeping up to date (N=573; 39%) and gathering data (N=515; 35.1%) represented the majority of the intentions reported by respondents, as seen in Table 3. Not surprisingly, when respondents managed their own personal information, they rated their trust level highest (M=6.94). Respondents also reported that they trusted information highly when they engaged in information activities in order to produce (M=6.50)

or share (M=6.48) content. On the other hand, when respondents selected information with the intention of evaluating something (M=6.13) or deciding about something (M=6.00), they rated their trust toward that information lower than for any other intentions.

The analysis indicated that examining respondents' trust perceptions with respect to goals and intentions was meaningful. However, we were not able to run a statistical test for significance because of the big difference in the frequencies of goals and intentions.

4.2. Topicality and Believability

Research Question 2: To what extent does the topic of information affect people's credibility perceptions of traditional media content (TMC) and user-generated content (UGC)?

In Study 2, every time subjects completed each of the four tasks within their condition (information search or content creation), they were asked to rate the "believability" of the information they rated in the website that was given to them. Subjects were asked to rate believability with respect to three questions presented in the post-task questionnaire: Being trustworthy, accurate, and reliable with a scale of 1 (not at all) to 7 (very).

Table 2. Information Activity Goals and Trust

Goals	N	% of Goals	Trust M (SD)	Trust Ranking
Entertain	293	24.7	6.09 (1.22)	11
Buy	257	21.6	6.25 (1.05)	8
Connect with people	205	17.3	6.28 (1.06)	7
Perform work-related task	156	13.1	6.48 (0.85)	3
Plan for future	88	7.4	6.55 (0.79)	2
Get employed	57	4.8	6.25 (0.97)	9
Help other people	39	3.3	6.15 (1.01)	10
Perform school-related task	31	2.6	6.29 (0.82)	6
Self-express	24	2.0	6.33 (0.76)	5
Maintain household and electronics	23	1.9	6.39 (0.94)	4
Sell	15	1.3	6.73 (0.46)	1
Total	**1188**	**100**	**6.27(1.04)**	

Table 3. Information Activity Intentions and Trust

Intentions	N	% of Intentions	Trust M (SD)	Trust Ranking
Keep up to date	573	39.0	6.31 (0.91)	6
Gather data	515	35.1	6.31 (1.03)	5
Learn	114	7.8	6.29 (0.94)	7
Evaluate	96	6.5	6.13 (1.01)	8
Manage personal information	66	4.5	6.94 (0.24)	1
Decide	45	3.1	6.00 (0.98)	9
Verify	28	1.9	6.32 (0.98)	4
Share	21	1.4	6.48 (0.81)	3
Produce	10	0.7	6.50 (0.71)	2
Total	**1468**	**100**	**6.33 (0.95)**	

We wanted to investigate to what extent the topicality of task (health, news, products, and travel) affect people's credibility perceptions of user generated content (UGC) and traditional media content (TMC). Overall, as shown in Table 4, the subjects of this study gave lowest believability ratings to health UGC (M=3.06) while giving highest believability ratings to health TMC (M=6.03). The difference in believability ratings for the three constructs of believability – being trustworthy, accurate, and reliable – between health UGC and health TMC was significant. In the case of news information, subjects overall rated TMC higher than UGC. They rated the trustworthiness and reliability of TMC significantly higher than UGC when using

news information. Although subjects still rated the accuracy of news information from TMC (M=5.24) higher than that from UGC (M=4.54), the difference in ratings was not significant. In the case of using product information, subjects rated TMC higher than UGC in terms of all three believability constructs, but none of the believability ratings between product TMC and product UGC were significantly different. Assessing the believability of travel information using TMC and UGC was mixed. There was virtually no difference in subjects' believability perceptions between travel UGC and travel TMC. It means that subjects of this study accepted travel UGC as almost equally reliable, accurate, and trustworthy compared to travel TMC.

Table 4. Credibility Constructs by Content Type Across the Four Topics

Credibility Construct	Health				News				Products				Travel			
	UGC M (SD)		TMC M (SD)		UGC M (SD)		TMC M (SD)		UGC M (SD)		TMC M (SD)		UGC M (SD)		TMC M (SD)	
Trustworthy	**3.06** (1.91)	<	**6.03** (1.15)		**4.27** (1.66)	<	**5.47** (0.86)		4.47 (1.41)	<	4.93 (1.53)		5.06 (1.16)	<	5.13 (1.67)	
Accurate	**3.40** (1.79)	<	**6.03** (1.15)		**4.54** (1.77)	<	**5.24** (0.87)		4.56 (1.27)	<	5.07 (1.26)		5.09 (1.12)	>	5.07 (1.60)	
Reliable	**3.03** (1.85)	<	**6.00** (1.11)		**4.24** (1.64)	<	**5.27** (0.87)		4.50 (1.37)	<	4.87 (1.48)		5.00 (1.24)	<	5.06 (1.41)	

Note. Boldface indicates that the difference between the two means is statistically significant (paired t-test, p<.05).

Figure 1 presents the comparison of UGC believability perceptions across four topics. Among the four topics we examined, subjects rated the believability of travel UGC highest compared to product UGC, news UGC, and health UGC. It may be because people tend to trust the UGC provided by other users who have first-hand experiences with certain locations or events when using travel information. Product and news UGC were perceived to be somewhat more believable than health-related UGC.

As shown in Figure 2, when using TMC, subjects believed health information most than information about other topics. With the exception of health, subjects' believability ratings for news, travel, and product TMC did not seem to differ to a great extent. Putting Figure 1 and Figure 2 together, we learned that topic matters more when subjects assessed believability of UGC than for believability of TMC.

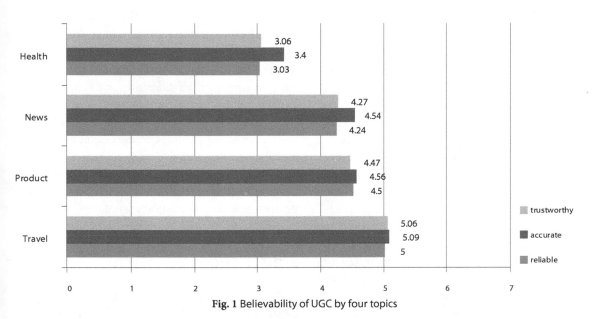

Fig. 1 Believability of UGC by four topics

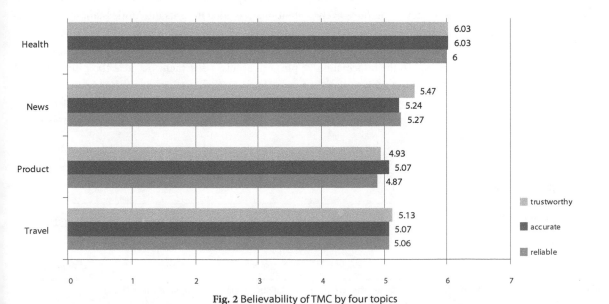

Fig. 2 Believability of TMC by four topics

4.3. Credibility Assessment in Search and Creation Contexts

Research Question 3: To what extent does the amount of effort that people invest in credibility assessment differ depending on the type of online activity (information search vs. content creation)?

We examined the differences in the amount of effort subjects exerted for credibility judgments depending on their activity types (information search and content creation). In this study, two kinds of judgments people make in the process of information activity were investigated: predictive judgment and evaluative judgment. According to Rieh (2002), predictive judgment denotes predictions reflecting what people expect before accessing webpages, whereas evaluative judgment is made when people actually interact with the webpages.

Table 5 presents a comparison of the means and standard deviations for effort exerted for predictive judgment and for evaluative judgment across the two activity types. Overall, subjects reported that they made more effort both in predictive judgment and evaluative judgment when performing a search activity than for a creation activity. In particular, effort exerted for predictive judgment was statistically different depending on the activity type. It means that study subjects put significantly more effort into the process of deciding which websites to visit (predictive judgment) when they were searching for new information than when they were creating new online content. We speculate that those subjects in the information search condition perceived searching as a primary task, and they were more likely to be concerned about finding credible information because information evaluation could come across as one of the primary actions encompassed in the information search process. On the other hand, those subjects in the content creation condition could perceive that they were dealing with two sub-tasks, as they have to first find

information and use that information in order to create their own content. Therefore, they may consider creating content to be a more cognitively demanding task, and thus, may put more effort into the actual content creation process while investing less effort in the preparatory activities of deciding which websites to visit and evaluating information from those websites.

We also investigated whether the topic of a task influences the amounts of effort that subjects invested in the two activity types. Figure 3 summarizes the results of an analysis of the effect of activity type on credibility judgment effort exerted across the various topics. With the exception of travel, subjects exhibited a consistent pattern across the topics, investing more effort in making credibility judgments when performing a search activity. In particular, the differences in the effort exerted for predictive judgment between search and creation were found to be statistically significant for the topics of health, news, and products. In the case of travel, however, subjects demonstrated an opposite trend, exerting more effort in making credibility judgments when performing a content creation activity; however, these differences were not statistically significant.

5. DISCUSSION

The major findings and implications of this study can be summarized as follows. First, comparing people's trust perceptions across various kinds of goals and intentions provided insights into understanding credibility assessment. The findings demonstrated that numeric ratings of trust perception did not say much about people's credibility assessment because the ratings tended to be consistently high, showing that the lowest average score was still higher than 6.0 with a scale of 1 (not at all) to 7 (very much). Therefore, rather than relying on

Table 5. Credibility Judgment Effort by Activity Type

Credibility judgment effort	Search M (SD)	Creation M (SD)
Effort for predictive judgment	**4.60** (1.60)	**3.91** (1.80)
Effort for evaluative judgment	4.52 (1.64)	4.14 (1.70)

Note. Boldface indicates that the difference between the two means is statistically significant (paired t-test, p<.05)

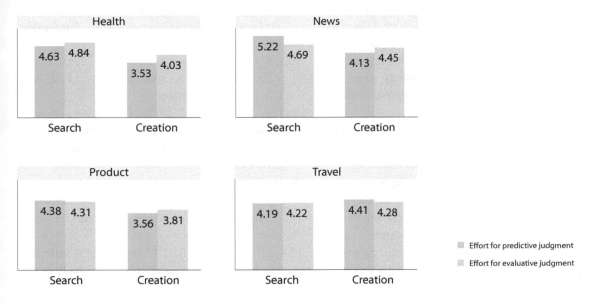

Fig. 3 Credibility judgment effort across four topics

numeric scores, it was more important to characterize people' credibility assessment with respect to a variety of contexts in which people use online information in their everyday life.

Second, people's assessment of the credibility of UGC was influenced by the topic of the task in which they are engaged. On the contrary, credibility of TMC was less influenced by the topic of information. For instance, when using health and news information, subjects in this study had greater reservations regarding UGC. With travel-related and product-related UGC, however, subjects rated the credibility of UGC as the same or higher than for TMC. This finding has direct practical implications for web designers. The designers of health- and news-related websites may want to present TMC and UGC separately within a web page, explicitly labeling UGC so that users are not confused regarding the type of content with which they are interacting. On the other hand, the findings indicate that TMC and UGC can complement one another for the topics of travel and products. Users may wish to have both of these types of content available side by side so that they can validate the information across these two content types. Users' credibility perceptions regarding travel UGC and product UGC can be even enhanced

by presenting this UGC side-by-side with related TMC.

Third, the results of this study indicate that people indeed invest different amounts of effort when they engage in content creation activities versus information search activities. Surprisingly, people tend to exert more effort when they look for information than when they create content. We provided some speculations concerning such findings above in Section 4.3.

6. CONCLUSIONS

Examining credibility assessment in various contexts including goals, intentions, topicality, and information activities is a major theoretical contribution of this study. While goals, intentions, and topicality have been often considered as information seeking and use contexts in previous studies, we believe that including different types of information activities – searching and content creation – is an important contribution to the field of information science. While the majority of web credibility research has been conducted with respect to information seeking or news reading activities (e.g., Johnson & Kaye, 2000; Metzger, Flanagin & Medders, 2010; Rieh, 2002), little previous research has looked at people's credibility assessment within the process of content creation, except for a couple of recent publications (St. Jean et al., 2011; Rieh et al., 2014). By conducting the study within the context of both information searching and content creation, we demonstrated that credibility assessment can be seen as a process-oriented notion rather than a matter of simple binary evaluation.

We hope that the findings of this study can help researchers and practitioners gain insights into how we might help users to judge the credibility of UGC more effectively in the course of their everyday information activities, rather than merely determining whether users do or should believe UGC or not. As UGC will be only increasing in number in online environments, more studies are needed in the future to examine how users select and assess UGC credibility efficiently and effectively in various information seeking and use contexts. Future research could also include more diverse types of information activities beyond searching and content creation. For instance, we can examine people's credibility assessment of online information when they ask questions in online communities, social networking sites, or social Q&A sites.

ACKNOWLEDGEMENTS

The author wishes to thank the members of the Credibility 2.0 Project – Beth St. Jean, Ji-Yeon Yang, Grace YoungJoo Jeon, and Yong-Mi Kim – for research assistance. The John D. and Catherine T. MacArthur Foundation supported this project.

REFERENCES

Arazy, O., & Kopak, R. (2011). On the measurability of information quality. *Journal of the American Society for Information Science and Technology, 62*(1), 89-99.

Borlund, P. (2000). Experimental components for the evaluation of interactive information retrieval systems. *Journal of Documentation, 56,* 71-90.

Courtright, C. (2007). Context in information behavior research. *Annual Review of Information Science and Technology, 41,* 273-306.

Flanagin, A. J., & Metzger, M. J. (2010). *Kids and credibility: An empirical examination of youth, digital media use, and information credibility.* Cambridge, MA: The MIT Press.

Fogg, B. J. (2003). *Persuasive technology: Using computers to change what we think and do.* San Francisco, CA: Morgan Kaufmann.

Hilligoss, B., & Rieh, S. Y. (2008). Developing a unifying framework of credibility assessment: Construct, heuristics, and interaction in context. *Information Processing & Management, 44*(4), 1467-1484.

Hovland, C. I, Janis, I. L, & Kelley, H. H. (1953). *Communication and persuasion; Psychological studies of opinion change.* New Haven, CT: Yale University press.

Johnson T. J. & Kaye, B. K. (2000). Using is believing: The influence of reliance on the credibility of online political information among politically interested internet users. *Journalism & Mass Communication Quarterly, 77,* 865–879.

Johnson, T. J., & Kaye, B. K. (1998). Cruising is believing?: Comparing Internet and traditional sources on media credibility measures. *Journalism and Mass Communication Quarterly, 75*(2), 325-340.

Lim, S. (2013). College students' credibility judgments and heuristics concerning Wikipedia. *Information Processing & Management, 49,* 405-419.

Metzger, M. J., Flanagin, A. J., & Medders, R. B. (2010). Social and heuristic approaches to credibility evaluation online. *Journal of Communication, 60*(3), 413-439.

Rieh, S. Y. (2010). Credibility and cognitive authority of information. In M. Bates & M. N. Maack (Eds.), *Encyclopedia of Library and Information Sciences* (3rd ed., pp. 1337-1344). New York: Taylor and Francis Group, LLC.

Rieh, S. Y. & Danielson, D. R. (2007). Credibility: A multidisciplinary framework. In B. Cronin (Ed.), *Annual Review of Information Science and Technology, 41,* 307-364.

Rieh, S. Y., Jeon, G. Y-J, Yang, J., & Lampe, C. (2014). Audience-aware credibility: From understanding audience to establishing credible blogs. Proceedings of the Eight International AAAI Conference on Weblogs and Social Media (ICWSM 2014), 436-445.

Rieh, S. Y., Kim, Y. M., Yang, J. Y., & St. Jean, B. (2010). A diary study of credibility assessment in everyday life information activities on the Web: Preliminary findings. *Proceedings of the 73rd Annual Meeting of the American Society for Information Science and Technology, 47.*

Rieh, S. Y. (2002). Judgment of information quality and cognitive authority in the Web. *Journal of the American Society for Information Science and Technology, 53*(2), 145-161.

Saracevic, T. (2010). The notion of context in "Information Interaction in Context." Proceedings of the Information Interaction in Context (IIiX 2010).

St. Jean, B, Rieh, S. Y., Yang, J. Y., & Kim, Y. M. (2011). How content contributors assess and establish credibility on the Web. *Proc. of the 74rd Annual Meeting of the American Society for Information Science and Technology, 48.*

Sundin, O., & Francke, H. (2009). In search of credibility: Pupils' information practices in learning environments. *Information Research, 14*(4), paper 418.

Wang, P., & Soergel, D. (1998). A cognitive model of document use during a research project. Study I. Document selection. *Journal of the American Society for Information Science, 49*(2), 115-133.

Xie, I. (2008). *Interactive information retrieval in digital environments.* Hershey, PA: IGI Global.

Xu, Q. (2013). Social recommendation, source credibility, and recency: Effects of news cues in a social bookmarking website. *Journalism & Mass Communication Quarterly, 90*(4), 757-775.

7

Age and Gender in Reddit Commenting and Success

S. Craig Finlay *

Franklin D. Schurz Library
Indiana University South Bend, U.S.A.
E-mail: scfinlay@iusb.edu

ABSTRACT

Reddit is a large user generated content (USG) website in which users form common interest groups and submit links to external content or text posts of user-created content. The web site operates on a voting system whereby registered users can assign positive or negative ratings to both submitted content and comments made to submitted content. While Reddit is a pseudonymous site, with users creating usernames but providing no biographical data, an informal survey posted to a large shared interest community yielded 734 responses including age and gender of users. This provided a large amount of contextual biographical data with which to analyse user profiles at the first level of Computer Mediated Discourse Analysis (CMDA), articulated by Susan Herring. The results indicate that older Reddit users both formulate more complex writing and enjoy more success when rated by other users. Gender data was incomplete and as such only tentative results could be proposed in that regard.

Keywords: Computer mediated discourse analysis, CMDA, Reddit, Computer mediated communication, CMC, Age, Gender

1. INTRODUCTION

While a good deal of work has been done using Computer Mediated Discourse Analysis (CMDA) to determine differences in computer mediated communication behaviours as noted when looking at gender or structure within the communicative dynamic, the subject differences in age groups is largely unexplored. This is likely due to the difficulty of obtaining a large dataset wherein the users being

*Corresponding Author: S. Craig Finlay
Scholarly Communication Librarian
Franklin D. Schurz Library
Indiana University South Bend, U.S.A.
E-mail: scfinlay@iusb.edu

studied provide age information. When this has been done, such as in work by Kapidzic and Herring (2011) or Subrahmanyam and Greenfield (2004) in examining teen computer-mediated communication (CMC), the age context was made possible by studying teen chat rooms. While this approach provides researchers with a focused study on a particular age group, it also necessarily precludes likely participation by other age groups, preventing comparative analyses. Coupled with the fact that age is infrequently included in user profiles, the opportunity to look at how age differences manifest themselves in CMC is limited. This study makes use of a unique dataset: an informal request by a member of a message board within the website Reddit for age, gender, and nationality of message board subscribers. The resulting discussion thread included 734 responses. These responses were collected, and a sampling of comments from users was analysed according to the first level of CMDA (Herring, 2004). The first level of CMDA, corresponding to the four domains of language, is structure, with "phenomena [which] include the use of special typography or orthography, novel word formations and sentence structure" (Herring, 2004). The other three levels are listed as meaning, interaction, and social behaviour (Herring, 2004).

For this study, the following research questions were formulated:

R1: Is there an observable relationship between age and the phenomena classified by Herring (2004) as belonging to the structural level of CDMA, as quantifiable by examination of comment length, word length, and utterance length? If greater age may be associated with greater educational attainment and social development, one might expect to see an increase in complexity concurrent with advanced age.

R2: Is there a correlation between age and success of submitted links and comments as calculated by overall link and comment karma (the cumulative net total of link and comment scores, which are themselves the summation of a the Reddit voting system whereby other users rate the quality of submitted links and comments). Based on earlier analyses of Reddit comments, users seem to react more positively to longer, complex comments. Thus, there may also be a positive correlation between age and karma score.

Age as a topic of study is currently poorly under-

stood in regard to effect on various aspects of CMD. While researchers have studied and learned about teen constructions of gender, sexuality, and overall usage, it is as yet unknown how and at what rate CMC evolves along with a user's age. The difficulty of studying CMC in context of gender and age is articulated by Androutsopolous (2006), who notes that user anonymity, coupled with the lack of the "main type of linguistic variable in the correlative paradigm … phonetics/phonology" results in fewer readily available dependent variables for researchers to analyse (p. 425). However, he notes that the diligent researcher can obtain this information, yielding textured, valuable results. This study is such an undertaking of computer-user biographical data which will hopefully shed light on issues of age and CMC. An important implication of this study is that there may be a reliable mechanism by which a user's age can be inferred purely from textual analysis. This should be of interest to CMC researchers as well as those engaged in advertising on the web. This study provides a foundation for important research into this area. If a system whereby age (or gender) can be inferred with a low error rate, the implications for CMC research could be enormous, as researchers would no longer have to manually mine biographical information.

2. REDDIT

Reddit is a popular user-generated content web site which allows users to submit links or original content to "subreddits," self-organized communities of interest created by users themselves. While membership within the site is not necessary to view posts, it is necessary to post links and comment on posted links. No content is hosted on Reddit itself. Links are usually either to news stories, or to images hosted on Imgur, a simple image sharing web site that generates short, random, persistent URLS for any uploaded image. Users may subscribe to these subreddits, and when signed in the web site recognizes user subscriptions and supplies popular content from those users' subscriptions. Some of these subreddits are quite general, such as "pics," a photo hosting board with (as of the time of writing), 1.28 million subscribers. Some subreddits more unique to Reddit include "todayilearned," with approximately 800,000 subscribers. Users post interesting and obscure facts to this subreddit, leading to the common acronym "TIL," used throughout the web site. Another is the "F7U12," or "rage comic" subreddit, in which readers create simple comic strips using Reddit's own drag-and-drop template to tell personal amusing stories. The data for this survey was taken from r/atheism, a message board of atheists from around the world that describes itself as the largest such community on the internet.

A unique aspect of Reddit is the option to provide a simple assessment of approval or disapproval on any submitted content or on any comment posted in response to content (or to an existing comment). Known as "upvoting" or "downvoting," the system is democratic in that a user may only vote once for any given link or comment. Thus, a user cannot repeatedly up or downvote a post, though a user may replace an upvote with a downvote if so desired. The net ratio of upvotes minus downvotes is displayed next to a link or comment as a "score." That score is automatically assigned to a user's profile as that user's "karma." Users have two different karma ratings for submitted links and submitted content. Within the community, high karma scores are seen as status symbols, and may be seen, from the researcher's perspective, to be indicative of a Redditor's success on the site. Since most comments are not highly upvoted, comment karma, a cumulative score of many comments with one or two points apiece, may also be said to correlate to a user's activity level. Because of the importance Redditors place on karma scores, they have important implications for CMDA when used to study communication on this site.

3. LITERATURE REVIEW

Computer mediated discourse analysis (CMDA) is broadly outlined in Herring (2004), which explained the approach to studying computer mediated communication (CMC) as "applying to four domains or levels of language, ranging prototypically from smallest to largest linguistic unit of analysis: 1) structure, 2) meaning, 3) interaction, and 4) social behaviour" (p. 3). The first level, structure, focuses on word usage, sentence structure, typography, and orthography. It is this level

which concerns the present study. As the first step toward studying this data set, establishing the structural characteristics is a prerequisite toward more qualitative analyses.

A number of studies have looked at specific age groups and their use of computer mediated communication. Suzuki and Calzo (2004) looked at teens who sought advice on sex and health from two message boards. The study collected 273 questions and responses and found that teens were willing to ask questions regarding sex and sexual health in an online setting that they were unwilling to ask face-to-face from an adult. Gross (2004) looked broadly at online behaviour, using surveys. Gross found that boys and girls alike tended to use CMC to communicate on intimate topics with friends whom they knew outside of their online lives. Subrahmanyam, Greenfield, and Tynes (2004) looked at teen CMC and found that adolescents were taking advantage of the "screen" provided by the medium as a way to engage with others on topics of sexuality and gender, as part of their developmental processes. They also found that adolescents utilized CMC as a way to "practice" participating in different kinds of relationships with others.

The wealth of information provided by mining comment boards and collaborative websites has recently allowed researchers to look at various aspects of human communication. Ioannou (2011) examined how wikis facilitate collaborative creation by web users. Three researchers recently looked at comment ratings on message boards to examine the spread of ideas. Koteyko, Jaspal and Nerlich (2013) looked at user comments on UK tabloid news sites to examine evolving attitudes toward the climate change debate. Chiluwa (2009) innovatively applied CMDA to study the popularly termed "419" emails – hoaxes which attempt to convince recipients to pay money by informing them of large lottery winnings or other large sums of money that may be claimed.

A more recent look at gender was undertaken by Kapidzic and Herring (2011), who looked at gender and CMC in English-language teen chat sites. They found that gender differences manifest on a number of levels. Males were found to participate in more "invite" acts, requesting behaviour of females, whereas female users tended to react to those assertive behaviours. They also found that male communications were often more overtly sexual in nature than those of their female counterparts. The study also looked at differences in self-representation in terms of posted profile photos. Herring (2010) looked at the concept of the "floor" in regard to gender, specifically in terms of success in gaining responses and controlling the floor of the conversation. That study found that males were more successful in garnering responses in message boards, probably due to higher rates of message posting. Such is of particular importance to the present study in that the dataset provides an opportunity to determine "success" as a Redditor (as evidenced by karma score), in the context of gender. In addition, such an approach may equally be applied to age.

The wealth of data (tens of thousands of comments) makes possible other analyses of writing not attempted here. For example, Herring and Paolillo (2006) looked at the "gender" of weblog genres using the Gender Genie program. In regard to the program itself, the researchers found it had mixed success in identifying author gender. The concept of automatically identifying age is an ultimate goal of this project, and the massive potential dataset offered by the Reddit interface providing all comments ever posted by each user means substantial steps could be taken toward this goal. In short, the large amount of work done identifying the ways in which gender is manifested in CMC provide a blueprint for studying age. Much of the work done in regard to the former focus on notions of power (see Herring, 2003) and gender, specifically manifestations of sexism on the internet. Obviously this dynamic would not manifest itself as such in the interactions of different age groups. However, the social position occupied by certain age groups, such as middle-school students as opposed to working adults, may well influence interactions in an online environment.

4. METHODOLOGY AND DATA COLLECTION

The methodology of analysis of this data set is CMDA, specifically the first level of CMDA as outlined in Herring (2004). The dataset for this study was collected from an informal survey posted to the r/atheism subreddit on December 17, 2011. User "xtimrs" posted to r/atheism a message wondering as to the demographic makeup of the subreddit, which at the time had a little less than 500,000 subscribed readers. While the original post simply asked for suggestions on workshopping a possible demographic survey, users began responding with largely "age, sex, location" comments. Of the 998 comments in the threads, 734 responded to the survey. This information was collected manually. While age is the primary focus of this study, there was a sufficient population of female respondents to enable a gender-based analysis of submitted comments [Table 1].

Gender, along with age and location data, was manually collected and assembled into a spreadsheet and then used as the basis for further data collection, starting with manual collection of user comments and link karma. Recall that comment karma may be broadly associated with user activity, as most comments are not highly upvoted and therefore a user's comment karma score grows slowly, over time. Also, as high karma scores are seen as status symbols, they may also be said to indicate a user's "success" as a Redditor. Comment and link kar-

Table 1. Self-Reported Gender of Reddit Users in r/atheism

Gender	Number	Percent
Male	470	64.03%
Female	122	16.62%
No response	141	19.21%
Other	1	0.14%
Total	734	

ma for each responding user was collected manually by clicking on each responding user's name in turn.

Among the publicly available information on Reddit is past activity by a user. Clicking on a user's name will display a list of every comment and link that user has ever posted to Reddit. Initially, it was envisioned that an automated crawler would be constructed that could gather this data in its entirety. Such a crawler could not be constructed in time, and as such comment collection was also manual. This meant that complete collection was impossible, as for most users the number of comments posted is likely to be in the dozens and often in the hundreds. To exhaustively document all activity by the 734 survey respondents would mean collecting tens of thousands of comments and links and their associated metadata (posting time, scores, etc.). It was thus decided to collect a sample of comments from users across all age groups, thereby enabling comparative analysis, if not presenting a necessarily accurate picture of the community as a whole. To do this, the first page of comments by each responding user was manually copied and pasted into an Excel sheet. Clicking a user's name brings up all comments by that user, divided into pages. To do this, bins were first created which may be said to roughly correspond to certain commonly accepted educational developmental periods [Table 2].

The logic behind this that Reddit is a U.S. based website and the ages in these bins commonly correspond in the United States to certain stages of educational prog-

ress. Those individuals in group 1 would be expected to be in grades 6-10 (middle school through mid-high school), group 2 to high school seniors, group 3 to college undergrads, group 4 to recent college grads, those entering the workforce and those in graduate school, 5 to young adults settling into professional career paths and 6 to adults firmly established in the workforce. Group 6 is by far the largest in terms of timespan, covering ages from 36 to 67. It is also the smallest group. For each group, the average comment and link karma was calculated, to provide a baseline for the "average" user of that demographic [Table 3]. Then, for each age group, the first five users with comment karma above and below this baseline were selected as that demographic's representative age group. This population of 60 was later expanded to 90 to include more female users, allowing for another level of comparative analysis. In all, data for 30 female users was collected. For each of these users, the most recent five comments posted were collected for a dataset of 450 comments. After collection, comments were analysed by manually counting all comments for number of utterances. Additionally, content was analysed with the Microsoft Word spelling and grammar check to determine average word length and readability statistics. Further studies will be conducted utilizing a crawler to automate data collection, enabling broader conclusions. The present results should be considered a compass pointing out future research directions.

Table 2. Age Bins of Reddit Survey Respondents

Group	Age	Number	Percent
1	12-16	120	16.35%
2	17-18	114	15.53%
3	19-22	204	27.79%
4	23-27	150	20.44%
5	28-35	83	11.31%
6	36+	59	8.04%
	No response	4	0.54%
	Total	734	100%

Table 3. Average Link and Comment Karma, By Age Bin

Age	Number	Average link karma	Average comment karma
12-16	120	321	649
17-18	114	534	1280
19-22	204	586	1307
23-27	150	497	2342
28-35	83	356	2979
36+	59	569	3006
No response	4	4	N/A
Overall	734	508	1699

5. RESULTS

The average Reddit r/atheism user may be described as a male in his late teens to mid-20s. Female users are very much in the minority, at some 16.6% of respondents. However, 19% of respondents neglected to include age in their comments, and as such the gender demographics of the Reddit r/atheism population may vary some from the proportions seen here. Far more complete was the age data, with only 4 users neglecting to provide information. We can see in Table 2 that a majority of Redditors fall within the 12-16 (16.3%), 17-18 (15.5%), 19-22 (27.7%) and 23-27 (20.4%) age groups. Users over the age of 28 are a distinct minority, although enough data was collected to enable meaningful analysis. In Table 3 it is apparent that there is a positive correlation between user age and comment karma score. Each age group revealed higher average comment karma than the group below it, although the difference between the 28-35 and 36+ groupings is minimal. The relationship is especially striking when visualized in bar graph form [Figure 1].

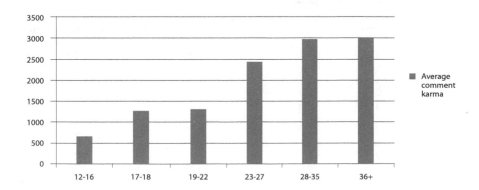

Fig. 1 Age differences in Reddit karma score

The average karma of the two highest age groups is so similar as to be functionally identical for the purposes of this study (2979 and 3006). Together, they have a population of 142, making them more or less equal in size as a demographic (albeit a very, very diverse one), to the other age bins. It is striking that the average karma score for this highest age bracket (or brackets) is on average over 4.5 times higher than for those in the youngest age bracket. The 12-16 year old age bracket displayed an average comment karma of only 649, a little over half that of the next age bracket, the 17-18 year olds, which displayed an average karma of 1280. This total was very similar to the 19-22 year old group, with an average karma score of 1307. Interestingly, this is identical in size to the gap between the two highest age groups. There is a large gap between the 19-22 year olds and the next age group, the 23-27 year olds, which had an average karma score of 2342. No substantial differences were observed in link karma among the age groups.

Comment karma was also examined in the context of gender [Table 4]. While male respondents were found to have a higher comment karma score (1737) than female respondents (1257), both were lower than the average score computed for the 141 who declined to include gender information. It must be assumed that the inclusion of missing gender data would alter the results and as such these numbers should be taken with the proverbial grain of salt.

When the average length of comments was analysed, age and gender differences were apparent as well [Table 5]. The average overall comment length was 28.1 words. While not as striking as the differences in user karma, a similar pattern is evident, with higher age groups writing longer comments. The 12-16 and 17-18 age groups wrote similar-length posts, 22.8 and 23, respectively. Users aged 19-22 years old wrote com-

Table 4. Karma in the Context of Self-Reported Gender

Gender	Number	Average link karma	Average comment karma
Male	470	517	1737
Female	122	352	1257
No response	141	493	1944
Other	1	N/A	N/A
Total	734	508	1699

Table 5. Average Comment Length by User Age (Number of Comments per Age bin = 75)

Age	Average comment length
12-16	22.8
17-18	23
19-22	26
23-27	32.1
28-35	32.9
36+	32.2
Overall	28.1

ments 26 words long on average. The 23-27, 28-35 and 36+ age groups all wrote comments, on average, of 32 words long, with decimal-size variation. When averaged together, the two highest age groups write around 10 more words per comment than the two smallest age groups.

When examined according to age, the length of the average comment by males was found to be similar to the two smallest age groups, at 23.3 [Table 6]. Females, by contrast, wrote posts similar in length to the three highest age groups, at 32.4. Again the group which neglected to provide gender information had the highest result, with an average number of 34.5, greater than any single age group.

To consider a unit of writing utterance in this study was it is a clause, as articulated by Condon and Cech (1996). The number of utterances per comment for the sampled data was manually counted and revealed to be 4.7, with an average overall utterance length of 5.8 words [Table 7]. While the average utterance length did not vary widely among age groups, the number of utterances per comment increased according to age. This follows when considering the longer average posts by those in the higher age brackets. Average word length was found to be broadly similar across all age groups.

The same analysis was applied to gender, and it was found that male Redditors write fewer utterances (4.7) and shorter utterances (4.9 words) than their female counterparts (5.4 and 6 words). Those users who neglected to provide gender data displayed a slightly higher number of average utterances (5.6), and identical words per utterance as the female respondents [Table 8].

Table 6. Average Comment Length by Reported Gender

Gender	Number	Average comment length
Male	470	23.3
Female	122	32.4
No response	141	34.5

Table 7. Utterances per Comment, Words per Utterance, and Average Word Length, By Age Group

Age	Number	Utterance/comment	Words/utterance	Word length
12-16	120	3.9	5.8	4.3
17-18	114	3.7	6.1	4.3
19-22	204	4.2	6.1	4.2
23-27	150	5.4	5.9	4.3
28-35	83	5.8	5.65	4.3
36+	59	5.6	5.6	4.2
No response	4	N/A	N/A	N/A
	734	4.7	5.8	

Table 8. Utterances Examined by Gender Identification

Gender	Number	Utterance/comment	Words/utterance	Word length
Male	470	4.7	4.9	4.3
Female	122	5.4	6	4.2
No response	141	5.6	6	4.2

6. DISCUSSION

In an earlier study on Reddit comments, looking at 94 comments posted to a single discussion thread in response to a rage comic in the F7U12 subreddit, users were arbitrarily binned according to comment karma, with length of comments and utterance data analysed in that context [Table 9]. That study found that users in the higher karma brackets tended to write longer posts with a greater number of utterances, and with longer utterances, than users with lower average karma. While the numbers analysed in that study were too small to draw more than preliminary conclusions, those would appear to have been confirmed by this study. Users with higher karma scores tend to write longer comments. Whether this is because longer comments are better received, or because more experienced users feel more comfortable writing longer comments cannot be determined at this time, and no causality should be assumed.

To recap the research questions formulated above:

R1: Is there an observable relationship between age and the phenomena classified by Herring (2004) as belonging to the structural level of CDMA, as quantifiable by examination of comment length, word length,

and utterance length? If greater age may be associated with greater educational attainment and social development, one might expect to see an increase in complexity concurrent with advanced age.

R2: Is there a correlation between age and success of submitted links and comments as calculated by overall link and comment karma (the cumulative net total of link and comment scores, which are themselves the summation of a the Reddit voting system whereby other users rate the quality of submitted links and comments). Based on earlier analyses of Reddit comments, users seem to react more positively to longer, complex comments. Thus, there may also be a positive correlation between age and karma score.

An important result of this study is the identification of differences in computer mediated communication among individuals of different age groups. Consistently, younger users have lower karma scores and write shorter posts than older users. They also write less complex comments, with a smaller number of utterances. This could indicate that as individuals attain more education their confidence and writing ability increases and this is manifested in their online communications. Therefore, R1 and R2 are answered in the affirmative: a positive correlation exists be-

Table 9. A Previous Study Examining Commenting Behaviour According to Karma Score

Population (by user comment karma)	Words per comment	characters per word	number of utterances	words/utterance
bottom third (n=25)	14.3	4.1	2.07	6.9
middle third (n=24)	15.41	4	2.56	6.01
top third (n=24)	21.82	4.1	2.68	8.147

tween success of submitted comments and age, and age differences manifest themselves at least at the level of comment length. It is interesting that no striking differences exist between age groups in terms of link karma, the aggregate score of all links submitted to Reddit. This would indicate that age has no bearing on the success of submitted content. This may be because the users' increased intellectual ability has less opportunity for expression in the short description space allowed by Reddit when submitting a link than in the comparatively freer platform of commenting.

7. LIMITATIONS

It is disappointing that the gender data was so incomplete, and the type of analysis conducted in Herring (2010) could not be repeated here. That more respondents neglected to include gender data than self-identified as female likely renders any conclusions tentative at best. Evidence of this may be seen in the fact that males had higher average karma scores but much shorter average comments. The lower number of utterances and shorter utterances per comment for males also indicates a decreased complexity of comments. However, those individuals who did not respond with gender information had both higher comment karma and longer average comments than either males or females, which seems to confirm earlier conclusions. More data needs to be collected to enable drawing a conclusion one way or the other.

8. FUTURE WORK

Much more work remains to be done with this dataset. The first level of CMDA was not exhausted here, not to mention issues of topicality, interactivity, or politeness. It has been established that at least some age-based differences are manifested in online communication. With further research, other differences will undoubtedly surface. The next task must be to exhaustively collect all comments and links submitted by all users within the dataset. Then researchers may begin the long task of applying higher levels of CMDA to what will be a very large corpus of data.

REFERENCES

Chiluwa, I. (2009). The discourse of digital deceptions and '419' emails. *Discourse Studies, 11*(6), 635-660. doi:10.1177/1461445609347229

Condon, S., & Cech, C. (1996). Discourse management strategies in face-to-face and computer mediated decision making interactions. *The Electronic Journal of Communication, 6*(3). Retrieved from http://www.cios.org/EJCPUBLIC/006/3/006314.HTML.

Gross, E. (2004). Adolescent internet use: What we expect, what teens report. *Applied Developmental Psychology, 25*, 633-649.

Herring, S. C. (2010). Who's got the floor in computer-mediated conversation? Edelsky's gender patterns revisited. *Language@Internet, 7*, article 8. Retrieved from http://www.languageatinternet.org/articles/2010/2857.

Herring, S. C., & Paolillo, J. C. (2006). Gender and genre variation in weblogs. *Journal of Sociolinguistics, 10*(4), 439-459. Preprint retrieved from http://ella.slis.indiana.edu/~herring/jslx.pdf.

Herring, S. C., & Martinson, A. (2004). Assessing gender authenticity in computer-mediated language use: Evidence from an identity game. *Journal of Language and Social Psychology, 23*(4), 424-446. doi: 10.1177/0261927X04269586

Herring, S. C. (2004). Computer-mediated discourse analysis: An approach to researching online behaviour. In S. A. Barab, R. Kling, & J. H. Gray (Eds.), *Designing for Virtual Communities in the Service of Learning* (pp. 338-376). New York: Cambridge University Press. Preprint retrieved from http://ella.slis.indiana.edu/~herring/cmda.pdf.

Herring, S. C. (2003). Gender and power in online communication. In J. Holmes & M. Meyerhoff (Eds.), *The Handbook of Language and Gender* (pp. 202-228). Oxford: Blackwell Publishers. Retrieved from http://ella.slis.indiana.edu/~herring/gender.power.pdf.

Ioannou, A. (2011). Online collaborative learning: The promise of wikis. *International Journal Of Instructional Media, 38*(3), 213-223.

Kapidzic, S., & Herring, S. C. (2011). Gender, communication, and self-presentation in teen chatrooms revisited: Have patterns changed? *Journal of Computer-Mediated Communication, 17*(1), 39-

59. Retrieved from http://onlinelibrary.wiley.com/doi/10.1111/j.1083-6101.2011.01561.x/full.

Koteyko, N., Jaspal, R., & Nerlich, B. (2013). Climate change and 'Climategate' in online reader comments: A mixed methods study. *Geographical Journal, 179*(1), 74-86.

Subrahmanyam, K., Greenfield, P., & Tynes, B. (2004). Constructing sexuality and identity in an online teen chat room. *Applied Developmental Psychology, 25*, 651-666.

Suzuki, L., & Calzo, J. (2004). The search for peer advice in cyberspace: An examination. *Applied Developmental Psychology, 25*, 685-698.

8

Internal Structure of Information Packages in Digital Preservation

Seungmin Lee *

Department of Library and Information Science
Sookmyung Women's University, Requblic of Korea
E-mail: ableman@sookmyung.ac.kr

ABSTRACT

The description of preserved resources is one of the requirements in digital preservation. The description is generally created in the format of metadata records, and those records are combined to generate information packages to support the process of digital preservation. However, current strategies or models of digital preservation may not generate information packages in efficient ways. To overcome these problems, this research proposed an internal structure of information packages in digital preservation. In order to construct the internal structure, this research analyzed existing metadata standards and cataloging rules such as Dublin Core, MARC, and FRBR to extract the core elements of resource description. The extracted elements were categorized according to their semantics and functions, which resulted in three categories of core elements. These categories and core elements were manifested by using RDF syntax in order to be substantially applied to combine metadata records in digital preservation. Although the internal structure is not intended to create metadata records, it is expected to provide an alternative approach to enable combining existing metadata records in the context of digital preservation in a more flexible way.

Keywords: Digital preservation, Information package, Metadata record, Internal structure

*Corresponding Author: Seungmin Lee
Assistant professor
Department of Library and Information Science
Sookmyung Women's University, Requblic of Korea
E-mail: ableman@sookmyung.ac.kr

1. INTRODUCTION

With the rapid increase of resources in digital formats, there is growing attention to the preservation of those resources. In this changed information environment, the importance of digital preservation is now becoming a hot issue in many communities, including the library and information science field. The preservation of traditional resources in printed formats has long been done in systematic ways. However, that of digital resources seems to be extremely different from the traditional archiving of resources.

In its initial stage, the major object of digital preservation was born-digital resources. With the advantages of digital preservation in preserving resources, however, any type of resources, including printed materials, is now the object of digital preservation. These resources in analog formats are transformed or converted into digital formats and preserved in digital archives.

The process of digital preservation consists of multiple phases that many experts from various fields need to participate in, including acquisition, archiving processes, storage, and dissemination of the resources preserved. In each phase, the target resource of digital preservation needs to be described in order to provide additional information. Therefore, the description of preserved resources is considered as the core of digital preservation. It can support an effective and efficient approach to resource management which is optimized for digital preservation.

Resource description is generally created in the format of metadata records using metadata standards. Digital preservation has also adopted various metadata standards, including rights, technical, administrative, and structural metadata, in order to provide detailed descriptions of preserved resources. In each phase of digital preservation, many metadata records are used to fully support the preservation process, which generates different types of information packages. However, these metadata standards adopt heterogeneous elements and the records generated based on these standards are considered as independent records. This has resulted in inefficiency in generating information packages and may not fully support each phase of the process of digital preservation.

In order to support efficient administration and management of digital preservation, heterogeneous metadata records need to be combined in a more flexible way during the process of digital preservation. From this perspective, this research proposes an approach to combine metadata records generated by heterogeneous metadata standards and to support the generation of information packages in digital preservation. This approach considers a set of metadata records as an independent unit which can also be used as an information package that can support the process of digital preservation. In order to constitute information packages, an internal structure of the information packages needs to be constructed based on the elements used in a set of metadata records.

To achieve this goal, this research analyzes the core elements used in metadata records in the context of digital preservation. By extracting the core aspects of resource description in the process of digital preservation, the criteria for combining different metadata records can be established. Based on the core aspects, an internal structure for combining metadata records is constructed. This research also adopted Resource Description Framework (RDF) in order to manifest the internal structure of information packages, which can be substantially applied in the combination of metadata records and the generation of information packages. This internal structure can clearly show the components of information packages and establish the relationships between metadata records optimized for digital preservation.

2. CONCEPTUAL FOUNDATIONS

2.1. Concept of Resource Description and Digital Preservation

With the development of Information and Communication Technology (ICT), various types of information resources are rapidly increasing and have been published in digital format on the Web. In addition, ICTs can play an important role in support of the use of those resources. In this changed information environment, the importance of digital preservation gains more weight in the management and re-use of information resources.

Although there are a variety of formats of information resources, most resources in both printed and digital formats are generally preserved in digital format because digital formatting has advantages in preserving resources from the perspective of retention and re-use of those resources.

Digital preservation refers to the series of managed activities necessary to ensure continued access to digital resources for as long as necessary (Digital Preservation Coalition, 2012). It includes all of the actions required to maintain access to digital resources beyond the limits of media failure or technological change (Gomes, Miranda & Costa, 2011).

In order to process digital preservation, it is required to identify and retrieve all related components for the purpose of preserving a digital object. From this perspective, the process of digital preservation is inseparable from accessing the preserved object, which can be supported by resource description (Vardigan & Whiteman, 2007). For these reasons, the object needs to be re-created in a surrogate form, which is mainly generated in the format of metadata records.

In order for successful digital preservation, fundamental principles for resource description need to be established. More specifically, metadata standards that can support the description of the preserved resources may be the core of the process of digital preservation. However, there are many limitations in establishing appropriate disciplines that can be applied to digital preservation. From this perspective, many research efforts have been conducted to address these challenges and to develop digital preservation activities.

According to Heslop, Davis, and Wilson (2002), the object preserved in digital archives is often not an original physical object but a conceptual or virtual object that contains, replicates, or embodies the original object's significant properties or essential qualities. It refers to the characteristics that need to be preserved as descriptive records. For these reasons, many research studies have made standardized conceptual models for supporting the description of preserved objects that can suit the purpose of their communities (Lynch, 2003).

However, it is possible that a preserved resource can change its format during its conversion or transformation process in order to be included in digital preservation. Metadata is required in this process and describes every aspect related to the resource from its origins to the current status in the digital preservation process. At this point, one important thing is that every change or property needs to be described in a standardized and formal way (Calhoun, 2006). The description of preserved resources is the core of digital preservation. In order to support resource description in digital preservation, many reference models and strategies have been proposed, including the Open Archival Information System (OAIS) Reference Model and DCC Curation Lifecycle Model.

In digital preservation communities, there have been many efforts to efficiently conduct digital preservation by standardizing the process of preserving resources in any format, including both born-digital and digitized resources. OAIS Reference Model is a representative model designed to support the overall process of digital preservation. The process provided by OAIS model consists of six steps. Each step requires different packages of additional information or metadata, and also needs different values for the same elements according to the purpose of each step, although they describe the same resource. From this perspective, the OAIS Reference Model defines long-term preservation in terms of the concept of an information package, for example, digital content and its associated metadata as a single package moving into (Submission Information Package: SIP), through (Archival Information Package: AIP), and out of (Dissemination Information Package: DIP) the archival system (Lane, 2012). Different metadata records may constitute different information packages. However, current approaches lack a well-defined architecture to support the use of preserved resources.

2.2. Challenges in Resource Description for Digital Preservation

Digital preservation is expected to provide a way of utilizing and reusing resources and the efficient long-term management of valuable resources. Because of arbitrary generation of information packages in the process of digital preservation, however, there are problems with resource description and the generation of information packages (IMS, 2003). In addition, because each set of metadata records is generated based on heterogeneous metadata standards and is independent from other records, they may not be efficiently reused when the process goes on. Therefore, each step may generate metadata records for the same resource redundantly. It may increase the complexity of the overall process of digital preservation. For these reasons, practical issues are considered in order to make appropriate use of resource description in the context of digital preservation. There is also a need to develop approaches and models for the re-use and connection of metadata records.

Resources for preservation go along with resource description. This description as additional information will have to be linked together in some way and methods of updating the resources and related information will have to be considered (NLII, 2003). From this perspective, a preserved resource is any resource that can be used to facilitate information activities and has been described using metadata. A resource cannot be regarded as a resource in digital preservation until it is made explicit through the addition of metadata. For these reasons, there is a growing awareness that preserving information resources will need to be expanded to include appropriate description through information packages by combining interrelated and relevant metadata records (Beagrie, 2002; Crow, 2002).

To fully support resource description in the context of digital preservation, metadata records that deal with every aspect of the preserved resource should be generated in each phase of digital preservation (Hedstrom, 1998). Because the same resource is described based on different metadata standards, the description can vary according to the unique purpose of each phase in the process of digital preservation. In the current status of digital preservation, however, the adoption of heterogeneous metadata standards has resulted in the inefficiency of generating information packages. This is mainly because the current reference models provide heterogeneous metadata records in each phase. For this reason, each metadata record is considered as an independent unit that may be isolated in each phase and may not be able to be fully reused in other phases

3. METHODOLOGY

To overcome the limitations and problems in resource description when preserving various resources, it is required to have a standardized way for resource description that can be applied to the overall process of digital preservation. The purpose of this research is to manifest a conceptual framework that represents each aspect of a variety of resources and supports the process of digital preservation by providing detailed resource description.

This research consists of three phases: (1) analysis of

the core aspects of metadata records in the context of digital preservation, (2) conceptualization of the internal structure of information packages optimized for digital preservation processes, and (3) the manifestation of internal structure to generate information packages.

This research begins with a review of the concept and role of resource description. This may be the foundation of digital preservation because it provides detailed description of preserved resources. In digital preservation, each resource description is not independent but interrelated with each other and provides a set of descriptions to support each phase of digital preservation. By reviewing the core aspects of resource description, the embedded meanings and the substantial functions of the description can be identified. Based on the reviews of resource description, the combination of metadata records can be achieved in a more flexible way and can support the overall process of digital preservation.

Based on the notion of resource description, the essential components of metadata records in digital preservation would be extracted. The existing metadata standards can be used to extract the core elements of metadata records for digital preservation. The identified elements are categorized according to their intended use and the relationships among the elements. These categories constitute the basic framework of the internal structure with multi-layered structure for generating information packages.

A structured framework for combining metadata records is constructed on the basis of the internal structure of information packages. This framework is not for acquiring metadata interoperability, but is a conceptual foundation that can combine existing metadata records in order to satisfy the purpose of each phase of the process of digital preservation. Each of the core elements that constitute the internal structure can be used as a reference point that provides a flexible combination of metadata records and generates various information packages applied in digital preservation.

In order to manifest the internal structure of information packages, this research adopts Resource Description Framework (RDF) so that the existing metadata records can be combined in a flexible way, which is an optimized way for each phase of digital preservation.

The approach proposed in this research might be helpful to clarify the internal structure of information packages, so that the management and description of resources contained in digital archives can be supported.

4. CONSTRUCTION OF INTERNAL STRUCTURE OF INFORMATION PACKAGE

To provide more efficient ways of utilizing information packages and to support digital preservation, metadata records applied to each phase need to be combined according to the unique purpose of each phase. In order to achieve the combination of metadata records, the internal structure of information packages should be established.

4.1. Layers of Metadata Records

The combination of metadata records requires a set of elements that can uniquely identify each metadata record. The element set can be used as primary keys of connecting metadata records. By using the key elements, heterogeneous metadata records can retain their intrinsic elements that may fully satisfy the purpose of each phase. In addition, each metadata record can be applied in a more flexible way in generating information packages whenever it is required. In setting up a set of elements as primary keys, however, the core elements used in metadata records should be identified, which can be manifested as the internal structure of metadata records.

An element can be related to other elements if they share some meanings. This establishes element relationships. This relationship makes the meaning and functions of each element clear. Each element can have attributes that describe certain aspects of the element and prescribe the range of the meaning of the element. These attributes can be also considered as components of resource description. However, most of these attributes can be applied to only one element, although some attributes can be broadly applied to other elements. The attribute may not be important in constructing the internal structure of information packages because it does not establish relationships with other elements and the range of the meaning is relatively narrow. Therefore, this research does not consider the attribute as the component of information packages.

The elements traditionally used to describe an information resource are linearly enumerated in one-dimensional structure. Although this linear structure can clearly show the meanings of the elements embedded in information packages, it cannot fully show the relationships among elements if one element has multiple relationships with other elements. In some cases, hierarchical structure can be more efficient to show the relationships among elements. However, not all elements do have a hierarchical relationship and the hierarchical structure may not provide the space for the enumeration of the meaning of each element.

In this research, a hybrid approach was used that combines linear and hierarchical structure. It can have multiple layers with enumeration of elements. Each element in each layer has hierarchical relationships with other elements in other layers. This multi-layered structure can enumerate the meanings of elements in detail and can also show the hierarchical relationships among elements.

4.2. Identification of Core Elements for Information Packages

In order to construct the internal structure of information packages, the components of an information package need to be transformed to a set of descriptive elements that can be substantially applied to the description of preserved resources. The elements of information packages can be transformed from each aspect of the information resources.

The elements of an information package may be similar to the traditional descriptive elements for information resources. However, they may be related to other elements in multiple layers. This is because an information package is a group of metadata records that share the same contents. In order to comprehensively combine different metadata records for the same resource, the elements used in metadata records should be tied in a structured format.

In order to extract the core elements for resource description in the context of digital preservation, this research used two existing metadata standards (Dublin Core and MARC) and one cataloging rule (FRBR). Dublin Core is one of the most representative metadata standards across communities and provides core elements in describing resources in any format. Although MARC was originally designed for printed materials in the library community, it is now applied to any format of resources both in printed and digital formats. These metadata standards are expected to identify the elements that can be essentially used in the resource description for digital preservation. Functional Requirements for Bibliographic Records (FRBR) is not a metadata standard, but a kind of cataloging rule. However, it provides a conceptual structure in describing resources and in supporting the establishment of relationships between elements used in resource description. It can be also used to combine inter-related elements when describing resources. By analyzing these three standards, the essential elements for digital preservation can be extracted (see Appendix 1). The core elements that can be applied to generate information packages appear to be nine elements (see Table 1).

Although these elements may be used as a set of core elements in digital preservation, each element cannot properly identify the preserved resources. Therefore, a set of core elements need to be connected as an independent unit. By using the set of elements, it can properly function as core elements that can support the generation of information packages.

4.3. Multi-Layered Element Relationships for Information Packages

The internal structure of an information package with semi-hierarchical structure proposed in this research consists of three layers with hierarchies: content, carrier, and publication. The layer 'content' can be defined as a set of bibliographic elements that describes specific aspects of a resource related to the content of the resource, such as title, creator, and subject. The layer 'carrier' is a set of elements that describes the medium of resource which manifests and communicates its contents. Representative elements contained in the 'carrier' layer include medium, language, date, and identifier. The bibliographic elements that represent the information related to the publication of the content and media are categorized in the 'publication' layer. It includes the elements such as publisher and edition, which are related to the publication of the resource.

These layers were based on the categories of inter-related elements extracted from the three standards. Each layer contains related elements as sub-elements and establishes certain types of relationship with one or more elements. These relationships are established when one element has effect on the meaning of the related elements in constructing an internal structure of the information package.

This research adopted the social network theory when establishing element relationships. The social network theory seems to be useful to identify the relationship between elements in information packages because each element can be seen as a component of element relationships within bibliographic description. The relationship between elements in information packages can be divided into three main types according to strength of relations: strong, medium, and weak ties. The strength

Table 1. Core Elements of Information Packages

Core Element	Definition
Creator	A group of creators responsible for the content of individual information resources that share the same or variation of the original content
Title	A group of names of information resources that share the same or a variation of content
Subject	A set of one or more terms that represent the content contained in an information package
Publication	Information related to the manifestation of the same or a variation of content in individual information resources
Language	Specific languages used to represent the same or a variation of content contained in an information package
Edition	A certain version of individual information resources contained in an information package
Identifier	A set of characters assigned to individual information resources contained in an information package
Date	Information related to the date of individual resources contained in an information package
Medium	Formats of individual information resources contained in an information package

of relationship refers to the closeness between two or more components and the range of the function of each component. This strength of relationship can represent the detailed relationships with related elements and can play an important role in constructing the internal structure of information packages.

4.3.1. Content layer

Among the nine elements provided in Table 1, Creator and Title are connected with strong ties. The element Title also establishes a strong tie with the element Subject (see Fig. 1). These two strong ties establish a weak tie among the elements Creator and Subject. These three elements are the ones that describe the content of the information package. The content of the information package is not changed or affected by other parts of the information package, no matter what forms the information package takes. The three elements that describe the content do not describe or prescribe other elements.

This means that the meaning of these three elements is not changed or affected by other elements. They can be considered to be grouped together because they are all related to the content of the information package.

4.3.2. Carrier layer

The elements Language, Identifier, Date, and Medium specify each aspect of the carrier of information resources. They only describe and prescribe the elements in other layers. The meanings of these elements can be changed according to context and the element value can be also changeable. These elements can be grouped together because they are related to the carrier of the information package. However, there is no direct relationship among these elements. These elements can only be connected through other elements. This type of connection establishes weak ties among these elements (see Fig. 2).

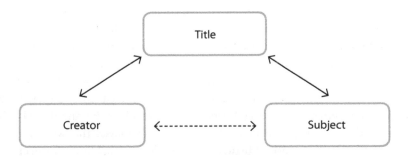

Fig. 1 Element relationships in Content layer

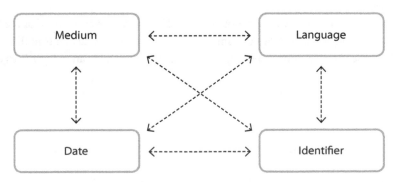

Fig. 2 Element relationship in Carrier layer

4.3.3. Publication layer

The elements Publisher and Edition share many characteristics and can be considered as similar elements in the context of digital preservation. This is because Edition is also a kind of publication of an information resource. In terms of bibliographic information, however, these two elements describe different aspects of information resources. Therefore, Publisher and Edition should be considered as different elements in the internal structure of information packages. These two elements are described by other elements, and simultaneously describe and prescribe the meaning of other elements. These elements represent the process of publishing information resources in order to transmit and communicate information. Therefore, these elements can be considered as a manifestation of the carrier of information. They are also related to the content of an information package. The elements Publisher and Edition establish a strong tie and can be grouped together because they are related to the publication process of information packages (see Fig. 3).

4.4 Construction of Internal Structure

The internal structure of information packages can be divided into two parts: layer-level and element-level. The relationships in layer-level construct the framework of the internal structure of an information package. The layer-level relationship concentrates on creating layers by combining elements that have the same or similar meanings and representing the relationships between the layers. The layer relationship adopts a hierarchical structure that can clearly represent hierarchical relationships among elements in different layers. This hierarchical structure is also useful to represent multiple relationships if an element establishes relationships with more than one element.

Linear structure is used to represent element relationships in each layer in element-level. Each layer enumerates elements that have the same or similar meaning and

functions. The linear structure is efficient to describe the detailed meanings and characteristics of each element in element-centered aspects which hierarchical structure cannot clearly represent. In addition, the element relationships that do not establish hierarchical relationship can be clarified by using linear structure.

By using the structure that combines hierarchical and linear structure, the meanings and functions of the elements in information packages can be clearly represented. The proposed internal structure of information packages consists of three layers: Content layer, Publication layer, and Carrier layer. Each layer adopts linear structure to enumerate the embedded elements. The enumerated elements are connected with other elements by establishing specific relationships (see Fig. 4).

The Content layer is placed on the top of the internal structure. The elements embedded in the Content layer are connected with each other by establishing strong ties with the element Title. Although the elements Creator and Subject are not directly connected, the weak ties are established through the element Title. The elements in the Content layer are described and prescribed by the elements in other layers.

The Publication layer is placed in the middle of the internal structure. It functions as a mediator that connects the Content layer and the Carrier layer. The two elements embedded in the Publication layer establish strong relationships and describe the element Title in the Content layer. The two elements in the Publication layer do not establish any direct relationship with the elements Creator and Subject in the Content layer, thus weak relationships are established with those elements through the element Title. Therefore, the Publication layer can be considered to describe the Content layer. The Publication layer is also described by the Carrier layer.

The Carrier layer is placed at the bottom of the internal structure. The elements in this layer describe all elements in the Publication layer. This element relationship

Fig. 3 Element relationship in Publication layer

is established by medium ties between the Publication and the Carrier layers. The elements in the Carrier layer also describe the elements in the Content layer. Therefore, the Carrier layer establishes medium ties with both the Publication layer and weak ties with the Content layers. However, not all of the elements in the Carrier layer describe all of the elements in the Content layer. Therefore, the relationship between the Content and Carrier layers is not a layer-level relationship. The relationship can be considered as an element-level relationship. Although the elements embedded in the Carrier layer are mainly related to represent the characteristics of the carrier of information, these elements are also used to describe the elements in the Publication and the Content layers. The elements in the Carrier layer play important roles in connecting all components of the information package through certain types of relationships.

Synthetically, the layer-level relationship constructs the framework of the internal structure of the information package. This layer relationship is established by the relationships between the elements embedded in each layer. Therefore, the element relationship among elements embedded in each layer provides the foundation of constructing the internal structure of the information package. The elements function as internal nodes that

connect each layer. They can also function as external nodes to connect other information packages that contain the same element values.

5. MANIFESTATION OF INTERNAL STRUCTURE

The proposed internal structure of information packages identifies the core elements that constitute an information package and the element relationships that connect the components of the information package. The internal structure can clearly identify the meanings and functions of the elements of information packages.

Once the categories of core elements are established, they can be used to combine a set of metadata records in digital preservation. However, these categories and elements are not designed for substantially describing resources. They are intended to be used to combine metadata records that describe preserved resources in a standardized way. In order to achieve the combination of records, the categories and core elements need to be manifested in a formal format of metadata. This research applied Resource Description Framework (RDF) based on eXtensible Markup Language (XML) and con-

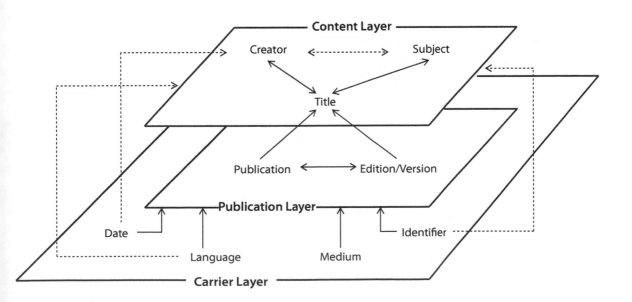

Fig. 4 Proposed internal structure of information package

verted the internal structure into a metadata framework.

In the RDF syntax, each category of core elements functions as an RDF Class. Because the core elements that are expected to be used to combine metadata records are categorized and set up as element categories, each Class needs to be represented as a category, not an element. Class Category defines the categories as Classes in the proposed RDF schema. Class Category functions to indicate each layer in the internal structure of information packages and contains Content, Carrier, and Publication as sub-Class (see Fig. 5).

However, these Classes are nothing but the representation of categories in RDF syntax if they are used to categorize the core elements. Therefore, the core el-

ements need to be manifested as a set of attributes that specify each aspect of the information package. In order to manifest the attributes in a formal format, the relationships between core elements should be syntactically represented. This is manifested as external properties (see Fig. 6).

Each core element functions as a property of the categories converted into RDF Classes. By using these Classes and Properties, the internal structure of information packages can be manifested as a metadata framework in RDF. It can be used to combine existing metadata records in digital preservation in a flexible way. The RDF syntax for these categories and core elements are manifested in Fig. 7.

```
<rdfs:Class rdf:about="#Category">
   <rdf:type rdf:resource="http://www.w3.org/2000/01/rdf-schema#Class"/>
</rdfs:Class>
<rdfs:Class rdf:about="#Content">
   <rdf:type rdf:resource="http://www.w3.org/2000/01/rdf-schema#Class"/>
   <rdfs:subClassOf rdf:about="#Category"/>
</rdfs:Class>
<rdfs:Class rdf:about="#Carrier">
   <rdfs:type rdf:resource="http://www.w3.org/2000/01/rdf-schema#Class"/>
   <rdfs:subClassOf rdf:about="#Category"/>
</rdfs:Class>
<rdfs:Class rdf:about="#Publication">
   <rdfs:type rdf:resource="http://www.w3.org/2000/01/rdf-schema#Class"/>
   <rdfs:subClassOf rdf:about="#Category"/>
</rdfs:Class>
```

Fig. 5 Class definition of information package

```
<rdf:Property rdf:ID="Relationship">
   <rdfs:range rdf:resource="#Resource"/>
   <rdfs:domain rdf:resource="#Resource"/>
</rdf:Property>
```

Fig. 6 Property definition of information package

As shown in Fig. 7, the nine core elements function as properties of the Class Category. Each property is expected to function as a mediator that combines the external elements used in the overall process of digital preservation. Based on the core elements as properties, the elements in information packages can be inter-related with each other and can provide more detailed resource description according to the phases of the overall process of digital preservation.

The elements can also integrate all the aspects of preserved resources that most of the types of the current resources contain. Therefore, the proposed structure can support the description of preserved resources optimized for each phase of the process of digital preservation. It can also clearly represent the details of preserved resources and establish relationships across metadata records created during the preservation process.

Although the internal structure of information packages are manifested using RDF syntax, this structure can be used to connect external metadata records created in other communities. Because the core elements are extracted from the existing metadata standards that

```
<rdf:Property rdf:ID="creator">
    <rdfs:range rdf:resource="#Content"/>
</rdf:Property>
<rdf:Property rdf:ID="title">
    <rdfs:range rdf:resource="#Content"/>
</rdf:Property>
<rdf:Property rdf:ID="subject">
    <rdfs:range rdf:resource="#Content"/>
</rdf:Property>
<rdf:Property rdf:ID="publication">
    <rdfs:range rdf:resource="#Publication"/>
</rdf:Property>
<rdf:Property rdf:ID="language">
    <rdfs:range rdf:resource="#Carrier"/>
</rdf:Property>
<rdf:Property rdf:ID="edition">
    <rdfs:range rdf:resource="#Publication"/>
</rdf:Property>
<rdf:Property rdf:ID="identifier">
    <rdfs:range rdf:resource="#Carrier"/>
</rdf:Property>
<rdf:Property rdf:ID="date">
    <rdfs:range rdf:resource="#Carrier"/>
</rdf:Property>
<rdf:Property rdf:ID="medium">
    <rdfs:range rdf:resource="#Carrier"/>
</rdf:Property>
```

Fig. 7 RDF definitions of information package

are commonly adopted in a variety of communities, the metadata records used in those communities can be applied to the generation of information packages via the core elements. From this perspective, the core elements and element categories can be considered as reference points to combine metadata records generated in communities other than digital preservation.

The Classes and Properties in the internal structure of information packages can also have a specific set of metadata elements from other metadata standards as a subset of each element. By adopting those external elements, the internal structure can provide more detailed descriptions for preserved resources. Therefore, the internal structure can be considered as an umbrella structure for both resource description in digital preservation and a conceptual structure for integrating metadata standards. With these strengths, the internal structure proposed in this research is expected to be used as a conceptual foundation for generating information packages that can be flexibly applied to satisfy specific purposes of resource description across communities.

6. CONCLUSION

With the rapid increase of information resources in digital format, the importance of digital preservation gains more weight across communities. Although many research efforts have been conducted to support the process of digital preservation and have provided standardized models and strategies, they have limitations because of inefficient and inconsistent description of preserved resources. In addition, the use of information packages in each phase of digital preservation may not fully support the unique purpose of digital preservation and/or resource description. To overcome these limitations and to address the current problems in digital preservation, this research proposed an internal structure of information packages generated in the process of digital preservation.

The internal structure is based on the core elements that are commonly used in creating metadata records across communities. The set of core elements describes the common characteristics of a variety of information resources and functions as a reference point in generating information packages in the context of digital preservation. The core elements were extracted from the existing metadata standards such as Dublin Core and MARC. In addition to these standards, a kind of cataloging rule, which is FRBR, is also analyzed to provide conceptual relationships across the extracted core elements. These extracted elements were categorized according to their semantics and functions in describing information resources. The categories of the core elements consist of three groups of elements, which are content-related, publication-related, and carrier-related elements. Each category constitutes a layer that can provide a space for enumeration of the core elements and can provide detailed description of preserved resources. The three layers also constitute a hierarchical structure in resource description for generating information packages.

Based on the constructed internal structure of information packages, this research manifested each category and core element in RDF syntax. This can provide a standardized format of converting the categories and core elements in a metadata format. Through the RDF syntax, the internal structure of information packages can be applied to substantially generate information packages by combining metadata records created during the process of digital preservation.

In digital preservation, information packages play an important role because they can satisfy the unique purpose of each phase of digital preservation and provide detailed description of preserved resources. The internal structure of information packages proposed in this research is designed to support the combination of metadata records for the same resource created by heterogeneous metadata standards. Although this approach is not intended to substantially describe actual information resources, it is expected to provide an alternative approach to combine existing metadata records in the context of digital preservation, and functions as a conceptual foundation of generating information packages in a more flexible way.

REFERENCES

Beagrie, N. (2002). *A continuing access and digital preservation strategy for the Joint Information Systems Committee (JISC), 2002-2005.* Retrieved September 18, 2014, from http://www.jisc.ac.uk/uploaded_documents/dpstrategy2002b.rtf

Calhoun, K. (2006). *The changing nature of the catalog and its integration with other discovery tools.* Washington, D.C.: Library of Congress. Retrieved September 29, 2014, from http://www.loc.gov/catdir/calhoun-report-final.pdf

Crow, R. (2004). *The case for institutional repositories: A SPARC position paper.* The Scholarly Publishing and Academic Resources Coalition, 2002. Retrieved October 15, 2014, from http://www.arl.org/sparc/IR/ir.html

Digital Preservation Coalition (2012). *Digital preservation handbook.* Retrieved October 27, 2014, from http://www.dpconline.org/advice/preservationhandbook/topic/168-introduction-definitions-and-concepts

Gomes, D., Miranda, J., & Costa, M. (2011). A survey on Web archiving initiatives. In *Proceedings of the 15th International Conference on Theory and Practice of Digital Libraries (TPDL '11): Research and Advanced Technology for Digital Libraries,* 408-420. Berlin: Springer-Verlag.

Hedstrom, M. (1998). Digital preservation: A time bomb for digital libraries. *Computers and the Humanities, 31,* 189-202.

Heslop, H., Davis, S., & Wilson, A. (2002). An approach to the preservation of digital records. *National Archives of Australia.* Retrieved October 22, 2004, from http://www.naa.gov.au/recordkeeping/er/digital_preservation/Green_Paper.pdf

IMS (2003). *IMS Digital Repositories Specification.* Retrieved October 15, 2014, from http://www.imsglobal.org/digitalrepositories/index.cfm

Lane, H. (2012). Models for the EU Arctic Information Centre: Engaging the polar libraries colloquy. In *Proceedings of the 24th polar libraries colloquy: Cold regions: Pivot points, focal points,* 169-170. Boulder, CO, USA, June 11-14.

Lynch, C. A. (2003). Institutional repositories: Essential infrastructure for scholarship in the digital age. *ARL Bimonthly Report, 226.* Retrieved September 15, 2004, from http://www.arl.org/newsltr/226/ir.html

NLII (National Learning Infrastructure Initiative) (2003). *Learning objects (NLII 2002-2003 Key Themes).* Retrieved September 20, 2014, from http://www.educause.edu/nlii/keythemes/LearningObjects.asp#nlii_research

Vardigan, M., & Whiteman, Cole. ICPSR meets OAIS: Applying the OAIS reference model to the social science archive context. *Archival Science, 7,* 73-87.

Appendix 1

Brief Comparison of Elements in Existing Bibliographic Standards: FRBR, Dublin Core, and MARC

	FRBR	Dublin Core	MARC
Creator	Name of person	Creator	1XX Author
	Dates of person	Contributor	7XX Contributor
	Title of person	-	-
	Name of corporate body	-	-
	Place of corporate body	-	-
	Date associated with the corporate body	-	-
Subject	Summarization	Subject	6XX Subject
	Term for the concept	Description	5XX Notes
Edition	Edition/issue	-	245 Title
Publication	Publication place/date	-	260 Publication
	Publisher/distributor	Publisher	-
Identifier	Identifier	Identifier	856 Identifier
Language	Language	Language	041 Language
Title	Title	Title	440 Series statement
	-	-	245 Title
Medium	Form	Format	246 Form of title
	Physical medium	Type	-
Date	Date	Date	-
	-	Relation	-
	-	Coverage	-
	-	Source	-
	-	Rights	-
	Intended termination	-	-
	Extensibility	-	-
	Extent	-	-
	Revisability	-	-
	Restriction	-	-
	Statement	-	-
	Responsibility	-	-
	Manufacturer	-	-
	Access authorization/restriction	-	-
	Availability	-	-
	Intended audience	-	-
	Context	-	-
	Term for the object	-	-
	Term for the event	-	-
	Term for the place	-	-

* This table does not show the entire MARC field set. It only provides the MARC elements that are matched with Dublin Core and FRBR elements.

9

Developing a Theory in Academic Research: A Review of Experts' Advice

Jacob Dankasa *

University of North Texas
Denton, USA
E-mail: jdankasa@gmail.com

ABSTRACT

Despite the number of developed theories, it still remains a difficult task for some established and emerging scholars in various academic fields to clearly articulate new theories from research studies. This paper reviews and collates the views of scholars on what a theory is and how a good theory can be developed. It explains the concept of a theory, and the different components that make up a theory. The paper discusses the different processes of theory development by emphasizing what theory is and what theory is not. This review found that scholars differ in their definition of a theory, which leads to using terms such as *model, paradigm, framework,* and *theory* interchangeably. It found the lack of theoretical constructs in a study to be one of the factors which explains why articles are rejected for publication. This paper may be of benefit to established researchers who may be struggling with theory development, and especially younger academics who are the future of scholarship in various academic fields, particularly in information science.

Keywords: Theory Development, Information Science, Review, Developing a Theory

1. INTRODUCTION

Studies with strong theoretical perspectives are often regarded as adding value to any field of learning. It is therefore essential for scholars and researchers in various academic fields to develop strong skills in theory development. A well-crafted theory supports logical thoughts and helps to make sense of the reality that re-

*Corresponding Author: Jacob Dankasa
University of North Texas
Denton, USA
E-mail: jdankasa@gmail.com

searchers struggle to present. Scholars of information science, for example, have developed various theories over the years (Chatman, 1999; Cole, 2011; Dervin, 1998; Kuhlthau, 1991), and new theories that point to new directions in the study of information science have also emerged (Spink & Heinström, 2011; Sin, 2011; Jaeger & Burnett, 2010). Despite the developed theories within this field, it still remains a difficult task for some emerging scholars to clearly articulate new theories from research studies (Pettigrew & McKechnie, 2001). Many researchers and scholars in various fields may be battling with similar problems because there is no one way or an agreed upon pattern of developing a theory. Various scholars provide variations in their methods of developing a theory (Smith & Hitt, 2005). The lack of a clear road map for theory development makes the process "one of the most frustrating and arduous tasks in which a scholar engages" (Cunningham, 2013, p. 3). The main objective of this paper is to bring together different ideas of scholars of theory development in order to help researchers find paths to follow in their process of developing a theory. In addition, in a highly competitive academic environment where *publish or perish* is the norm, it is essential for future scholars to be aware of factors that may increase their chances of getting their work published. The ability to design a study that contributes to theory is obviously a major factor.

This paper reviews literature to collate the different views of scholars on what makes a good theory and how it can be developed. The paper explains the concept of a theory and the different components that make up a theory. It discusses the different processes of theory development by emphasizing what a theory is and what a theory is not. A theory needs to benefit the progression of research. Therefore, this paper examines the role of theories in academic research and their importance to various academic fields, especially the field of information science. It contributes to the understanding of the process of theory development from different perspectives. It is hoped that this paper may be of benefit to established researchers who may be struggling with theory development, and especially younger academics who are the future of scholarship in the field of information science and other disciplines.

2. METHODOLOGY

Various searches were conducted to look for articles on theory development. Search terms such as *developing a theory, theory development, how to develop a theory,* and *theory development in information science* were used to identify studies conducted on this subject area. Electronic databases such as EBSCOhost, Google Scholar, and other institutional library databases were used in the search for materials. The major sources retrieved and used for this review were journal articles. Some books that contributed to the discourse on theory development were consulted. About 81 sources were collected but only 38 journal articles and 20 books were used for this review because of their relevance to the topic and scope of the paper. However, there was no limit set for the year of publication of the sources to be used because the process of theory development is as old as the research process itself. In addition, widening the scope of the publication period of sources to be included may help in gaining insights into diverse views on the subject and the changes in those views over time. The major sources included in this review were drawn from a variety of disciplines. It must also be noted that this paper is not a review of different theories; rather, it is a review of ideas presented by some scholars and researchers on what a theory is and the process of developing a theory.

3. CONCEPT AND COMPONENTS OF A THEORY

Different researchers have presented different definitions of a theory (Odi, 1982; Silverman, 2006; Vogt, 1993; Babbie, 1992; Schwandt, 1997; Merton, 1957). According to Corley and Gioia (2011), a theory is a relationship of concepts that shows how and why a phenomenon occurs. It is made up of "constructs linked together by propositions that have an underlying, coherent logic and related assumptions" (Davis, Eisenhardt, & Bingham, 2007, p. 481). Garver (2008) suggested that theories vary in their specifications. Some theories are termed as knowledge while others are contrasted with knowledge; some can be tested, others cannot; some theories are idea-based while others are application-based. While some theories help to further understanding, others can be barriers to understanding, Garver concluded. For Buckland (1991), a strong theory is based on perception; whatever theory matches one's perception becomes a good theory. Davis et al. (2007, p. 481) brought together the views of some scholars of theory development and enumerated four elements of a theory. These are

- constructs
- propositions that link those constructs together
- logical arguments that explain the underlying theoretical rationale for the propositions, and
- assumptions that define the scope of the theory.

In the same vein, Wacker (2004) identified four properties that should characterize a good theory: "formal conceptual definitions, theory domain, explained relationships, and predictions" (p. 631). Wacker defines a theory as a link that creates relationships of concepts. Various researchers define a theory based on their perception of what a theory does. According to Sutton and Staw (1995), the lack of a unified definition among scholars of what a theory is has often made it difficult to develop a strong theory. This is evident in many researchers' use of terms such as *model, paradigm, framework*, and *theory* interchangeably to denote the same thing. The distinction between a paradigm, a model, a framework, and a theory should be made so that readers can clearly understand the distinctions.

In order to develop a good theory, there are some identifiable features that must be considered in a study. Some of these features could be drawn from Wacker (2004) who proposed that a theory should be unique, in the sense that it should be clearly distinguished from other theories; it should be conservative by standing the test of time, which means it should only be replaced by a new *superior* theory. A good theory should be worthy of being generalized, applicable to other disciplines, and capable of producing hypotheses and generating models. An example of such a theory is the diffusion of innovation theory (Rogers, 1995), which led to developing more superior theories that shaped other theories. Diffusion of innovation theory has also been applied in a variety of disciplines (Durante, 2011; Osareh & Wilson, 1997; Patterson, Shaw, & Masys, 1997).

Schroeder (2008) is in agreement with Wacker (2004) that a good theory should be tested, confirmed,

refined, or even refuted. Glaser and Strauss (1967), however, have a rather stronger position on the elastic limits of a theory. They contend that a theory that is deeply rooted in data cannot be easily refuted or undone by another theory. Such theories stand the test of time regardless of whatever modifications or reformulations they undergo. Glaser and Strauss pointed to grounded theory, in contrast to theories that are based on ungrounded assumption which they referred to as products of logical deduction. They believe such theories are mostly altered by subsequent logic that counters their assumptions. Grounded theory has been used in many studies to develop new theories (e.g., Goodall, Newman, & Ward, 2014; Urquhart & Fernández, 2013; Wolfswinkel, Furtmueller, & Wilderom, 2013).

From the aforementioned assertions, Glaser and Straus seem to be more concerned with building theory using qualitative data rather than quantitative. However, many studies have applied quantitative data to build theories and such studies may not be simply dismissed as based on ungrounded assumptions as Glaser and Straus seem to suggest. Both qualitative and quantitative data can lead to good theories if processes of effective theory development are followed.

4. PROCESSES OF THEORY DEVELOPMENT

In developing a theory various considerations have to be made. The discussion below presents the views of researchers and scholars on the processes of developing a good theory.

4.1. Demonstration of Relationship among Variables

Sutton and Staw (1995) believe a strong theory should be simple and interconnected; it should be able to predict, to explain, and to delight. In other words, theories begin with insights that have to be developed into concepts and relationships. These concepts and relationships are then connected and integrated into a whole. Insight alone, without conceptual connections, cannot make a theory (Rindova, 2011). Therefore, developing a theory is more than merely drawing a list of variables; the relationship between or among the variables should be clearly demonstrated (Whetten, 1989). This means the author needs to have the readers in mind when constructing a theory. According to DiMaggio (1995), for a theory to be considered relevant, the author has to configure propositions that readers can comprehend. Propositions are the statements that help to explain the relationships between the different constructs of a study. Through these constructs hypotheses are drawn. Bacharach (1989) made the distinction between propositions and hypotheses which are oftentimes mistaken to be synonymous. According to Bacharach, "propositions state the relations among constructs, and on the more concrete level, hypotheses (derived from the propositions) specify the relations among variables" (p. 500). Therefore, it is very essential that an author should explain these propositions so that any theory developed can be understood based on the clear statements of its propositions.

Since a theory is a set of concepts, definitions, and propositions used to explain events and situations, Michie and Prestwich (2010) believe that a good theory should draw a systematic relationship. Such a relationship will advance the understanding of the situations and events it claims to explain. This can be done through the development of paradigms. A paradigm is something which makes sense of a particular area of learning. Through a paradigm, areas of studies and the process of carrying out the studies are determined. A paradigm serves as a guide to researchers in their various fields of study (Olsen, Lodwick, & Dunlap, 1992). Olsen et al. (1992) identified two types of paradigms with which theories can be developed: scientific paradigms and social paradigms. The scientific paradigm is the frame of thoughts that guide researchers with scientific perspectives. This paradigm is mostly applied by natural scientists in their intellectual activities. Social paradigms, on the other hand, are used to interpret how people make sense of their social lives in their communities or environments. This type of paradigm guides scholarship mostly in the social sciences and humanities. It must be noted that *paradigm* is a concept that has been used and explained differently by various scholars (Guba, 1990; Kuhn, 1970). There is no one way of defining a paradigm. However, a paradigm, as used here in relation to a theory, is the framework by which a theory can be developed.

Whetten (1989) mentioned four essential elements that are needed to make a theory complete. These elements are the *what, when, how,* and *why* of the theory.

The *what* looks at the judgments made in including the right factors to make up the theory. Two criteria can be used to determine the *what* of the theory. The first is the comprehensiveness of the theory: Does it contain all the necessary factors such as variables, concepts, or constructs? The second is parsimony: Are there irrelevant factors that add nothing new to the theory? If such factors exist, they must be removed. The *when* describes the factors that are added at the time of creating the theory. According to Whetten, "when authors begin to map out the conceptual landscape of a topic they should err in favor of including too many factors, recognizing that over time their ideas will be refined. It is generally easier to delete unnecessary or invalid elements than it is to justify addition" (p. 490). This means adding more factors such as constructs, variables, or concepts at the beginning of the research process and allowing for the possibility that they may be deleted later is better than adding fewer factors at the beginning, only to realize later that more are needed. Making justifications for such additions at a later stage may prove difficult. The *how* of the theory seeks to determine how the different factors are related. This is sometimes presented in a form of a diagram or by linking terms or variables using arrows. This is also known as a *model*. Graphical representation of thoughts can help to bring clarity to the meaning of concepts. The *why* of the theory will bring out an explanation of the purpose for which the factors were chosen. The big question to be asked here is: *Why should the theory be accepted or be seen as useful by those in the field who look at it?* According to Whetten (1989), the logic behind the creation of the theory is more significant than the data of the theory. The question that anyone developing a theory should ask is: *Do my propositions make sense in this field of studies?* Readers should be able to assess the theory based on the sense it makes, not on the data it presents, Whetten concluded.

Whetten's (1989) emphasis on the logic behind the creation of a theory rather than the data of the theory is a sharp deviation from the emphasis of the grounded theory of Glaser and Strauss (1967), which lets the data guide the development of the theory. These are two opposing views that present some challenges to researchers in their choice of research method. However, the method to be used depends on one's research orientation.

In presenting the four essential elements of a theory, Whetten describes variables, constructs, and concepts as factors of a theory but did not explain their meaning. It is unclear whether Whetten assumes that the factors he mentioned all meant the same thing in relation to theory. On the contrary, Bacharach (1989) advised that theorists should avoid using terms such as variables and constructs synonymously. According to Bacharach, "a construct may be viewed as a broad mental configuration of a given phenomenon, while a variable may be viewed as an operational configuration derived from a construct" (p. 500).

4.2. Clear Definition of Concepts

Kuhn (1959) proposed that, in order to understand and create a theory, the theorist must bring together previous knowledge and rearrange it. According to Kuhn, "the scientist must usually rearrange the intellectual and manipulative equipment he has previously relied upon, discarding some elements of his prior belief and practice while finding new significances in and new relationships between many others" (p. 22). This means in the process of developing a theory, some elements of the previous knowledge may be discarded, while newly found concepts are developed into significant relationships. Kuhn believes that new ideas come with some reordering of already known ideas. Therefore, for a paper to exhibit strong theory, it has to begin with a few conceptual statements that are built in a logical manner.

For a theory to be significantly developed using statistical data, for instance, concepts must be measured appropriately. In the process of theory development, attention must be given to the definition and progression of concepts (Wacker, 2004). Conceptual definitions must be given using the appropriate vocabularies which are representative of the field of inquiry. For example, in developing a user-centered theory in the field of information science, the definition of a *user* is necessary to give the perspective of the unique meaning of the word in the field. According to Wacker (p. 630), a good theory should define concepts (who and what a conceptual definition is), domain (the when and where the conceptual definitions apply), causal relationships (how and why the conceptual definitions are related to measurements), and lastly, make predictions (what should, could, and would happen when

formal conceptual definitions are used for measurement). This suggests that for a theory to be described as a good theory the flow of its progression must be consistent and reasonable, applying the rules of deduction or induction.

4.3. The Constituents of a Theory

Mills (1959) believes that developing a theory is an intellectual craft that involves the use of one's life experience. This means that the theorist enters into the intellectual work by personally getting involved in the product that is worked on. Throughout the process, the theorist will continue to examine and interpret the work by applying the life experience and knowledge acquired. This is to enable the researcher to apply all the necessary elements that constitute a theory. In order to have the elements needed in a theory, Mills presented the following suggestions to theory developers:

1. Make formal theory and build models as well as you can.
2. All facts and details, together with their relationship, should be well examined.
3. All works should be related closely and continuously to historical reality.
4. Make it your task to define the reality without assuming someone else will do it for you.
5. Formulate the problems in their own terms and try to provide solutions to the problems. (p. 224).

In order to highlight the constituents of a theory, Sutton and Staw (1995) outlined five elements of a research paper that are often mistakenly taken as theory while in the actual sense they are not. According to these authors: 1) references are not theory; 2) data are not theory; 3) lists of variables or constructs are not theory; 4) diagrams are not theory; 5) hypotheses or predictions are not theory. They argued that making references to a list of theories in an article is not in itself a theory because there is no explanation of the logical link between these references. According to Sutton and Staw (1995), when theoretical works are cited in an article or in a study, such theories should be shown to have a relationship to the new framework. Mere data presented in a study cannot be termed as theory in themselves. The data should be able to explain certain causal relationships in order to be called a theory. The authors believe that it is not enough to present data in a study; researchers also have to show what the data represent and explain their meaning.

Sutton and Staw (1995) insisted that when researchers present variables and constructs in a study, they must know that these are not theories. For constructs or variables to become theory, researchers have to show how they emerged and must explain their connections. Many theories are demonstrated through diagrams or models, but diagrams by themselves are not theories. The causal connections the diagrams represent must be explained and the relationships they established must be highlighted. Sutton and Staw concluded that mere predictions or hypotheses are not theories because a hypothesis only explains the *what* rather than the *why*. These authors believe explaining the *why* is the basis of a theory.

The views of Sutton and Staw above spur a debate among scholars on what constitutes a theory. Weick (1995) responded to Sutton and Staw on their assertions of *what theory is not*. According to Weick, the points raised by Sutton and Staw could make sense if one alludes to them as theory due to "laziness and incompetence" (Weick, p. 385). Weick believes that, in the early stages of theory development, the points that Sutton and Staw described as *not theories* are actually very important in enhancing the process. On this note, Weick accused Sutton and Staw of getting "lost in their concern with theory as a product rather than as a process" (p. 385). Weick contended that it is difficult to determine what a theory is by merely examining the product. The context of the product itself, which is the process of the theory creation, needs to be examined as well. In Weick's view, rather than Sutton and Staw tagging their five proposed assertions as *not theory at all*, they should instead be seen as the road to creating a theory. Weick asserts that developing a theory involves activities such as "abstracting, generalizing, relating, selecting, explaining, synthesizing, and idealizing" (p. 389).

The debate between Weick (1995) and Sutton and Staw (1995) brought out interesting points that express the need for researchers to pay attention to theory as both a product and a process. Therefore, there is a need to articulate clearly the level or the composition of the sample a researcher uses to develop a theory in a study in order to further the understanding of the applicability of the theory.

4.4. Level of a Theory

In building a theory, the levels at which the generalization is made need to be described clearly. Klein, Dansereau and Hall (1994) stated that, in trying to show the level of a theory, members of a group under study need to be either homogeneous, independent, or heterogeneous. This should be part of the prediction of the construct of the theory. If a group is chosen as the level of study for developing a theory, the prediction to be made should be based on the composition of the group. If there is similarity in the composition of the group, all members can be characterized together. The important factor here is the *group as a variable*, and not the individual members of the group. On the other hand, if the specification of the level of the theory is based on the individual, then the prediction should be made looking at the individual as independent of the influence of other group members. On a similar note, Kalnins (2007) also stressed the importance of the selection process in theory development. He argued that sample selection, when carried out appropriately, is capable of explaining the type of empirical relationship that takes place during the process of theory development. Considering selection issues first will help reveal data that are either consistent or on par with the actual cause of relationship observed during the research process.

Emphasizing the importance of sample determination in the process of theory development, Klein et al. (1994) suggested that, in order to add precision to the theory and remove confusion in the process of data collection and analysis, efforts should be made to specify correctly the levels of the theory. They proffered the following suggestions:

1. Theory building is enhanced by explicit specification and explication of the level of a theory and its attendant assumptions of homogeneity, independence, or heterogeneity. Specificity increases the clarity of theories.

2. Theory building may be enhanced by specification and discussion of the sources of the predicted homogeneity, independence, or heterogeneity of the constructs. Attention to these issues increases the depth and comprehensiveness of theories.

3. Theory building may be enhanced by explicit consideration of alternative assumptions of variability, which increases the creativity of theories. (p. 205).

In the field of information science, Pettigrew, Fidel, and Bruce (2001) hold that frameworks in research can be developed through cognitive, social, or multifaceted approaches. Various researchers have developed theories, especially in the area of information seeking behavior research, using these approaches. The cognitive viewpoint concentrates on the individual as the subject of research by looking at the attributes of that individual in order to understand his/her information behavior. By doing this, a framework is formed based on the emotional and cognitive elements that motivate an individual to behave in a certain way when seeking or using information. The social approach for creating a framework centers on the context in which a behavior is observed. Here, the social context is interpreted in order to establish meaning. Examples of such frameworks are those developed by Chatman (1999; 2000) in her formulation of the theories of information poverty, life in the round, and normative behavior. Scholars use the social approach to look at the dynamics of how humans interact among themselves to share and use information.

Due to scholars' dissatisfaction with using either the cognitive or social approach to develop a framework, a multifaceted approach was developed to integrate all approaches in order to better explain human information behavior. A notable importance of the multifaceted approach is that it allows a researcher to develop a theory from the combined theories of others (Pettigrew et al., 2001). The work of Pettigrew et al. is very important in the understanding of how to develop theory in information science research; however, it also uses the terms *frameworks, models,* and *theory* interchangeably. This tends to blur the clarity of the meaning of these concepts and how they differ.

5. THE ROLE OF THEORY IN ACADEMIC RESEARCH

Producing a paper that makes a contribution to theory depends on the ability of scholars to develop original ideas that bring something insightful into scholarship, and which can be applied to bring about fresh thinking (Corley & Gioia, 2011). Any work that is worthy of publication should have some theoretical perspective. Sharma (2011) points out that reviewers of

journal articles do not only look at a study's methodology but also what contribution the work makes to the field of study. According to Corley and Gioia (2011), assessment of publications in some top journals such as *Academic Management Review (AMR)* shows that "the idea of contribution rests largely on the ability to provide *original insight* into a phenomenon by advancing knowledge in a way that is deemed to have *utility* or usefulness for some purpose" (p. 15). Corley and Gioia believe that originality and utility are two major criteria for theoretical contributions: "Originality can be categorized as either (1) advancing understanding incrementally or (2) advancing understanding in a way that provides some form of revelation, whereas the utility dimension parses into (1) practically useful and (2) scientifically useful" (p. 16). When a research paper is perceived to make an insufficient contribution to theory, does not appear to fill any gap in the literature, or the connection between the theory that is proposed and the data presented is not properly made, its suitability for publication could be affected (Huy, 2012).

DiMaggio (1995) gives a summary of what different schools of thought consider a good theory in a research paper. These are: 1) the theory should make one or more generalizations that help in describing our world; 2) the theory should have elements of enlightenment that not only generalize but also create insights into new domains; 3) the theory should be able to give a narrative that is plausible, and should present accounts of actions that are used to make predictions; 4) good theory should be able to cause reality to be viewed in a new way (in what DiMaggio refers to as a process of de-familiarization). This process occurs when an individual is able to see his/her world in a new light that is significantly different from his or her preconceived notions because a theory has suggested an alternative mode of thinking. In other words, theory should bring clarity, not distortion. Therefore, Higgins (2004) advised that a theory in development should be cared for like a parent cares for a child. It should not be abandoned at the developmental stage; time should be devoted to its growth through further research.

In their view, Glaser and Strauss (1967) feel that a theory in academic research should help in predicting and giving explanations of behavior in order to make situations clearer and understandable. Similarly, Huy

(2012) felt that reviewers often view research that shows or offers vivid explanation of how data were collected and analyzed, and how the data are linked to concepts in the theory, as a sign of the rigorous application of a good method of data collection and analysis.

Glaser and Strauss (1967), like DiMaggio (1995), also advised that theory should serve as a guide for the selection of the approach to use in academic research. To achieve this, a good theory should be clear in its categories or propositions and hypotheses so that they can be verifiable in replicated research. Glaser and Straus added that theory developers must not try to force categories where there are none. Instead, categories should come naturally and be identified in the data used for the study. When created, the theory should give meaningful explanation to whatever behavior is studied. Thus, a good theory should not only be understood by the professionals in the field of study, but also by nonprofessionals, especially if it is a theory that is based on an observed behavior.

For a theory to make a significant contribution to a field, Whetten (1989) insisted that the study in which the theory is developed should be able to demonstrate what is new about the theory, what makes the theory relevant, and the plausibility of the evidence and logic. Researchers aiming to develop a theory from a study should ask: Is such a study well done, well written, thorough, and complete in thought and composition? Are the ideas presented new? Do they add to existing knowledge, making it so compelling as to be written at the chosen time? These questions are very important factors in the review process for publications. A lacking in these factors may militate against acceptance of papers for publication because they may be regarded as lacking in theoretical constructs.

6. IMPLICATIONS FOR EMERGING SCHOLARS

The inconsistencies concerning what constitutes a theory have shown themselves in the back-and-forth arguments among scholars. This further confirms the complicated nature of theory development. These complications are also evident in the field of information science, where even the definition of *information*

science has been a subject of debate. Several information scientists (Bates, 1999; Borko, 1968; Buckland, 2012; Saracevic, 1999) present different definitions of information science. Such variations in meaning may translate into difficulties in conceptualizing what a theory should be in the field. There are scholars who believe that the field of information science is lacking in good theories (Hjørland, 1998; Chatman, 1992). Consequently, Aspray (2011) acknowledged the ambiguity that comes with the attempt to establish what defines information science. He is of the opinion that, in defining or explaining information science, a single event is not sufficient for use as a perfect definition, since what constitutes information science changes over time. These changes pose some challenges to emerging scholars in the field. They must be conscious of the fact that the future of the discipline lies in the development of theories that explain realities in a new way.

Notwithstanding the lack of agreement about what constitutes a good theory, the lack of agreement over how to develop a strong theory shows there is a need for rigor in the process of developing a theory. The findings of this review show that one reason why studies are not published is their lack of theoretical constructs. There are researchers who try to publish studies that they perceive to have theoretical perspectives, only to find their work rejected. Sutton and Staw (1995) believe that some papers are rejected partly due to various misconceptions as to what constitutes a theory.

The disagreement between Weick (1995) and Sutton and Staw (1995) about what a theory is and what it is not further shows how complicated it is to determine a good theory from a research paper. Disagreements such as these demonstrate a need for researchers and scholars to be consistent in defining what constitutes the acceptable definition of a theory, and what makes a good theory. This idea was also corroborated by Pettigrew and McKechnie (2001), who found discrepancies in the way researchers describe what makes a good theory. These discrepancies may likely influence the decisions of reviewers, who may be divided on their perception of what constitutes a good theory in a research paper. Therefore, emerging scholars have to be cognizant of these divisions and aim toward developing theories based on the many informative processes suggested by expert researchers. They also need to be familiar with these disagreements because sometimes disagreements and/or varying viewpoints drive a field. Disagreements and varying viewpoints are important aspects of science and discovery.

This paper does not claim to review all work that has been done on theory development. It only concentrates on selected materials, especially journal articles. The aim is to point to the need of paying more attention to construction of good theories among established and emerging researchers, particularly in the field of information science, and to describe different views of experts on what constitutes a good theory. There are many books written on theory development (e.g., Dubin, 1978; Gibbs, 1972) which this review does not reflect. Further research may concentrate on reviewing the published books on the subject of theory development.

7. CONCLUSION

This paper discusses the concept and components of a theory, the process of developing a theory, the role of theories in academic research, and the implications to emerging scholars. It finds that in developing a theory, relationships among variables need to be demonstrated, concepts clearly defined, and elements of a theory explained. It also stresses the need to give more attention to the levels of a theory determined by the sample and population of the study.

The paper shows that scholars differ in their definition of a theory, which has led them to use terms such as *model, paradigm, framework,* and *theory* interchangeably. The elasticity of a theory has also been a subject of debate. Some scholars believe that good theories should be internally consistent but open to refutation. Others are of the opinion that a good theory, one that is worth its name, cannot be easily refuted or undone by another theory. However, scholars and researchers agree that a strong theory should stand the test of time.

REFERENCES

Aspray, W. (2011). The history of information science and other traditional information domains: Models for future research. *Libraries & the Cultural Record, 46*(2), 230-248. doi: 10.5555/lcr.2011.46.2.230

Babbie, E. (1992). *The practice of social research.* Belmont, CA: Wadsworth.

Bacharach, S. B. (1989). Organizational theories: Some criteria for evaluation. *Academy of Management Review, 14*(4), 496-515.

Bates, M. J. (1999). The invisible substrate of information science. *Journal of the American Society for Information Science, 50*(12), 1043-1050.

Borko, H. (1968). Information science: What is it? *American Documentation, 19*(1), 3-5. doi: 10.1002/asi.5090190103

Buckland, M. (1991). *Information and information systems.* Westport, CN: Greenwood.

Buckland, M. (2012). What kind of science can information science be? *Journal of the American Society for Information Science and Technology, 63*(1), 1-7. doi: 10.1002/asi.21656

Chatman, E. A. (1992). *The information world of retired women.* Westport: Greenwood Publishing Group.

Chatman, E. A. (1999). A theory of life in the round. *Journal of the American Society of Information Science, 50*(3), 207-217.

Chatman, E. A. (2000). Framing social life in theory and research. *The New Review of Information Behaviour Research, 1,* 3-17.

Cole, C. (2011). A theory of information need for information retrieval that connects information to knowledge. *Journal of the American Society for Information Science and Technology, 62*(7), 1216-1231. doi: 10.1002/asi.21541

Corley, K. G., & Gioia, D. A. (2011). Building theory about theory building: What constitutes a theoretical contribution? *Academy of Management Review, 36*(1), 12-32.

Davis, J. P., Eisenhardt, K. M., & Bingham, C. B. (2007). Developing theory through simulation methods. *Academy of Management Review, 32*(2), 480-499. doi: 10.5465/AMR.2007.24351453

Dervin, B. (1998). Sense-making theory and practice: an overview of user interests in knowledge seeking and use. *Journal of Knowledge Management, 2*(2), 36-46.

DiMaggio, P. J. (1995). Comments on "what theory is not." *Administrative Science Quarterly, 40*(3), 391-397.

Dubin, R. (1978). *Theory building* (revised ed.). New York: Free Press.

Durante, C. (2011). Active citizenship in Italian cohousing: A preliminary reflection. *Everyday Life in the Segmented City, 11*, 307-333.

Garver, N. (2008). What theory is. *Journal of Folklore Research, 45*(1), 63-70.

Gibbs, J. P. (1972). *Sociological theory construction.* IL: Dryden Press.

Glaser, B., & Strauss, A. (1967). *The discovery of grounded theory: Strategies for qualitative inquiry.* Chicago: Aldine.

Goodall, K., Newman, L., & Ward, P. (2014). Improving access to health information for older migrants by using grounded theory and social network analysis to understand their information behaviour and digital technology use. *European Journal of Cancer Care, 23*(6), 728-738. doi: 10.1111/ecc.12241

Guba, E. G. (1990). *The paradigm dialog.* Newbury Park, CA: Sage Publications.

Higgins, E. T. (2004). Making a theory useful: Lessons handed down. *Personality and Social Psychology Review, 8*(2), 138-145. doi: 10.1207/s15327957pspr0802_7

Hjørland, B. (1998). Theory and metatheory of information science: A new interpretation. *Journal of Documentation, 54*(5), 606–621.

Huy, Q. N. (2012). Improving the odds of publishing inductive qualitative research in premier academic journals. *Journal of Applied Behavioral Science, 48*(2), 282-287. doi: 10.1177/0021886312438864

Jaeger, P. T., & Burnett, G. (2010). *Information worlds: Social context, technology, and information behavior in the age of the Internet.* New York: Routledge.

Kalnins, A. (2007). Sample selection and theory development: Implications of firms' varying abilities to appropriately select new ventures. *Academy of Management Review, 32*(4), 1246-1264. doi: 10.5465/AMR.2007.26586802

Klein, K. J., Dansereau, F., & Hall, R. J. (1994). Levels issues in theory development, data collection, and analysis. *Academy of Management Review, 19*(2), 195-229.

Kuhlthau, C. C. (1991). Inside the search process: Information seeking from the user's perspective. *Journal of the American Society of Information Science, 42*(5), 361-371.

Kuhn, T. (1959). The essential tension: Tradition and innovation in scientific research. In C. W. Taylor (Ed.), *The third University of Utah research conference on the identification of scientific talent.* Salt Lake City: University of Utah Press.

Kuhn, T. S. (1970). *The structure of scientific revolutions* (revised ed.). Chicago: The University of Chicago Press.

Merton, R. K. (1957). *Social theory and social structure.* New York: Free Press.

Michie, S., & Prestwich, A. (2010). Are interventions theory-based? Development of a theory coding scheme. *Health Psychology, 29*(1), 1-8. doi: 10.1037/a0016939

Mills, C. W. (1959). On intellectual craftsmanship [Appendix]. In *The sociological imagination* (pp. 195-226). London: Oxford University Press.

Odi, A. (1982). Creative research and theory building in library and information sciences. *College and Research Libraries, 43*(4), 312-19.

Olsen, M. E., Lodwick, D. G., & Dunlap, R. E. (1992). *Viewing the world ecologically.* CO: Westview Press Boulder.

Osareh, F., & Wilson, C. S. (1997). Third World Countries (TWC) research publications by disciplines: A country-by-country citation analysis. *Scientometrics, 39*(3), 253-266.

Patterson, T. L, Shaw W. S, & Masys, D. R. (1997) Improving health through computer self-help programs: Theory and practice. In P. F. Brennan, S. F. Schneider, & E. Tornquist (Eds.), *Information networks for community health* (pp. 219-246). New York: Springer.

Pettigrew, K. E., & McKechnie, L. E. (2001). The use of theory in information science research. *Journal of the American Society for Information Science and Technology, 52*(1), 62-73.

Pettigrew, K. E., Fidel, R., & Bruce, H. (2001). Conceptual frameworks in information behavior. *Annual Review of Information Science and Technology, 35*(43-78).

Rindova, V. (2011). Moving from ideas to a theoretical contribution: Comments on the process of developing theory in organizational research. *Journal of Supply Chain Management, 47*(2), 19-21. doi: 10.1111/j.1745-493X.2011.03221.x

Rogers, E. M. (1995). *Diffusion of innovation theory.*

New York: Free Press.

Saracevic, T. (1999). Information science. *Journal of the American Society for Information Science, 50*(12), 1051-1063.

Schroeder, R. G. (2008). Introduction to the special issue on theory development in operations management. *Production and Operations Management, 17*(3), 354-356.

Schwandt, T.A. (1997). *Qualitative inquiry: A dictionary of terms.* Thousand Oaks, CA: Sage Publication.

Sharma, R. (2011). Research methods and the relevance of the IS discipline: a critical analysis of the role of methodological pluralism. *Journal of Information Technology, 26*(4), 306-312. doi: 10.1057/jit.2011.27

Silverman, D. (2006). *Interpreting qualitative data: Methods for analyzing talk, text and interaction.* Thousand Oaks, California: Sage Publication.

Sin, S. J. (2011). Towards Agency–Structure integration: A person-in-environment (PIE) framework for modelling individual-level information behaviours and outcomes. In A. Spink and J. Heinström (Eds.), *New directions in information behaviour* (pp. 181-209). UK: Emerald Group Publishing Limited.

Spink, A., & Heinström, J. (Eds.). (2011). *New directions in information behaviour.* UK: Emerald Group Publishing.

Sutton, R. I., & Staw, B. M. (1995). What theory is not. *Administrative Science Quarterly, 40*(3), 371-384.

Urquhart, C., & Fernández, W. (2013). Using grounded theory method in information systems: The researcher as blank slate and other myths. *Journal of Information Technology, 28*(3), 224-236. doi: 10.1057/jit.2012.34

Vogt, W. P. (1993). *Dictionary of statistics and methodology: A non-technical guide for the social sciences.* Newbury Park, California: Sage Publications

Wacker, J. G. (2004). A theory of formal conceptual definitions: Developing theory-building measurement instruments. *Journal of Operations Management, 22*(6), 629-650. doi: 10.1016/j.jom.2004.08.002

Weick, K. E. (1995). What theory is not, theorizing is. *Administrative Science Quarterly, 40*(3), 385-390. doi: 10.2307/2393789

Whetten, D. A. (1989). What constitutes a theoretical contribution? *Academy of Management Review, 14*(4), 490-495. doi: 10.5465/AMR.1989.4308371

Wolfswinkel, J. F., Furtmueller, E., & Wilderom, C. P. (2013). Using grounded theory as a method for rigorously reviewing literature. *European Journal of Information Systems, 22*(1), 45-55. doi: 10.1057/ejis.2011.51

10

Challenges and Opportunities of Knowledge Management in University Library: A Case Study of Dhaka University Library in Bangladesh

Sk. Mamun Mostofa *

Department of Information Science and Library
Management, Faculty of Arts, University of Dhaka
Bangladesh
E-mail: sk_mostofa@yahoo.com, mostofa@du.ac.bd

Muhammad Mezbah-ul-Islam

Department of Information Science and Library
Management, Faculty of Arts, University of Dhaka
Bangladesh
E-mail: mezbah2000@yahoo.com

ABSTRACT

Knowledge Management (KM) has become a fundamental process for all types of institutions in society. Academic libraries are also an integral part of the knowledge system, these institutions being one of the forms that contribute to knowledge development. This study aims to find out the challenges and opportunities associated with KM practices in Dhaka University Library (DUL). The specific objectives were to ascertain the understanding of KM concepts among library professionals of DUL, to explore an overview of KM and its role, and to identify the rationale behind not practicing KM properly at DUL. Appropriate methods were employed. The findings indicate that limited expertise and lack of clear guidelines are the major challenges for the implementation of KM in DUL.

Keywords: Knowledge Management (KM), Dhaka University Library (DUL), Knowledge, Academic Library, Bangladesh

*Corresponding Author: Sk. Mamun Mostofa
Lecturer
Department of Information Science and Library
Management, Faculty of Arts, University of Dhaka,
Bangladesh
E-mail: sk_mostofa@yahoo.com, mostofa@du.ac.bd

1. INTRODUCTION

Academic libraries have transformed significantly from Machine Readable Catalogue (MARC) and circulation desks to metadata, from interlibrary loans to online databases, from bibliographic instruction to information literacy, from information management to Knowledge Management (KM), and so on. KM is a viable means by which academic libraries can improve their services in the knowledge economy. This can be achieved through creating an organizational culture of sharing knowledge and expertise within the library. However, organizations face innumerable challenges in nurturing and managing knowledge. The challenges occur because only a part of knowledge is internalized by the organization; the other is internalized by individuals (Bhatt, 2002). Organizations, including academic libraries, can create and leverage their knowledge base through initiation of appropriate KM practices. TFPL (1999) argued that "for organizations to compete effectively in the knowledge economy they need to change their values and establish a new focus on creating and using intellectual assets." The success of academic libraries depends on their ability to utilize information and staff knowledge to better serve the needs of the academic community. Academic libraries as constituents of the parent university should rethink and explore ways to improve their services and become learning organizations in which to discover how to capture and share tacit and explicit knowledge within the library. The changing role of academic librarians as knowledge managers emphasizes the need to constantly update or acquire new skills and knowledge to remain relevant with today's library environment. Academic libraries may need to restructure their functions, expanding their roles and responsibilities to effectively contribute and meet the needs of a large and diverse university community.

The Dhaka University Library (DUL) started as a part of the DU on the first of July, 1921 with 18,000 books. At present the DUL has 6 lacs and 80 thousand books and magazines. Besides that the library has 30,000 rare manuscript: 20,000 old and rare books and large numbers of tracts (booklets, leaflets, pamphlets, and folklore puthi poems). Some rare books and documents have also been preserved in microform. In the same way, rare books and reports, puthis, Bengali tracts, and private collection of Buchanan on Bengal have been acquired from the British Museum (Nowrin & Mostofa, 2015). However, the rest of the paper is structured as follows: Section 2 presents aims and objectives; Section 3 reviews the related literature; Section 4 discusses research methodology; Section 5 interprets and analyses data; Section 6 proposes the KM model; Section 7 provides recommendations for the implementation of KM in DUL; and the final section concludes the paper with a brief summary.

2. OBJECTIVES OF THE STUDY

The aim of the study was to explore an overview of KM and its role in DUL. The specific objectives were to:
i.   determine the understanding of the KM concept among library professionals at DUL
ii. find out the reasons for practicing KM
iii. discover the challenges associated with KM practice
iv. identify the rationale behind not practicing KM properly at DUL
v.   give recommendations and propose a model for better implementing KM at DUL.

3. LITERATURE REVIEW

3.1. Definition of KM

Malhotra (2006) reported that "KM refers to the critical issues of organizational adaptation, survival, and competence against discontinuous environmental change. Essentially it embodies organizational processes that seek synergistic combination of data and information processing capacity of information technologies, and the creative and innovative capacity of human beings."

According to Drucker (1989), "Knowledge is information that changes something or somebody – either by becoming grounds for action, or by making an individual (or an institution) capable of different or more effective action." There are two types of knowledge: explicit and tacit knowledge. Explicit knowledge is documented and articulated into a formal language. It is rule-based, stored in certain media, and easily communicable and shared; examples are organizational databases, web-pages, subject-portals, policies, and manuals. Tacit knowledge is personal, hard to document, and it is knowledge in action used by people to perform their tasks every day. Tacit knowledge has a personal quality, which makes it hard to formalize and communicate. Tacit knowledge is deeply rooted in action, commitment, and involvement in a specific context (Nonaka, 1994). KM is the management of knowledge that is critical for a person to work more efficiently, inclusive of both tacit and explicit knowledge.

3.2. Barriers to Implementing KM in Academic Libraries

Every library professional who works in an academic, public, or any special library wants to use the techniques of KM to achieve organizational goals and provide better service to its users, but due to some of the following barriers they are not able to use them: Raja and Sinha (2009) reported the barriers of academic libraries are: i) There is no co-operation between senior and junior staff; ii) Generally, the junior staff cannot share their knowledge and ideas when they feel there is no benefit to this in terms of salary increases; (iii) Not every library can participate in terms of modern technology and its management; (iv) Lack of communication skills; (v) Lack of staff training; (vi) Lack of sufficient budgets / funds; (vii) Lack of tools and technologies; and (viii) Lack of centralized library policies.

A literature review provides a systematic review of existing knowledge in the field and provides a necessary guide for the successfulness of this study. We tried hard to collect documents from journals articles and conference papers to enrich this paper. The related literature includes the following:

A study was carried out by Nazim and Mukherjee (2011) based on a literature review and the results of a web-based survey of sixty-four library professionals of thirty academic libraries in India. Their findings suggest that the term 'KM' is familiar to most of the professionals but the ways of knowing and degrees of their understanding are varied. They focused primarily on management of explicit knowledge and their roles were perceived as basic information management activities. Professional education and training programs, community of practices, information technology, and knowledge sharing were identified as the important tools of KM in academic libraries. Misunderstanding of KM concepts and lack of a knowledge sharing cul-

ture, top management commitment, incentives and rewards, financial resources, and IT infrastructure are the major challenges faced by library professionals in incorporating KM into library practices.

Jain (2012) identified the main reasons for KM adoption as: to improve library services and productivity, to produce more with less due to financial constraints, to leverage already existing knowledge, to manage information explosion, to manage rapid knowledge decay, to make informed decisions, to establish best practices, and to avoid duplication of efforts. This study also identified the major challenges in practicing KM as: constant budget decline, lack of incentives, inadequate staff training, limited expertise, lack of clearly defined guidelines on KM implementation, insufficient technology, and a lack of a knowledge sharing culture. A lack of cooperation among juniors and seniors and of tracking the materials from departments did not appear to be major challenges.

Now the main challenges faced by the knowledge practicing university libraries are discussed. Raja, Zubair, and Sinha (2009) reported how information technology and related automated systems can support librarians' endeavors toward better implementation of KM. Provision of adequate budgetary support, professional training, and a pro-active outlook are key factors for an effective KM strategy.

Maponya (2004) mentioned that the success of academic libraries depends on their ability to utilize information and staff knowledge to better serve the needs of the academic community. This requires academic librarians to reappraise their functions, and to expand their roles and responsibilities to effectively contribute and meet the needs of a large and diverse university community. KM is a viable means by which academic libraries may improve their services in the present knowledge era. This is a report of the results of a case study conducted to establish the ways in which the academic librarians of the University of Natal, Pietermaritzburg Libraries could add value to their services by engaging with KM.

Judith and Patrick (2011) presented the results of a study to find out how knowledge is identified, captured, shared, and retained in order to enhance performance and improve the quality of service in the Metropolitan College of New York (MCNY) library. The findings indicate that the MCNY library practices are not deliberately informed by KM principles, but are amenable to KM principles. The study also recommended that KM, with its potential to turn individual knowledge into organizational knowledge, should be used in positioning the MCNY library in a changing information environment.

Agarwal and Islam (2014) revealed that at the moment technology is an enabler for KM and the technology tools are not adequate. A combination of physical environment and technology-enabled tools is essential. They also suggest that the more tools that a library espouses, the more would be the learning required for all employees.

Hamid, Nayan, Bakar, and Norman (2007) did a KM adoption and implementation readiness case study of the National Library of Malaysia (NLM). The study investigated the status of KM at the NLM, with the objective of discovering how the organization went about creating, disseminating, and applying knowledge internally. It revealed the importance of capturing tacit knowledge that resides in employees' heads. The recommendations that resulted from the study included the need to define and document the organization's policy for KM, documenting best practices and the expertise required for KM practice, and a system that allows for the easy location of specific knowledge and expertise.

According to Sinotte (2004) and Wen (2005) KM has been seen as a survival factor for libraries to overcome the challenges that library professionals face in the changing and competitive environment.

Teng and Al-Hawamdeh (2002) believed that libraries can also improve their knowledge-based services for internal and external users through creating an organizational culture of sharing knowledge and expertise within the library.

Sarrafzadeh (2005) found that KM has also been seen as a threat for library professionals to survive in a competitive and complex academic and professional environment. If library professionals remain reluctant to gaining new skills they will become irrelevant to their organization and will probably lose out in competition for employment to people from other fields.

The role of library professionals and their involvement in KM programs has been widely discussed in the Library and Information Science (LIS) literature. Most of the professionals involved in KM programs are playing key roles such as design of information infrastructure, development of taxonomy, or content management, development of Intranet and institutional repositories, embedding information literacy instruction in curriculum, and applying Web 2 tools for knowledge sharing (Ajiferuke, 2003; Branin, 2003; Clarke, 2004; Roknuzzaman et al., 2009).

Sarrafzadeh, Martin, and Hazeri (2010), and Roknuzzaman and Umemoto (2009) in their respective studies have focused on the relationship between KM and libraries. Wen (2005) demonstrated the need for KM in libraries and Maponya (2004) expressed the necessity of KM in academic libraries. Siddike and Islam (2011) also illustrated librarians' awareness or perceptions of KM.

The review of related literature shows that there are many challenges for library professionals in implementing KM in academic libraries. The major challenges are lack of skills and competencies, reluctance of library professionals to accept the change, misunderstanding of KM concepts, lack of a knowledge sharing culture and top management commitment, and lack of collaboration. The review of literature indicates that there is a gap of literature on KM in academic libraries of Bangladesh.

4. METHODOLOGY

The study employed a descriptive research design utilizing a case study approach. A Deputy Librarian, Assistant Librarian, Junior Librarian, Research Officer, and Senior Cataloguer of DUL were selected as participants for the study. These information professionals were selected because of their key roles and functions in the library. Initial contact was made with each of the potential interviewees and each interview lasted for about 15-20 minutes. The study used questionnaires and interviews to collect data. The questionnaires were also sent to 25 respondents and among them 22 completed questionnaires were returned. The quantitative data were analyzed using SPSS version 16.

5. RESULTS

The following sections premeditated the results of the survey conducted as part of this research and data analysis has been conducted on responses to the questionnaire.

Gender plays a vital role in all research. This study also tried to show the percentage of male and female professionals who took part in this study. In total 22 respondents responded to the questionnaire, of whom 13 (59.1%) were male and 9 (40.9%) were female (Fig. 1). So, this is an indication that males largely dominate the profession.

In terms of educational background the figure shows that a large proportion of respondents (77.27%) completed their M.A. degree from the Department of Information Science and Library Management at University of Dhaka and the rest (22.73%) completed B.A. (Hon's) and M.A. degrees from the same department and the same university (Fig. 2). This show the demands of the profession in terms of keeping skills in progress. Also some of the professionals replied that they keep updating their skills, especially when new library software is installed in the library.

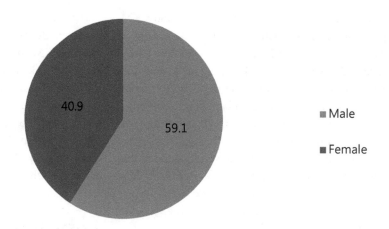

Fig. 1 Respondents' gender

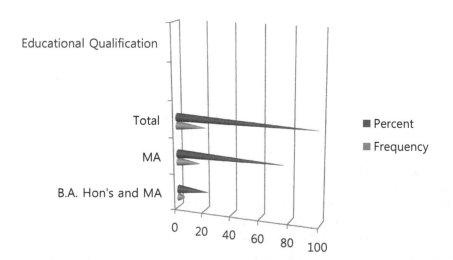

Fig. 2 Educational qualifications

Knowledge and experience of library staff are the intellectual assets of any library and should be shared between employees of the library (Lee, 2000).The respondents were asked to indicate their working experience. The results indicate that most of the respondents, i.e. 59.09%, have working experience at an academic library of 1-5 years, while 27.27% have 11-15 years, and the rest (13.64%) have 6-10 years of working experience at an academic library.

Sharing knowledge with each other assists professionals in creating new knowledge and ideas. In this regard respondents were asked to comment about their thinking as to how knowledge sharing can benefit them. Data presented in Fig. 4 reveals that the respondents share their knowledge with their colleagues, and it was formal sharing for 54.5%, followed by 27.3% informal, while the rest (18.2%) do not share their knowledge.

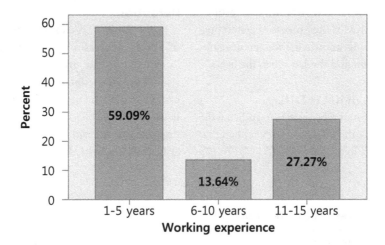

Fig. 3 Experience of the respondents

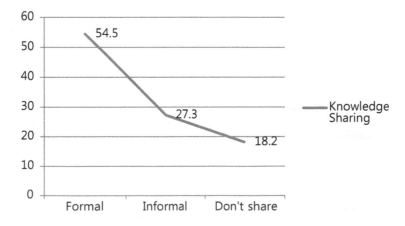

Fig. 4 Sharing knowledge with colleagues

5.1. Understanding the Concept of KM by the Library Professionals of DUL

The majority of the participants seemed to understand the concept of KM, and the KM concept was well-defined by the participants. In general comments, one respondent mentioned, "KM is a system of managing knowledge and it's better to provide." Others mentioned that "KM is the process of capturing, developing sharing, and effectively using organizational knowledge"; "KM is the systematic process that manages the conception, dissemination, and consumption of knowledge." It refers to multi-closely controlled approaches to achieving executive objectives by making the best use of knowledge that proliferates within the organization. It includes economics and philosophy librarians, and so on: "KM is the process of generating, maintaining and utilizing knowledge for the development of the organization and the service to the users."

5.2. Current Status of KM in DUL

The library professionals were asked to indicate the present status of KM in the DUL and they replied that it is in the introductory age.

5.3. Rationale for Not Properly Practicing KM in DUL

From Table 1 it can be seen that more than 31% of library professionals agreed that lack of organizational initiatives in the organization is the main factor for not practicing KM in the DUL properly, while 27.3% of professionals reported that poor technological infrastructure is the other reason for not practicing KM in the DUL properly; the rest (18.2%, 13.6%, and 9.1%, respectively) said that lack of awareness, lack of qualified professionals, and inadequate budget are another factor for other rationales for not practicing KM in the DUL properly.

5.4. Problems Related to Knowledge Retention

From Table 2, it can be seen that more than 63% of library professionals agreed that poor sharing of knowledge in the organization is the main problem related to knowledge retention, followed by 27.27% of professionals who reported that information overload is the main problem related to knowledge retention; the rest (9.09%) said that lack of information is another factor for knowledge retention.

Table 1. Rationale for Not Properly Practicing KM in DUL

Rationale for not properly practicing KM in DUL	Frequency	Valid Percent
Lack of awareness	4	18.2
Inadequate budget	2	9.1
Lack of qualified professionals	3	13.6
Poor technological infrastructure	6	27.3
Lack of initiatives by the authority	7	31.8
Total	22	100.0

Table 2. Problems Related to Knowledge Retention

Knowledge retention	Frequency	Valid Percent
Lack of information	2	9.09
Information overload	6	27.27
Poor sharing of knowledge in the organization	14	63.64
Total	22	100.0

5.5. Reasons for Practicing KM

The respondents were asked to indicate the reasons for practicing KM in the academic library. The results indicate that the largest group of library professionals, i.e. 36.4%, replied that improving library services and managing information explosion are the reasons for practicing KM in the library, while 22.7% indicated to improve library productivity, and the rest (4.5%) reported that managing rapid knowledge decay is the reason for practicing KM in an academic library (see Table 3).

5.6. Challenges in KM Practices

The study identified the major challenges in practicing KM as limited expertise (31.8%) and lack of clear guide lines (31.8%). Inadequate staff training (9.1%), lack of a knowledge sharing culture (9.1%), constant budget decline (9.1%), insufficient technology (4.5%), and lack of cooperation among juniors and seniors (4.5%) did not appear to be major challenges. In addition, the findings indicate that there is a lack of awareness of KM in the library. In most of the cases academic libraries do not systematically or formally manage their KM activities (see Table 4).

5.7. Improving Performance of Library Professionals

From Table 5, it can be seen that 90.9% of the library professionals agreed that KM practices in the library can improve the performance of library professionals. Only 9.1% said that KM practices in the library cannot improve the performance of library professionals.

Table 3. Reasons for Practicing KM

Reasons for practicing KM	Frequency	Valid Percent
To improve library services	8	36.4
To improve library productivity	5	22.7
To manage information explosion	8	36.4
To manage rapid knowledge decay	1	4.5
Total	**22**	**100.0**

Table 4. Challenges in KM Practice

Challenges of KM	Frequency	Valid Percent
Constant budget decline	2	9.1
Inadequate staff training	2	9.1
Limited expertise	7	31.8
Lack of clear guide lines	7	31.8
Insufficient technology	1	4.55
Lack of knowledge sharing culture	2	9.1
Lack of cooperation among juniors and seniors	1	4.55
Total	**22**	**100.0**

5.8. Relation Between Working Experience and Perception of Satisfaction

The findings showed that working experience is not closely associated with perceptions of satisfaction and the differences were statistically insignificant (X^2- 8.125 (4); p > .087) (see Table 6).

5.9. Relation Between Sex and Sharing Knowledge with Others

The findings revealed that gender is not closely associated with sharing knowledge and the differences were statistically insignificant (X^2- 2.006 (2); p >.367) (see Table 7).

5.10. Proposed KM Model for DUL

The five basic statements underlying our model (Fig. 5) for the implementation of KM at DUL and also for other academic libraries are:

Table 5. Improving Performances of Library Professionals

Improve performances	Frequency	Valid Percent
Yes	20	90.9
No	2	9.1
Total	22	100.0

Table 6. Relation Between Working Experience and Perception of Satisfaction

	Perception on Satisfaction			Total
Working experience	Suitable	Medium	Not suitable	
1-5 years	0	5	8	13
6-10 years	0	2	1	3
11-15 years	1	5	0	6
Total	1	12	9	22

Pearson Chi-Square X^2- 8.125 (4) ; p > .087
Fisher's Exact Test 8.365

Table 7. Relation Between Sex and Sharing Knowledge with Others

	Sharing knowledge with others			Total
Sex	Formal	Informal	Don't Share	
Male	6	5	2	13
Female	6	1	2	9
Total	12	6	4	22

Pearson Chi-Square X^2-2.006 (2); p >.367
Fisher's Exact Test 2.002

- **Processes of Knowledge Creation, Organization, Dissemination, Use, and Sharing:** The knowledge and expertise on which activities such as knowledge organization and preservation, information search, retrieval, and dissemination and development of value-added information products and services are based are essential organizational assets for libraries and information services.
- **Human Resources:** Human resource management (including here a number of elements such as communication, organizational learning, knowledge sharing, communities of practice, and organizational culture) is a fundamental element for the process of KM.
- **Technological Infrastructure:** Technology plays a key role in creating a culture and an infrastructure for promoting and supporting access to and sharing of knowledge.
- **Networks and Partnerships:** Networks and partnerships with other public libraries are a solution for creating extended access to knowledge, for a more creative use of knowledge and for increasing the quality of products and services which libraries and information services make available for users.
- **Knowledge Manager:** The creation of a knowledge manager position of the CKO (Chief Knowledge Officer) type considerably increases the chances of successful implementation of this new feature in academic libraries.

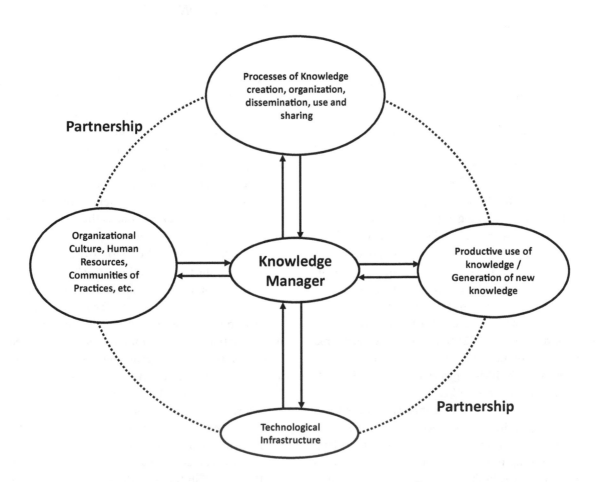

Fig. 5 Proposed KM model for DUL (*Source*: Porumbeanu, 2009)

The model of implementation of KM in DUL allows:

- Identification of the most important processes, products, and services of libraries and information services and their evaluation;
- Identification of knowledge resources and skills in the organization in order to exploit these resources; and
- Identification of potential external partners for collaboration.

To implement the proposed KM model in DUL there should be:

- Achievement of a more extensive collaboration in order to use knowledge in the most effective and creative way;
- Achievement of a joint or common database with all sections regardless of type, which would allow a permanent and full access to the stock of knowledge stored; and
- Establishment of partnerships for KM with each section.

6. DISCUSSION

The results on experience of library staff in this study authenticate the statement of Lee (2000) that knowledge and experience of library staff are the intellectual assets of any library and should be shared with others in the library. Respondents were asked to indicate their working experience and how sharing knowledge with their colleagues benefits them. The results indicate that most of the respondents, i.e. 59.09%, have working experience at an academic library and they also share their knowledge with their colleagues, with both formal and informal shares. Gender based analysis also validates the statement of Islam and Hossain (2012) that more males compared with females dominate the profession. From the data received from the library professionals at DUL, it was clear that they understood KM concepts but degrees of their understanding of the concepts are varied, and they focused primarily on management of explicit knowledge, which they have been doing for a long time. According to the respondents this study shows that KM practices in the library can improve the performance of library professionals. The respondents were asked to indicate the reasons for practicing KM in the academic library. The results indicate that the largest group of library professionals, i.e. 36.4%, agreed that improving library services and managing information explosion are the reasons for practicing KM in the library. Library professionals pointed out that poor sharing of knowledge in the organization is the main problem related to knowledge retention and they also indicated that limited expertise and lack of clear guidelines are the major challenges for the implementation of KM in academic libraries in Bangladesh. Finally, the authors suggest that further studies should consider respondents from numerous universities inside Dhaka Division, possibly including those at both the apex and bottom staff levels of the library, to ensure more generality of the findings.

7. RECOMMENDATIONS

This study provides the following recommendations for better implement of KM in DUL:

i.   **Patronization:** Patronization is essential for any type of organization for its development. So, parent organizations should take KM seriously and allocate sufficient financial resources in order to provide needed KM infrastructures.

ii. **Training:** To understand and adapt KM effectively, rigorous training is essential for library professionals of DUL. Therefore, a training program should be carried out as this will enhance the quality of library services.

iii. **Incentives:** The higher authorities should be aware of the value of KM practice in the library. There should be adequate incentives for academic librarians to motivate them for KM practice and to create a knowledge sharing culture.

iv. **Infrastructure:** The library should strengthen the existing KM environment and information technologies to maximize the use of information and knowledge at the DUL. Declared alternatively, the library should enhance the value and use of organizational knowledge. Recognizing knowledge and information as organizational assets requires the involvement of the library; in this way, the service value of the latter will be enhanced.

v. **Use of ICT tools:** Librarians have to find ways to use new technologies to their best advantage, as advised by Anderson (2007). The library should use collaborative and interactive work spaces such as the wikis that are available for locating and sharing specific knowledge and expertise. Internet communication technologies can provide a collaborative learning environment that can encourage the teaching and learning community to make more vigorous use of the DUL.

ACKNOWLEDGEMENTS

We express our deepest thanks to Dr. Md. Shiful Islam, Associate Professor, Department of Information Science and Library Management, University of Dhaka for his assistance and support regarding this paper. We also thank the professionals of DUL who have participated for completing the questionnaire and making this study possible.

REFERENCES

Agarwal, N. K., & Islam, M. A. (2014). Knowledge management implementation in a library: Mapping tools and technologies to phases of the KM cycle. *VINE, 44*(3), 322-324.

Ajiferuke, I. (2003). Role of information professionals in knowledge management programs: Empirical evidence from Canada. *Informing Science Journal, 6*, 247-257.

Anderson, P. (2007). All that's glitter is not gold: Web 2.0 and the librarian. *Journal of Librarianship and Information Science, 39*(4), 195-198.

Bhatt, G.D. (2002). Management strategies for individual knowledge and organizational knowledge. *Journal of Knowledge Management, 6*(1), 31-39.

Branin, J.J. (2003). Knowledge management in academic libraries: Building the knowledge bank at the Ohio State University. Retrieved from http://kb.osu.edu/dspace/bitstream/1811/187/1/KBJAL.pdf.

Clarke, R. (2004). KM in the main library of the university of West Indies, Trinidad. *Information Develop-ment, 20*(1), 30-35.

Drucker, P. (1989). *The new realities*. New York: Harper & Row.

Hamid, S., Nayan, J.M., Bakar, Z.A., & Norman, A.N. (2007). Knowledge management adoption and implementation readiness: A case study of the National Library of Malaysia. In *Building an information society for all: Proceedings of the International Conference on Libraries, Information and Society, ICOLIS 2007*, Armada Hotel, Petaling Jaya.

Islam, M.A., & Ikeda, M. (2014). Convergence issues of knowledge management in digital libraries: Steps towards state-of-the-art digital libraries. *VINE: The Journal of Information and Knowledge Management System, 44*(1), 140-159.

Islam, M.A., & Hossain, M.J (2012). Access and use of Internet among undergraduate students in the Faculty of Arts, University of Dhaka, Bangladesh. *Pakistan Journal of Library & Information Science, 13*. Retrieved from http://pu.edu.pk/home/journal/8.

Jain, P. (2012). An empirical study of knowledge management in university libraries in SADC countries. *New Research on Knowledge Management Applications and Lesson Learned*. Retrieved from http://www.intechopen.com/books/new-research-on-knowledge-management-applications-and-lesson-learned/an-empirical-study-of-knowledge-management-in-university-libraries-in-sadc-countries.

Judith, M., & Patrick, N.(2011). Exploring the use of knowledge management practices in an academic library in a changing information environment. Retrieved from http://sajlis.journals.ac.za.

Lee, H.W. (2000). The role of libraries in knowledge management. Retrieved from http://szlibszptt.net.cn/download/km_n_lib.ppt.

Malhotra, Y. (2006). Worldwide impact on information technology and knowledge management practices. Retrieved from http://www.brint.com/casestudies.html.

Maponya, P.M. (2004). Knowledge management practices in academic libraries: A case study of the University of Natal, Pietermaritzburg Libraries. Retrieved from http://citeseerx.ist.psu.edu/viewdoc/download?doi=10.1.1.137.8283&rep=rep1&type=pdf.

Nazim, M., & Bhaskar, M. (2011). Implementing

knowledge management in Indian academic libraries. *Journal of Knowledge Management Practice,* *12*(3).

Nonaka, I. (1994). A dynamic theory of organizational knowledge creation. *Organization Science,* *5*(1), 14-37.

Nowrin, S., & Mostofa, SK.M. (2015). Expected web-based library services from faculty of business studies students: A study of Dhaka University Library. *Kelpro Bulletin, 19*(1), 1-20.

Porumbeanu, O.L. (2009). Strategic model for implementing knowledge management in libraries and information services. Retrieved from www.lisr.ro/en13-porumbeanu.

Raja, W., Ahmad, Z., & Sinha, A.K. (2009). Knowledge management and academic libraries in IT era: Problems and positions. Retrieved from http://crl.du.ac.in/ical09/papers/index_files/ical-124_198_418_2_RV.pdf.

Roknuzzaman, M., Kanai, H., & Umemoto, K. (2009). Integration of knowledge management process into digital library system: A theoretical perspective. *Library Review, 58*(5), 372-386.

Roknuzzaman, M., & Umemoto, K. (2009). How library practitioners view knowledge management in libraries: A qualitative study. *Library Management, 30*(8/9), 643–656.

Sarrafzadeh, M. (2005). The implications of knowledge management for the library and information professions. *Online Journal of Knowledge Management, 2*(1), 92-102.

Sarrafzadeh, M., Martin, B., & Hazeri, A. (2010) Knowledge management and its potential applicability for libraries. *Library Management, 31*(3), 198–212.

Siddike, K., & Islam, M.S. (2011). Exploring the competencies of information professionals for knowledge management in the information institutions of Bangladesh. *International Information and Library Review, 43*(3), 130-136.

Teng, S., & Al-Hawamdeh, S. (2002). Knowledge management in public libraries. *Aslib Proceedings, 54*(3), 188-197.

TFPL (1999). *Skills for knowledge management: Building a knowledge economy.* London: TFPL. Retrieved from http://www.lic.gov.uk/publications/executive-summaries/kmskills.pdf.

11

Digital Libraries: Analysis of Delos Reference Model and 5S Theory

Abdulmumin Isah*

Department of Library and Information Studies
University of Botswana, Gaborone
E-mail: abdulmumin.isah@yahoo.com

Athulang Mutshewa

Department of Library and Information Studies
University of Botswana, Gaborone
E-mail: mutshewa@mopipi.ub.bw

Batlang Comma Serema

Department of Library and Information Studies
University of Botswana, Gaborone
E-mail: batlang.serema@mopipi.ub.bw

Lekoko Kenosi

Department of Library and Information Studies
University of Botswana, Gaborone
E-mail: kenosils@mopipi.ub.bw

ABSTRACT

The proliferation of digital libraries (DL) in the twenty-first century has revolutionized the way information is generated and disseminated. This has led to various practical and research models of DLs. This paper discusses the concept and development of digital libraries, and examines various components and characteristics of DLs. It further identifies various models and theories of digital libraries with a special focus on the DELOS Reference Model and 5S Theory. The relationship between the two focused frameworks is analyzed for better understanding of their application in the DL universe.

Keywords: Digital libraries, DL Initiatives, ICT, DELOS reference model, 5S framework

1. INTRODUCTION

The advent of information and communication technology (ICT) has revolutionized the way information is generated and disseminated in modern times. As a result, many organizations have moved from

*Corresponding Author: Abdulmumin Isah
Lecturer
Department of Library and Information Studies
University of Botswana, Gaborone
E-mail: abdulmumin.isah@yahoo.com

paper-based systems to become more digital-oriented organizations. This wave of change has also been observed within libraries. According to the British Library Digitization Strategy Plan 2008- 2011 (2008), "the advent of the Internet and the ability to digitize large quantities of text and images and make them available over the Web has transformed ways of working" (p. 1). The need to harness the numerous benefits of this modern technology has given rise to various digital library (DL) initiatives across the globe. Libraries, especially academic libraries, are now investing heavily on electronic library services with a view to providing seamless access to library collections. The traditional methods of collecting, storing, processing, and accessing information have undergone a massive transformation due to the growth of virtual libraries, digital libraries, online databases, and library and information networks (Varatharajan & Chandrashekara, 2007). Information users in the present digital era can access the vast digital collection of libraries by using computers connected to the Internet to search and retrieve needed information from electronic catalogues, e-journals, and large databases of digitized scholarly information (Marcum & George, 2003).

This new trend in library practice has generated a great deal of challenges in the areas of design, application, acceptance, and the use of technology by potential library users. Another major challenge to libraries in the digital era is the difficulty surrounding DL *interoperability*- that is, the ability of two or more systems to exchange information and use the information that has been exchanged (Gradmann, 2009). Athanasopoulos et al. (2011) attributed this problem to the lack of a common model and single interoperability solution or approach that is generic and powerful enough to serve all the needs of digital library organizations and digital library systems. Candela (2003) stressed the need for a common model that will address these new emerging issues. Several models and theories of digital libraries have been developed with a view to guiding digital library designers towards building digital libraries that will meet the information needs of various users. There is a need to examine some of these models and theories for better understanding of their validity and reliability in the digital library universe. This paper, therefore, sets out to analyze models and theories of

digital libraries with special focus on the DELOS Reference Model and 5S Theory.

2. THE CONCEPT OF THE DIGITAL LIBRARY

The digital library is not a new concept in librarianship. However, its evolution in the modern era has opened up a new chapter in the history of information generation, processing, preservation, and dissemination. The goal of the DL is to facilitate easy and remote access to library collections. Roknuzzam et al. (2009), quoting Gapen (1993), defined the DL as "the concept of remote access to the contents and services of libraries and other information resources, combining an on-site collection of current and heavily used materials in both print and electronic form, with an electronic network which provides access to, and delivery from, external worldwide library and commercial information and knowledge sources" (p. 374). According to Mutula and Ojedokun (2008) an ideal DL should be able to provide users with access to electronic information resources via electronic means. This is reflected in a recent definition of DL by IFLA (2010) as a "collection of digital objects, of assured quality, that are created or collected and managed according to internationally accepted principles for collection development and made accessible in a coherent and sustainable manner, supported by services necessary to allow users to retrieve and exploit the resources" (p. 2).

This development in library practice had been predicted by Vannever Bush, who envisioned a device which he called the 'memex,' a mechanized system based on microfilm technology which would be able to store large amount of books, records, and communication, with the ability to be consulted and retrieved with exceeding speed and flexibility (Bush, 1945). This prediction was further made clearer by Licklider (1965) in his book titled *Libraries of the Future,* where he demonstrated future roles of computer and digital technologies in the development of library practice. He envisioned a future library system that would extend further into the process of generating, organizing, and using knowledge with the application of digital technology. These various definitions presented a common element of the digital library as a collection of digital information that has to be collected or created, processed, and managed to provide universal access to digital content. Therefore, for a library to be referred to as digital library its collection needs to cut across various forms of digital resources and provide universal access to digital content.

3. COMPONENTS OF DIGITAL LIBRARIES

DLs are comprised of various components that interact together to serve information needs of end users. The literature shows that digital libraries, like traditional libraries, share common functional components such as content, digital object, metadata, repository, identifier, Internet and Intranet, digitization, and user interface (Arms, 1995; Magnussen, 2003; Pandey, 2003; Altman, 2006; Bhuyan, 2007). These components can be grouped into five core element which include content, organization, service, technology, and people (Carter, 2002). Each of these five elements is discussed in the paragraphs that follow:

Content: The core function of any library is dissemination of the right content to its community. The dissemination of content, in traditional libraries, comes in the form of physical objects such as books, journals, and audio and video tapes. These physical objects are integrated into digital libraries either through conversion or creation of newborn digital objects of the old contents. Digital objects also come in different formats such as data sets (e.g., a table of results, the genomic information for an individual), or multimedia information (an image, graphic, animation, sound, musical performance, or video) (Fox, 2002). DL contents, just like the practice in the traditional library where contents are catalogued and shelved for easy access, are also catalogued in the form of metadata and managed in the digital repository for easy accessibility. According to Henry (2012), one means of providing reliable access is to mirror (i.e., replicate) the DL in multiple locations so that if there is a problem at one location, the mirrored site can provide continued access to the digital contents and services.

Organization: Organizing information resources to facilitate easy access to a collection has been the major task of libraries for several decades (Chowdhury & Chowdhury, 2003). Libraries and other information institutions have used different types of knowledge organizational schemes to provide easy access to their collections. Following the emergence of digital technology, organization of content in the DL, as in traditional systems, required a bibliographic record mechanism called metadata. Metadata is structured information that surrogates the real described object (NISO, 2007). Metadata is expected to provide vivid description of digital content for easy discovery and integration across various digital repositories. The Internet is a tool that has greatly increased access to digital materials. However, it has done little for the integration of materials across these repositories. It lacks organizational control of the available search tools and search engines. In the case of DLs, contents are organized for easy and seamless access through the application of metadata.

Service: Services to users in traditional libraries such as reference services and selective dissemination of information (SDI) are designed to assist users in their efforts to navigate library collections. In the DL system, remote users can also enjoy personalized services such as online reference services, which are rendered to digital library users in order to solve or address their information search problem (e.g. "ask a Librarian"). Several reference and information services are now available on the web and many of these services are provided by non-library organizations. Some web sites provide listings of libraries that offer real-time reference services. The services use such specific software as live interactive communication tools, call centre management software, bulletin board services, and other Internet technologies (Parida, 2004). These services also guide and assist users in navigating the various information repositories.

Technology: The role of technology in digital environments is to support other elements. These elements include content, organization, and service. The use of appropriate technology when designing a DL determines the level of functionality of the system with respect to digital object processing, organization, preservation, and dissemination. Different technologies have been applied to achieve DL growth; these technologies include locally developed databases, network connections that aid access to other databases, computer hardware with audio-visual capability and video conferencing kits (Parida, 2004).

People: The human elements of DLs make decisions about content, design, and modification of organizational structures. The categories of people in the domain include librarians, repository managers, and system administrators. These people ensure that the system works in accordance with the mission and goals of the library and information institution. The librarians select the content they are interested in making available based on the mission of the parent institution. In addition, they assist end-users with searching techniques that facilitate easy usage of digital libraries (Tibenderana, 2010). In the same vein, the repository managers may adopt policies that implicitly select the digital objects that can be deposited into the repository. The system administrators maintain the index server and select the digital objects that are indexed in the server (Logoze & Fielding, 1998)

DLs are still developing and most of the components identified by various researchers in the field of digital libraries focus on the above five core elements of digital libraries. The goal of any information institution is to meet the information needs of its parent body or community. Therefore, digital objects must be properly selected based on the needs of potential users and organized for easy accessibility. DL architecture provides good user interfaces that enable users to navigate the vast numbers of digital objects in the library repositories with ease.

4. CHARACTERISTIC OF DIGITAL LIBRARIES

DLs have unique characteristics. Their unique characteristics have been discussed in various conferences and fora in many parts of the world, such as: European Conference on Research and Advanced Technology for Digital Libraries (ECDL); International Conference on Asia-Pacific Digital Libraries (ICADL); and International Conference on Theory and Practice of Digital Libraries (TPDL), just to mention few. Several researchers have equally examined the various characteristics of digital libraries against the features of traditional libraries (Cleveland, 1998; Chowdhury, 2003).

These characteristics show the flexibility, portability, and accessibility of DLs over traditional libraries.

DLs generally share the following common characteristics:

- They provide round the clock services to users within and without the library environment. Users can access digital objects at any time 24/7.
- They provide a coherent view of all information contained within a library, no matter its form or format (e.g. text, audio, and video).
- Contents in digital libraries can only be accessed through the help of computers.
- Several users can access a digital object at the same time in different locations.
- Digital libraries do not require large spaces, unlike traditional libraries where physical space is needed for building and maintaining collections.

These characteristics show a shift from traditional library practice, where users need to physically visit library buildings to have access to collection. The dynamics of services in digital libraries has over the years attracted several models and theories of DLs proposed to serve as a framework for building digital libraries that will meet the information needs of users in the new global environment. As pointed out by Gonçalves et al. (2004), formal models and theories are crucial in order to specify and understand clearly and unambiguously the characteristics, structure, and behavior of complex information systems. In line with this assertion, different practical and research efforts towards models and theories of digital libraries have been developed. The Digital Library Initiative (DLI) projects in the USA and the eLib projects in UK have been the major drivers of these efforts through research and practical projects. There are now a number of models of digital libraries that can serve as a framework for best practices.

5. MODELS AND THEORIES OF DIGITAL LIBRARIES

5.1 Models and Theories

The terms *models* and *theories* are used interchangeably in the context of this paper. This is in line with the position of Minshull (1975), as quoted by Coleman

(2002), that "a model can be a theory, law, hypothesis, structured idea, a role, relation, equation, reasoning, or synthesis of data" (p. 1). A model, according to the Business Online Dictionary (2012), is a "Graphical, mathematical (symbolic), physical, or verbal representation or simplified version of a concept, phenomenon, relationship, structure, system, or an aspect of the real world" (p. 1). In the same vein, Dulle (2010) defined a model as any abstract representation of some portion of the real world, constructed for the purpose of understanding, explaining, predicting, or controlling a phenomenon being investigated. A model can be used for better understanding of a phenomenon, therefore models and theories of digital libraries will be analyzed for better understanding of their application in the design and development of digital libraries.

The DL is one of the byproducts of the evolution of digital technologies in the late twentieth century. In effect, it has witnessed a great deal of development in the areas of design, application, and use. Most of the institutions and agencies that have embraced DLs have adopted various approaches. Some have employed a system-oriented approach while some embraced user-centered approaches. These developments have driven the need for common foundations that foster best practices to shape development in the field of DLs (Candela et al. 2011). Over the years, various models and theories have been developed with the aim of addressing issues generated from the development of DLs. Examples of such efforts include the DELOS Digital Library Reference Model, the International Committee for Documentation of the International Council of Museums (CIDOC), the Conceptual Reference Model, the Cornell Reference Architecture for Distributed Digital Libraries (CARDDL), and the 5S Theory.

These models of DLs are some of the on-going efforts in the DL universe towards providing a framework for standards and best practices. The DELOS Reference Model and 5S Theory are general attempts toward a conceptual framework, while the CARDDL and CIDOC Conceptual Reference Models focus on specific domains of digital libraries. The DELOS Reference Model and 5S Theory, apart from being general models, are also the two prominent models of digital libraries (Gonçalves et al. 2004; Candela et al.

2007; Shen et al. 2008; Murthy et al. 2010). They are therefore analyzed for better understanding of their application in the digital library universe.

6. THE DELOS DIGITAL LIBRARIES REFERENCE MODEL

The DELOS Digital Library Reference Model is a conceptual framework aimed at addressing major entities and their relationships in the digital library universe. The DELOS DL reference model is one of the results of the DELOS Network of Excellence, a DL project partially funded by the European Commission. The DELOS project aims at integrating and coordinating the ongoing research activities of the major European teams working in DL-related areas with the goal of developing the next generation DL technologies. Among the objectives of the project are to:(i) define unifying and comprehensive theories and frameworks over the life-cycle of DL information; and (ii) build interoperable multimodal/multilingual services and integrated content management ranging from the personal to the global for the specialist and general population (Casarosa, 2007). In achieving these objectives, the DELOS Reference Model was designed as a framework for the development of appropriate systems. The model is built on six main domains: content, user, functionality, quality, policy, and architecture. These are briefly discussed:

(1) *Content* – represents the information managed in the DL. The most general concept in the Content Domain is "Information Object", which includes text documents, images, sound documents, multimedia documents, and 3D objects, including games and virtual reality documents, as well as data sets and databases. (2) *User* – represents the actors interacting with the system; the DL connect users with information content that supports them in meeting their information needs. (3) *Functionality* – represents the facilities supported which aid in services rendered by DLs to end users. This is to ensure that the system functions reflect the particular needs of the DL community. (4) *Policy* – represents the rules and conditions, including digital rights, governing the operation of the elements of the

DL. For example, policy specifies acceptable user behavior, digital rights management, privacy, and so on. (5) *Quality* – represents the aspects of digital library systems to be considered from a quality point of view and general functionality of the system. (6) *Architecture* – represents the software (and hardware) constituents concretely realizing the whole.

The DELOS Reference Model is a product of brainstorming workshops of stakeholders in the digital libraries field. This led to the drafting of the Digital Library Manifesto with the aim of identifying the cornerstone concepts within the DLs community. The manifesto introduced a three tier framework:

- Digital Library Management System (DLMS)
- Digital Library System (DLS)
- Digital Library (DL)

The interconnectivity of these three systems and the six main domains of the reference model is graphically shown in Figure 1.

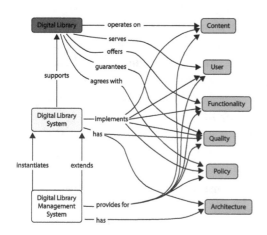

Fig. 1 The DELOS Reference Model Concept Map (Candela et al 2011)

The first tier, Digital Library Management System (DLMS), is a generic piece of software providing basic functionality required by the particular DL. The second tier, Digital Library System (DLS), is built on top of DLMS and enriches it with specific functionality and/or configurations required by the digital library. Finally, the third tier, Digital Library (DL), is understood as an organization collecting and preserving digital content and giving access to it (Murthy et al. 2010). This three-tier framework interacts with the six domains of the DELOS Reference Model (content,

user, functionality, quality, policy, and architecture) to provide allembracing DL services. The players in the DL universe include End users, Designers, System Administrators, and Application Developers. These individuals play a significant role in DL design and application.

For almost a decade after its emergence, the DELOS Reference Model has made significant strides in defining the essential DL concepts and relationships (Candela et al. 2007). It has provided a common vocabulary to facilitate communication between researchers, users, and designers of digital libraries. It has also laid out the digital library concepts in a clear and structured way. However, the model was heavily revised with guidance and contributions from the international members of a range of DL working groups during the DL.org project (Candela et al. 2011). Apart from its comprehensive and explicit illustration of DLs domain, the model provides a conformance checklist that can serve as a benchmark or assessors to determine whether or not their library is compliant with the DELOS digital library reference model. The model has identified players in the DL universe which can equally serve as a guide to any library, organization, and individual intending to embark on a DL project. Evidently the application of the DELOS Reference Model will guide designers of DLs in how to address various components of digital libraries.

7. The 5S Theory

The 5S Theory is a product of efforts aimed at providing theoretical and practical unification of digital libraries. It provides a foundation for the definition of the digital library through the use of five (5) fundamental abstractions, namely Streams, Structures, Spaces, Scenarios, and Societies. The 5S Theory defines a "core" or a "minimal" DL, i.e., the minimal set of components that make a DL, without which a system/application cannot be considered a DL (Murthy et al 2007, 2010). Its flexibility as an instrument for analyzing DL development and organization has been demonstrated in several respects (Shen et al. 2008; Murthy, et al. 2010). Table 1 shows how 5S constructs can be employed to describe key concepts of DLs such as digital objects, metadata, collections, and services.

Table 1. The 5S Framework

5S	Examples	Objectives
Streams	Text; video; audio; image	Describes all types of content, as well as communications and flows over networks. Streams describe properties of DL content such as encoding and language for textual material or particular forms of multimedia data.
Structures	Collection; catalog; hypertext; document; metadata	Specifies organizational aspects of the DL content, that is, the way in which parts of a whole are arranged or organized. Structures can represent hypertexts, taxonomies, system connections, user relationships, and so on.
Spaces	Measurable distance; spatial, topological, vector etc.	A space is a set of objects together with operations on those objects that obey certain constraints. Spaces define logical and presentational views of several DL components, and can be of type measurable, measure, probability, topological, metric, or vector space.
Scenarios	Searching, browsing, recommending	A scenario is a sequence of events that also can have a number of parameters. Events represent changes in computational states; parameters represent specific variables defining a state and their respective values. Scenarios detail the behavior of DL services.
Societies	Service managers, learners, teachers, archaeologists, etc.	A society is "a set of entities and the relationships between them" and can include both human users of a system as well as automatic software entities which have a certain role in system operation. Describes managers, responsible for running DL services; actors, that use the services; and relationships among them.

These abstractions provide a formal foundation to define, relate, and unify concepts in the DLs. They are used to define other DL constructs such as digital objects, metadata specification, collection, repository, and services (Doerr et al. 2007). For example, a digital object may be defined in terms of its structured storage stream and structured metadata specification. The interplay of the 5S constructs and how each of the constructs leads to a minimal digital library system is illustrated in Figure 2.

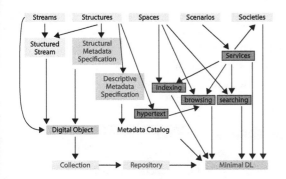

Fig. 2 5S Framework (Gonçalves et al. 2004)

The 5S framework describes minimal requirements for a DL and how the 5S constructs relate with the various components of DLs. For example, digital objects are composed of streams. These include: data; struc-

tured streams (tables of contents, chapters, etc.); and structural metadata specification (which describe each digital object for easy retrieval). Scenarios, according to Gonçalves (2004), consist of "sequences of events or actions that modify the states of a computation in order to accomplish a functional requirement" (p. 2). The scenarios as shown in Figure 2 link the DL services and the societies it serves. The 5S framework focuses on defining the minimal set of features belonging to a digital library. The minimal DL is defined as a quadruple (Repository, Metadata Catalogue, Services, Society) containing the core digital library components. The applicability, versatility, and unifying power of the 5S model are demonstrated through its use in three distinct applications: building and interpretation of DL taxonomy, informal and formal analysis of case studies of digital libraries, and utilization as a formal basis for a DL description language (Gonçalves et al. 2004).

8. COMPARISON OF DELOS REFERENCE MODEL AND 5S THEORY

The DELOS Reference Model is intended as a roadmap to enable the wider digital library community to follow the same route and share a common understanding when dealing with the entities of the DL universe (Innocenti et al. 2011). In addition, the 5S Theory is built on this premise to provide a foundation for the definition of the digital library toward achieving theoretical and practical unification. The two models/theories have common objectives. These objectives are to provide a standard framework for DL projects. However, the methods employed in the presentation of DL frameworks are quite different, though their concepts still address the core components of DLs. While 5S Theory applies a rigorous definition of various concepts to DLs, the DELOS model focuses on identifying the main concepts and relationships encompassing the entire digital library. This is opposed to the 5S definition of individual DL aspects in terms of abstract entities, and these five levels of abstraction and their associated formalisms also render it difficult to adopt due to the complexities involved (Phiri, n.d.). The DELOS Reference Model's six (6) main domains: content, user, functionality, quality, policy, and architecture, are explicit and serve as a foundation for assessment of DLs. However, the organization of three distinct systems (Digital Library, Digital Library System, and Digital Library Management System) into one framework makes the DELOS model complex in nature. It also lacks strong emphasis on social aspects of digital libraries compared to 5S Theory (Fox et al 2003). There are some areas covered in the DELOS Reference Model's six main domains which are not distinctly represented in the 5S main constructs. They include policy and quality domains. 5S Theory provides a separate quality model which makes up for quality constructs not explicitly covered in the main 5S constructs.

Apart from the above differences there are some common relationships shared by these models. These common relationships are in such areas as Streams, Contents, Societies, and Users constructs. These two related concepts address the same component of a DL. The commonality of the two concepts can be vividly identified when applied to different DLs such as institutional based DLs (e.g. a University Digital Library) and a collaborative DL (e.g. the Networked Digital Library of Theses and Dissertations (NDLTD). For example, a university DL will serve the information needs of members of the university community, referred to as *societies* and *users* in 5S and DELOS

Reference models respectively. However, in the case of a collaborative DL like NDLTD the *societies* and *users* will be determined by a number of institutions that are members of the collaborative project. NDLTD is a collaborative project of various universities, libraries, and other supporting institutions towards electronic thesis and dissertations (ETDs). In effect, its collections will be made open to all members. In the same vein, in regard to the digital objects or collections referred to as *streams* and *contents* respectively, in the case of a university DL the streams or content will be tailored toward meeting information needs of the university community, while in the case of a collaborative DL the streams or contents will cut across the information needs of members of the collaborative project.

9. CONCLUSIONS AND FUTURE WORK

The proliferation of digital library initiatives with different patterns of application systems calls for a unified model that will shape the development of the DL universe. The DELOS Reference Model and 5S Theory are the two prominent attempts in that direction. They are developed to guide in the design of various digital library initiatives. The aim of this development is to guide DL designers towards building DLs that will meet the information needs of users in the new global environment. However, there is still a dearth of research on their application. Therefore there is a need to examine various digital library initiatives using either of these two models as a framework for better understanding of patterns of DL initiatives. The outcome of such research will help to validate the applicability and usefulness of such models.

REFERENCES

Athanasopoulos, G., Candela, L., Castelli, D., El Raheb, K., Innocenti, P., Ioannidis,Y., Katifori, A., & Vullo, G. (2011). Digital library technology & methodology cookbook: An interoperability framework, best practices & solutions.Retrieved November 5, 2012, from http://www.dlorg.eu/uploads/Booklets/booklet21x21_cookbook.pdf

Arms, W. Y. (1995, May). Key concepts in the architecture of the digital library. *D-Lib Magazine*. Retrieved August 25, 2012, from *http://www.dlib.org/dlib/July 95/07arms.html*

Altman, M. (2006). An overview of digital libraries: Issues and trends. Retrieved September 5, 2012, from http://dlissu.pbworks.com/f/DigitalLibrary Overview.pdf

Bhuyan, S. (2007). Digital library architecture: A case study. *In Proceeding of 5th Convention Planner-2007,* Gauhati University, Guwahati, December 7-8.

Bush, V. (1945). As we may think. *Atlantic Magazine.* Retrieved June 25, 2012, from http://www.theatlantic.com/magazine/archive/1945/07/as-we-may-think/3881/

Business Online Dictionary (2012). Model. Retrieved from http://www.businessdictionary.com/definition/model.html

Candela, L. (2003). Virtual digital libraries. PhD. Thesis submitted to Dipartimento di Ingegneria dell' Informazione Dottorato di Ricerca in Ingegneria dell'Informazione. Retrieved June 25, 2012, from www.scribd.com/doc/60548981/Peruzzo-PhD-Thesis

Candela, L., Athanasopoulos, G., Castelli, D., El Raheb, K., Innocenti, P., Ioannidis, Y., Katifori, A., & Ross, S. (2011). Digital library reference model In a Nutshell. Retrieved July 2, 2012, from http://www. dlorg.eu/uploads/Booklets/booklet21x21_nut-shell_web.pdf

Carter, D. S. (2002). Elements of digital libraries, present and future. Retrieved June 25, 2012, from http://www.dl.slis.tsukuba.ac.jp/DLjournal/No_22/1-superman/1-superman.html

Casarosa, V. (2007). DELOS Reference model for digital libraries. In Proceedings of Elag Conference, Barcelona. Retrieved December 5, 2012, from http://elag2007.upf.edu/papers/casarosa.pdf

Chowdhury, G. G. (2002). Digital libraries and reference services: present and future. *Journal of Documentation, 58*(3), 258-283.

Chowdhury, G. G., & Chowdhury, S. (2003). Introduction to digital libraries. Facet: London.

Cleveland, G. (1998). Digital libraries: Definitions, issues and challenges. Universal Dataflow and Telecommunications Core Programme, Occasional

Paper 8. *International Federation of Library Associations and Institutions (IFLA).* Retrieved June 5, 2012, from http://www.ifla.org/VI/5/op/udtop8/udtop8.htm

Coleman, A. S. (2002). Classification of models. Retrieved April 25, 2012, from http://arizona.openrepository.com/arizona/bitstream/10150/105432/1/iskoasc.pdf

Doerr, M., Meghini, C., & Spyratos, N. (2007). Leveraging on associations – A new challenge for digital libraries. In *Pre-Proceedings of the First International Workshop on Foundations of Digital Libraries in Conjunction with ACM IEEE Joint Conference on Digital Libraries.* Vancouver, Canada. Retrieved October 25, 2012, from http://146.48.87.21/OLP/UI/1.0/Disseminate/13470 26307Md8LWE8f6q/a221347026307GfwWD NWK

Dulle, F. W. (2010). An analysis of open access scholarly communication in Tanzanian public universities. University of South Africa. PhD. Thesis in Information Science. Retrieved April 25, 2012, from http://uir.unisa.ac.za/bitstream/handle/10500/3684/thesis_dulle_f.pdf sequence=1

Fox, E. A. (2002). Overview of digital library components and developments. Retrieved December 2, 2012, from http://eprints.cs.vt.edu/archive/0000 062301/OASdl12refs.pdf

Fox, E. A., Suleman, H., Madalli, D., & Cassel, L. (2003). Digital libraries. In Singh, M. P. (Ed.), *Practical Handbook of Internet Computing,* CRC Press, p. 4-11.

Gonçalves, M. A., Fox, E. A., Watson, L. T., & Kipp, N. A. (2004). Streams, Structures, Spaces, Scenarios, Societies (5S): A formal model for digital libraries. *ACM Transactions on Information Systems, 22*(2), 270 312. Retrieved July 5, 2012, from http://146.48.87.21/OLP/UI/1.0/Disseminate/1339020480 IrReHIvNgT/a221339020480T2vJs fSa

Gradmann, S. (2009). Interoperability challenges in digital libraries. ECDL. Retrieved October 5, 2012, from http://www.dlorg.eu/uploads/Workshop %20Corfu/Interoperability%20Challenges% 20in%20Digital%20Libraries_Gradmann.pdf

Henry, G. (2012). *Core infrastructure considerations for large digital libraries.* Washington, DC: CLIR

Publication. Retrieved December 5, 2012, from www.clir.org/pubs/reports/pub153/pub153.pdf

IFLA, (2010). *IFLA Manifesto for digital libraries.* Retrieved August 25, 2012, from http://www. ifla. org/en/publications/ifla-manifesto-for-digital-libraries

Innocenti, P., Smith, M., Ashley, K., Ross, S., Robbio, A., Pfeiffenberger, H., & Faundeen, J. (2011). Towards a holistic approach to policy interoperability in digital libraries and digital repositories. *The International Journal of Digital Curation,* 6(1), 111-124.

Licklider, J. C. R. (1965). *Libraries of the future.* Cambridge, MA: MIT Press.

Logoze, C. & Fielding, D. (1998, November). Defining collections in distributed digital Libraries. *D-Lib Magazine.* Retrieved July 4, 2013, from http://cdigital.uv.mx/bitstream/123456789/6080/2/Bibliotecas%20digiitales%20colecciones .pdf

Magnussen, A. (2003).Creating digital libraries: A model for digital library development. In *Proceedings of 10th Asia Pacific Special Health and Law Librarians Conference–Adelaide* 24–27 Aug 2003. Retrieved November 25, 2012, from: http ://conferences.alia.org.au/shllc2003/papers/008 .pdf

Marcum, D. B., & George, G. (2003). Who uses what? Report on a national survey of information users in colleges and universities. *D-Lib Magazine,* 9(10). Retrieved October 25, 2012, from http://.dlib.org /dlib/october03/george/10george.html

Murthy, U., Kozievitch, N. P., Leidig, J., Torres, R., Yang, S., Gonçalves, M., Delcambre, L., & Fox, E. A. (2010). Extending the 5S framework of digital libraries to support complex objects, superimposed information, and content-based imageretrieval services. Virginia Tech Computer Science Technical Report. Retrieved December 5, 2012, from http:// eprints.cs.vt.edu/archive/00001114/01/IJDL.pdf

Mutula, S. M. & Ojedokun, A. A. (2008). Digital libraries. In Aina, L.O., Mutula, S.M. & Tiamiyu, M.A. (Eds.), Information and knowledge management in the digital age: Concept, technologies and African perspectives. Ibadan: Third World Information Services Ltd. pp. 101-121.

National Information Standards Organization (2007). A framework of guidance for building good digital collections (3rd ed.). Baltimore: NISO. Retrieved December 5, 2012, from www.**niso.org**/publications/rp/framework3.pdf

Pandey, R. (2003). Digital library architecture. In DRTC Workshop on digital libraries: Theory and practice. Retrieved November 25, 2012, from www.dlissu.pbworks.com/w/file/fetch/44829234/ B_architecture.pdf

Parida, B. (2004). Emergence of digital library services in India. In *Proceedings of 2nd International Convention on Automation of Libraries in Education and Research Institutions (CALIBER),* New Delhi, February 11-13, pp. 199-205. Retrieved November, 25, 2012, from http://ir. inflibnet.ac.in/bitstream/handle/1944/334/04cali_ 26.pdf sequence=1

Roknuzzam, M., Kani, H., & Umemoto, K. (2009). Integration of knowledge management process into digital library system: A theoretical perspective. *Library Review* 58(5), 372-386.

Shen, R., Vemuri, N. S., Fan, W. & Fox, E. A. (2008). Integration of complex archeology digital libraries: An ETANA-DL experience. *Information Systems* 33(7-8), 699-723. Retrieved November 25, 2012, from http://www.sciencedirect.com/science/article/pii/S0306437908000173#

Tibenderana, P., Ogao, P., Ikoja-Odongo, J. & Wokadala, J. (2010). Measuring levels of end-users' acceptance and use of hybrid library services. *International Journal of Education and Development using Information and Communication Technology (IJEDICT),* 6(2), pp. 33-54.

Varatharajan, N. & Chandrashekara, M. (2007). Digital library initiatives at higher education and research institutions in India. Retrieved October 25, 2012, from http://digitalcommons.unl. edu/cgi/viewcontent.cgi?article=1158&context= libphilprac

12

Normalization and Valuation of Research Evaluation Indicators in Different Scientific Fields [+]

Abdolreza Noroozi Chakoli

Department of Knowledge and Information
Science and Scientometrics
Shahed University, Tehran, Iran
E-mail: noroozi.reza@gmail.com

Roghayeh Ghazavi *

Scientometrics Department
Isfahan University of Medical Sciences, Isfahan
Knowledge and Information Science
Shahid Chamran University of Ahvaz, Ahvaz, Iran
E-mail: r.ghazavi2011@gmail.com

ABSTRACT

Given the difference in research performance in various scientific fields, this study aims to weight and valuate current indicators used for evaluation of scientific productions (publications), in order to adjust these indicators in comparison to each other and make possible a more precise evaluation of scientific productions. This is a scientometrics study using documentary, evaluative, and survey techniques. The statistical population consisted of 106 top Iranian researchers, scientists, and scientific and research managers. Then their research résumé information was gathered and analyzed based on research questions. In order to compare values, the data gathered from research production performance of the population was weighted using Shannon entropy method. Also, the weights of each scientific production importance according to expert opinions (extracted from other works) was analyzed and after adjustment the final weight of each scientific production was determined. A pairwise matrix was used in order to determine the ratios. According to the results, in the area of engineering sciences, patents (0.142) in the area of science, international articles (0.074) in the area of humanities and social sciences, books (0.174), and in the area of medical sciences, international articles (0.111) had the highest weight compared to other information formats. By dividing the weights for each type of publication, the value of each scientific production compared to other scientific productions in the same field and productions of other fields was calculated. Validation of the results in the studied population resulted in very high credibility for all investigated indicators in all four fields. By using these values and normalized ratios of publication indicators it is possible to achieve precise and adjusted results, making it possible to feasibly use these results in realistic policy making.

Keywords: Valuation, Normalization, Research Evaluation Indicators, Scientific Fields, Scientific Areas, Scientific Production

*Corresponding Author: Roghayeh Ghazavi
Ph.D. Student
Isfahan University of Medical Sciences, Isfahan
Knowledge and Information Science
Shahid Chamran University of Ahvaz, Ahvaz, Iran
E-mail: r.ghazavi2011@gmail.com

[+] This article is derived from an MSc thesis.

1. INTRODUCTION

In order to develop scientific policies and advance scientific and research programs, it is necessary to have comprehensive and precise information about the potential scientific and technological capabilities of a country. Also, given the fact that science and technology is the driving force of today's science-based society, evaluation of these capabilities, and qualitative and quantitative analysis of scientific research, is unavoidable in national scientific policies and research management strategies, in order to obtain a comprehensive picture about the scientific structure and growth of the society (Moed, 2005).

By specialization of knowledge and expansion of science over time, various new disciplines have been created in science, engineering, humanities and social sciences, and medical sciences. Given the differences in the nature of these disciplines, it is not possible to achieve desirable policy making in any of the scientific fields without knowing these differences, because the most important goals of scientific policies are evaluation of research needs, evaluative analysis of researcher performance, validation of authors and their works, and development of main strategies for those scientific organizations which need to be mindful of these differences.

Therefore on one hand, due to the different situation of various disciplines, non-standard comparison between disciplines is not advised and on the other hand, due to the necessity of policy making and planning for all active disciplines in an academic or research institution, one needs to compare various disciplines. Therefore an operational and standardized method is needed for correct comparison between various disciplines.

As a result, it is necessary to develop tools and methods that provide a precise evaluation of a country's scientific situation by considering all different factors. In this regard bibliometrics and scientometrics fields have developed and expanded their theories, tools, and indicators in order to compare the scientific performance of different disciplines based on standardized and normalized indicators.

Therefore the goal of the current study is to investigate the value of all scientific productions in various scientific disciplines while comparing these values in different fields and data formats. In order to meet the study goal, it was conducted around three questions: 1. Which kind of scientific product is common in any of the studied areas? 2. How much is the value of each scientific production in each subject area compared to any scientific production in other subject areas? 3. How much is the equivalent amount of a specific type of scientific production in an area in relation to other types in another area?

2. LITERATURE REVIEW

By using scientometrics indicators some researchers have attempted to evaluate the research performance of various fields or disciplines.

Davarpanah's (2010) study investigated various field-base indicators and suggested that a scientific power index which normalizes publications and citations and simultaneously evaluates quality and quantity of scientific works is the best among all available indicators.

Rezaie, in a research study which used survey methods, showed that for researchers in the field of humanities indicators related to books are the most important, while researchers in the fields of natural and medical sciences place greater importance on indicators related to published articles, and those in the field of engineering sciences development place the most emphasis on indicators related to patents and research projects as the most suitable indicators for evaluation of different researchers (Rezaie 2012; Rezaie & Noroozi Chakoli, 2014). Waltman et al. (2011) in their article offer some criticism toward the current Crown indicator (CPP/FCS_m) used for normalization of citations in the Science and Technology Center of Leiden University of Netherlands, and then propose a Mean Normalized Citation Score (MNCS) that can be used as a replacement for Crown indicator.

Also in another study by Waltman et al. (2010), two formulations were used in order to analyze citation information in 8 subject categories in the Netherlands in 1999, comparing the results among 4 levels of research groups, research institutions, country level, and journal level. Based on their results, at higher levels such as research institutions or country level the difference between two indicators is negligible, while in lower levels such as research groups or journal level the difference between two indicators becomes apparent.

Waltman and his coworkers in the Science and Technology Center of Leiden University, as well as in other research, suggest some solutions such as field-base normalized indicators, and according to its deficiencies or different situations, offer some editions on these indicators which can measure and compare scientific disciplines fairly (Waltman et al., 2013; 2015).

Torres-Salinas et al. (2011) in their article present a bi-dimensional indicator as a methodology for classification of institute-discipline with regards to scientific productions and quality of productions. This index provides a comprehensive and goal oriented method for comparing the research output of different institutes in a certain discipline with the help of journal citations. This study also used this index for classification of leading Spanish universities in the fields of chemistry and computer science between the years 2000 and 2009.

Dorta-González et al. (2014) in their research suggest the citation potential mesurement in different fields according to the number of scientific productions, citations, and references in four disciplines. This result can be used in the selection and promotion of interdisciplinary research processes.

Chen et al. (2015), in regard to properties of humanities and social sciences showed the result that existing indicators are insufficient for evaluation of research performance in fields according to databases. So, using altmetrics was suggested to keep in account all formal and informal communication channels in these sciences.

Based on previous studies, applied indicators are only useful for comparing the disciplines within a field, and in other words, normalization methods have been applied uniformly for all scientific production formats. Also, weights of different formats in different disciplines have not been compared with each other.

3. MATERIALS AND METHODS

This applied study is a scientometrics study which was carried out in 2013 and uses documentary, evaluative, and survey techniques. The study population (424 individuals) are Iranian researchers that have been introduced as top researchers, scientists, and scientific

and research managers by the Ministry of Science, Research, and Technology between the years 2007 and 2010, and whose names were published in bulletins of various scientific gatherings as top researchers. Then the study sample was limited to 106 researchers who are faculty members in disciplines mentioned in Iran's Holistic Scientific Map with attention to the disciplines' priorities. Among these numbers, 34 were from medical science disciplines, 19 from humanities and social sciences, 23 from engineering sciences, and 30 from natural sciences. The scientific performance of all members of the study sample was determined by comprehensive searches in national (Magiran, SID, Noormags, and so on) and international (ISI Web of Science, Scopus, Pubmed, and so on) bibliometrics and citation databases separately, and completed based on the research resume of each researcher. This information was entered in predesigned checklists and the duplicate items from different databases were removed. Finally these checklists were verified by all 106 members of the sample, so the checklists were provided by using documentary and survey techniques.

To answer the first question of this research project, based on the total data obtained from the checklists, the ratios of any information formats in each subject area were calculated.

Then, in order to compare values (second question) and by using evaluative techniques, the data gathered from the research production performance of the population in regard to its dispersion was weighted using Shannon entropy method. Independently in each of the subject areas, the mentioned method's formula $(\Sigma Pi \times \ln (pi))$ was applied on the scientific production of each member. Using this method a weight (W_j) was determined for each type of scientific production in each field. Also, since the factor of "quantity" and "significance" are both important in calculating the final weight, with the experts' opinion (Rezaie, 2012) the values for this factor (λ_j) were also determined and used in the following equation (W_{j1}):

$$W_j = \frac{\lambda_j W_j}{\sum_{j=1}^{m} \lambda_j W_j}$$

Also in order to create comparability between the values of scientific productions of different fields, a weighted average method (W_j) was used to determine the weight of scientific productions in each field compared to other fields. Again the significance of these new weights was determined with the experts' opinion (λ_j) (Rezaie, 2012) and used in the above equation (W_{j2}). Finally the overall weight for each type of scientific production was determined as the product of two previous weights ($W_j = W_{j1} \times W_{j2}$) and all weights were normalized.

In order to answer the third question with the help of these weights, in accordance with paired comparison matrixes which are used in the Analytic Hierarchy Process (AHP), all types of scientific productions were valued compared to each other in all different fields. This matrix is able to measure and compare these values relative to each other. Then pairwise comparison matrixes were calculated for comparison between each two fields.

Figs. 1 and 2 were obtained by the Correspondence Analysis method in Minitab 16 software.

4. RESULTS

The most active scientific field in each type of publication is shown in Table 1 and Figure 1. As can be seen in Figure 1, the highest relation between different data forms in different fields is shown as the least distance between them.

Based on the obtained data, the field of medical sciences with 0.45 of all international articles was the most active field in this type of publication. In regards to Persian articles, again medical sciences with 0.44 of all publications was the most active field. In conference articles, engineering sciences with 0.49 of all publications was the most active field while humanities and social sciences with 0.49 of all book publications was the most active field in this type of publications. Also medical sciences with 0.4 of all research projects, and engineering sciences, with 0.63 of all patents, were the leading fields among these types of publications.

Then, according to research goals, the weight of each type of scientific publication in each field was determined using the number of publications and the significance of each type of publication in each field (Rezaie, 2012). The sum of all weights is equal to 1 in order to make it possible to compare different types of publications.

By investigating the calculated weights (Table 2), in the field of engineering sciences the highest weights in descending order belonged to patents (0.142), research projects (0.063), conference articles (0.046), international articles (0.02), Persian articles (0.007), and books (0.004). In natural sciences the highest weights belonged to international articles (0.074), conference articles (0.04), books (0.02), Persian articles and research projects (0.014), and patents (0.008), and in humanities and social sciences, the highest weights belonged to books (0.174), Persian articles (0.087), conference articles (0.012), research projects (0.009), and international articles (0.006). Finally, in the field of medical sciences, the highest weights belonged to international articles (0.111), Persian articles (0.061),

Table 1. The Proportion of Scientific Publications among Fields in Each Type

| No. | Fields | 1. Article | | | 2. Book | 3. Research Project | 4. Patents |
		International Articles	Persian Articles	Conference Articles			
1	Engineering Sciences	0.187	0.078	0.49	0.166	0.316	0.627
2	Basic Sciences	0.295	0.138	0.206	0.172	0.151	0.352
3	Humanities	0.07	0.345	0.115	0.49	0.137	0
4	Medical Sciences	0.448	0.439	0.189	0.172	0.396	0.021
Total	1	1	1	1	1	1	1

research projects (0.04), conference articles (0.03), patents (0.011), and books (0.007).

Fig. 2 shows the relation of each type of scientific publication with different fields. In this figure the closeness of each data form for each field is shown by considering its total weight.

By calculating the value for each type of scientific publication, it is possible to calculate the equal scientific production score of each field based on each publication type or other data forms in other fields. Therefore it will be possible to compare the scientific production of each field with other productions in the same field, as well as productions of other fields. For example, Table 3 shows the value of engineering scientific production based on the same field while Table 4 compares these scientific productions to those of natural sciences.

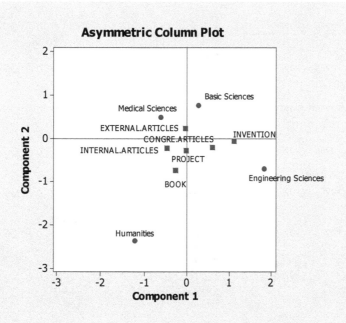

Fig. 1 The relation and importance of each type of scientific publication in different fields regarding its proportion

Table 2. The Weight of each Type of Scientific Publications of Fields in the Entire Complex

| No. | Fields | 1. Article | | | 2. Book | 3. Research Project | 4. Patents |
		International Articles	Persian Articles	Conference Articles			
1	Engineering Sciences	0.02	0.007	0.046	0.004	0.063	0.142
2	Basic Sciences	0.074	0.014	0.04	0.02	0.014	0.008
3	Humanities	0.006	0.087	0.012	0.174	0.009	0
4	Medical Sciences	0.111	0.061	0.03	0.007	0.04	0.011

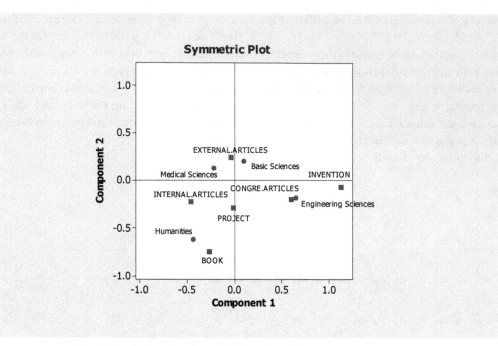

Fig. 2 The relation of each type of scientific publications with different fields

Table 3. The Proportion of Each Type of Engineering Scientific Production to other Types in the Same Field

Scientific Field			Engineering Sciences					
				Article		Book	Research Project	Patents
Scientific Field	Scientific Production		Int'l Articles	Persian Articles	Conference Articles			
Engineering Sciences	Article	Int'l Articles	1	2.823	0.438	4.541	0.318	0.142
		Persian Articles	0.354	1	0.155	1.608	0.113	0.05
		Conference Articles	2.283	6.445	1	1.367	0.727	0.325
	Book		0.22	0.622	0.096	1	0.07	0.031
	Research Project		3.141	8.867	1.376	14.262	1	0.447
	Patents		7.021	19.82	3.075	31.879	2.235	1

Table 4. The Proportion of Each Type of Engineering Scientific Production to Those of Natural Sciences

Scientific Field	Scientific Production		Natural Sciences					
		Scientific Field	Article			Book	Research Project	Patents
		Int'l Articles	Persian Articles	Conference Articles			
Engineering Sciences	Article	Int'l Articles	0.275	1.492	0.51	0.992	1.488	2.508
		Persian Articles	0.097	0.528	0.181	0.351	0.527	0.888
		Conference Articles	0.627	3.406	1.165	2.265	3.397	5.727
	Book		0.061	0.329	0.112	0.218	0.328	0.552
	Research Project		0.863	4.685	1.603	3.116	4.674	7.878
	Patents		1.929	10.472	3.584	6.964	10.447	17.609

5. DISCUSSION

Schubert and Braun (1996) state that it is not correct to use the sheer number of publications and citations for evaluation and that first it is necessary to standardize and normalize these data. By weighting the publications of top researchers in every field and determining the importance of each publication type according to the researchers, it is possible to obtain a weight for each scientific source which shows the value of each scientific production compared to all others. Since these weights are determined based on frequency and significance, if the significance of a certain type of publication increases in a certain subject area, its weight will also increase.

These weights enable us to determine the comparative net value of each data type based on other data types in the same or other subject areas, or the same data type in other subject areas. Therefore, as the matrixes presented in the findings show, it is possible to calculate the value of each data type compared to other data types. For example if we need to convert all publications of a certain researcher in a certain discipline just as engineering sciences to international articles, it is possible to obtain a number for each researcher in that discipline that is the equivalent of their publications in terms of international articles and then compare these numbers. By using the matrix presented in

table 3 which shows the ratio of each type of publication in this field compared to other publication types, normalization will be possible.

For example, in the field of engineering the number of international articles is multiplied by 1, the number of Persian articles is multiplied by 0.354, the number of conference articles is multiplied by 2.283, the number of books is multiplied by 0.220, the number of research projects is multiplied by 3.141, and the number of patents is multiplied by 7.021. Then these calculations are carried out for scientific productions of all researchers in the field (in all levels including research groups, departments, universities, and national level) and then the results are ranked. As Torres-Salinas et al. (2011) state in their work, it is necessary to compare the scientific productions of academic institutions. Also in this regard, Narin et. al. state that in scientometrics, the weights of n articles is equal to the weight of 1 book that is used repeatedly, and also emphasize that the value of n cannot be constant (as cited in Noroozi Chakoli, 2011). Archanbault and Gagne (2004) also state that in order to conduct a precise scientometrics evaluation of humanities and social sciences and to determine the coverage of these disciplines in international databases, especially those in English, it is useful to know the exact ratio of articles, books, conference reports, government reports, and other types of publications based on local tendencies of each discipline.

In order to determine these ratios, an extensive study on a number of local and international universities needs to be conducted which first concentrates on a small number of disciplines, extending its reach further as the need arises. Also in normalization studies one needs to consider the number of research efforts based on local tendencies and their influence on bibliometrics evaluations. Also, studies need to consider the ratio of location-oriented studies, especially those published in journals with limited distribution (Archanbault & Gagne, 2004). According to Larivière et al. (2006), by correctly calculating the share of each publication type in scientific communications, it is possible to evaluate the credibility of bibliometrics methods and ISI databases. By normalization of publications based on publication type and number of authors, Kyvik (1989) concludes that there was no significant difference between various disciplines.

6. CONCLUSIONS

There are several limitations that need to be overcome in order to achieve a detailed and precise evaluation of scientific productions. These limitations are on one hand due to differences in characteristics and philosophies and publication and citation behaviors of different fields, and on the other hand due to lack of tools, methods, and databases that can counter the effects of these differences. In order to make it possible to compare scientific production factors of various fields it is necessary to have adjusted and normalized scientometrics and bibliometrics indicators and tools. As shown above, to this day other than some suggestions about normalization of current indicators or the creation of a database that covers all sources and languages, which is a costly and ineffective method, no operational solution for countering these limitations exists. Therefore this study has aimed to offer an applicable solution for this problem by calculating normalized weights of different publication types. To this end, top Iranian researchers in engineering, natural sciences, humanities and social sciences, and medical sciences, and their research performances were investigated and the weights, values, and ratios obtained from this investigation were used in order to propose a method for comparing the research performance of

various fields.

The calculated weight of each type of scientific publication in each field presented in comparison tables makes it possible to compare scientific production components in different fields. Also, since the ratios are calculated by dividing the weight of each type of scientific publication in each field by the number of that type of publication, the effect of number of publications in each field is included in the calculated ratios.

In this study the research performance of the study population in different formats was investigated and the reported values and ratios consider these differences.

Therefore, by the special properties of the ratios and weights presented in this work, it is possible to normalize even indexes designed for comparing large levels such as Crown indicator, citation index, anti-logarithmic index, and other similar indexes. These results are also useful in normalization of comparison methods suggested by other researchers in order to compare various disciplines.

REFERENCES

Archanbault, E., & Gagne, E. V. (2004). *The use of bibliometrics in the social sciences and humanities* (Report). Montreal: Social Sciences and Humanities Research Council of Canada (SSHRCC).

Chen, K.-H., Tang, M.-C., Wang, C., & Hsiang, J. (2015). Exploring alternative metrics of scholarly performance in the social sciences and humanities in Taiwan. *Scientometrics, 102*(1), 97-112.

Davapanah, M. R. (2010). Scientific Power Indicator: A model to measure and compare the scientific performance of the fields. *Journal of Library and Information Science, 13*(3), 20-30.

Dorta-González, P., Dorta-González, M. I., & Suárez-Vega, R. (2014). An approach to the author citation potential: Measures of scientific performance which are invariant across scientific fields. *Scientometrics, 102*(2), 1467-1496.

Kyvik, S. (1989). Productivity differences, fields of learning, and Lotka's law. *Scientometrics, 15*(3), 205-214.

Larivière, V., Archambault, É., Gingras, Y., & Vignola-Gagné, É. (2006). The place of serials in referencing practices: Comparing natural sciences and engineering with social sciences and humanities. *Journal of the American Society for Information Science and Technology, 57*(8), 997-10.

Moed, H. (2005). *Citation analysis in research evaluation.* Dordrecht, NL: Springer.

Noroozi Chakoli, A. (2011). Introduction. In Scientometrics (*Foundations, concepts, relations & origins*). Tehran: Samt; Shahed University.

Rezaie, M. (2012). *Identification and validation of indicators to evaluate the productivity of researchers and universities* (Dissertation). Tehran: Shahed University.

Rezaie, M., & Noroozi Chakoli, A. (2014). Scientometrics, international special indexes, scientific productivity evaluation. *Information Processing and Management, 30*(1), 3-39.

Schubert, A., & Braun, T. (1996). Cross field normalization of scientometric indicators. *Scientometrics, 36*(3), 311-324.

Torres-Salinas, D., Moreno-Torres, J. G., Delgado-Lo´pez-Co´zar, E., & Herrera, F. (2011). A methodology for Institution-Field ranking based on a bidimensional analysis: The IFQ2A index. *Scientometrics, 88*(3), 771-786.

Waltman, L., van Eck, N. J., van Leeuwen, T. N., Visser, M. S., & van Raan, A. (2010). Towards a new crown indicator: An empirical analysis. *arXiv*:1004.1632v1.

Waltman, L., van Eck, N. J., van Leeuwen, T. N., Visser, M. S., & van Raan, A. (2011). Towards a new crown indicator: Some theoretical considerations. *Journal of Informetrics, 5*(1), 37-47.

Waltman, L., van Eck, N. J., van Leeuwen, T. N., & Visser, M. S. (2013). Some modifications to the SNIP journal impact indicator. *Journal of Informetrics, 7*(2), 272-285.

Waltman, L., & van Eck, N. J. (2015). Field-normalized citation impact indicators and the choice of an appropriate counting method. *Journal of Informetrics, 9*(4), 872-894.

13

Non-Governmental Organization (NGO) Libraries for The Visually Impaired in Nigeria: Alternative Format Use and Perception of Information Services

'Niran Adetoro *

Department of Library and Information Science
Tai Solarin University of Education, Ijagun, Ijebu-Ode
E-mail: adetoroaa@tasued.edu.ng, niranadetoro@yahoo.com

ABSTRACT

Nigeria's non-government organization (NGO) libraries for the visually impaired has over the years been at the forefront of information services provision to persons with visual impairment. This study adopted a survey research design to investigate use of alternative formats and perceptions of information services to the visually impaired, focusing on two purposively chosen NGO libraries for the visually impaired in Nigeria. Using a complete enumeration approach, data were gathered from 180 users of the libraries through the use of a structured questionnaire with a reliability score ($\alpha = 0.74$). Data from 112 (62.2%) of the 180 administered copies of a questionnaire that were retrieved were analysed. The study found that Braille materials had a high level of utilization ($\bar{x} = 4.46$) and were the most frequently utilized (90.9%). Perception of information services by the visually impaired was positive while use of alternative formats was significantly and positively related to users' perception of information services ($r = .041$; $p < 0.05$). The study recommends improved transcription and investment in alternative formats and in e-resources. It also recommends collaborations to widen access as well as constant evaluation of services.

Keywords: Non-governmental organizations, Libraries, Visually Impaired, Alternative formats, Information Services, Nigeria

*Corresponding Author: 'Niran Adetoro
Associate Professor
Department of Library and Information Science
Tai Solarin University of Education, Ijagun, Ijebu-Ode
E-mail: adetoroaa@tasued.edu.ng,
niranadetoro@yahoo.com

1. INTRODUCTION

An aspiration for library and information services to the visually impaired is that they be equally hospitable to users of all kinds and categories. Such services must essentially disregard artificial boundaries in terms of information (Davies, 2007). The visually impaired just like the sighted need to use and acquire information, but such information would only be relevant when available in alternative formats, which includes Braille, audio recordings/materials, large print, and electronic resources. The United Nations document on the equalization of opportunities for persons with disabilities (UN, 1993) and the UNESCO public library manifesto (1994) espouses that information is a primary and fundamental right for the disabled. With this, libraries have to play key roles in building an inclusive society.

It is crucial for the visually impaired, through the use of information, to become active participants in social life. Just like the sighted, information use will ensure that they partake in modern society's processes through the ability to identify, interpret, process, disseminate, use, and reuse information in order to make informed choices and reduce uncertainties (Singh & Mairangthem, 2010). The visually impaired will not achieve these ideals unless libraries provide services geared towards meeting their reading interests and information needs (Adetoro & Atinmo, 2012).

Library services for the visually impaired are known to vary from country to country. The services may not be part of the local or national library system but usually they run on low budgets, focusing on production of accessible formats with limited library services. A few of them have the capacity to leverage on new developments in digital library services. In many developing countries such as Nigeria, government investment in services to persons with disabilities has been minimal and therefore the space for information services to the visually impaired has been taken over by specialized libraries, especially a few non-governmental organization (NGO) libraries. The demand for information materials in alternative format in Nigeria by the visually impaired through libraries is high (Atinmo, 2007; Adetoro, 2010; Adetoro, 2012) However, the visually impaired perceive information services as weak with an inadequate resource base of limited and obsolete alternative information materials for use (Adetoro, 2010).

These perceptions underscore the need for services to be based on the reading interests and needs of the visually impaired and that such services must provide opportunities and support that will enable them become independent, active, and self-sustaining members of their communities. In Nigeria, some NGOs providing information services to the visually impaired go beyond materials production by establishing libraries specifically for the visually impaired. Notable among them are NigerWives, an association of foreign women married to Nigerian men, with the NigerWives library, the Anglo-Nigerian Welfare Association for the Blind (ANWAB) with ANWAB Library, and the Nigerian Society for the Blind with Inlaks Library for the Visually Handicapped. Niger-Wives and ANWAB have over the years been making available reading text for students. ANWAB have been making information available to tertiary level students and blind workers. ANWAB and Inlaks library for the visually handicapped both have an extensive library of Braille and audio recordings. Both libraries have also in recent times trained users in the use of computers and the Internet; they have provided Internet services to their users.

The libraries have a computerized Braille press for transcription of materials into alternative format. They also produce large print editions. Inlaks Library for the visually impaired have a well-equipped sound-proof studio for the production of audio recordings and carrels equipped with audio gadgets that facilitate individualized listening. This article further presents the statement of the problem, research questions and hypothesis raised to guide the study, a review of relevant literature, methods adopted, results, discussion of findings, and conclusions and recommendations.

2. STATEMENT OF THE PROBLEM

The responsibility of providing information services to the visually impaired in Nigeria has been shouldered by NGOs. This is because the education and provision of information services to disabled persons has not received the needed attention and investment from the government. There is no data or government statistic indicating this neglect; however, a few public libraries located in some states make available readable materials for the visually impaired in secondary schools and from neighboring towns. These libraries do not produce materials; they are more distributors of information materials in alternative formats. They are poorly equipped, and their materials are obsolete and mainly Braille and a few talking books. Their effort is minimal relative to the needs of the visually impaired in Nigeria (Adetoro, 2009; Atinmo, 2007).

The inadequacies of existing institutions has propelled these NGOs through their libraries to dictate the direction of service provision to the visually impaired in Nigeria. But how have these NGO libraries fared given the prevailing signs of weak capacity? The demand for information materials in alternative formats by the visually impaired is high in Nigeria (Adetoro, 2010). However, it is believed that the use of alternative formats for study and leisure purposes even in these libraries probably has its shortcomings especially in terms of level and frequency of use. The situation may explain the opinions or perceptions of many visually impaired persons that information services are generally weak and unable to adequately cater for their information needs for study and recreational purposes. These perceptions may have been shaped by factors relating to weak investment, lack of government support, and disjointed services, among others.

2.1. Research Questions and Hypothesis

The following research questions were investigated in this study:

i . What is the general level of use of alternative formats in NGO libraries for the visually impaired?

ii . How frequently do the visually impaired use the alternative formats in the NGO libraries?

iii. How do the visually impaired perceive the information services provided by the NGO libraries?

2.2. The Research Hypothesis was Validated at 0.05 Level of Significance

There is no significant relationship between use of alternative formats and perception of information services in the NGO libraries by the visually impaired.

3. LITERATURE REVIEW

A study on the use of alternative formats by Canadian college students with print disabilities (Anne, 2000) found that 56% of the students use tape recordings frequently, 31% use large print, and 19% use Braille frequently. This is an indication of the popularity of audio recordings among the students. Davis, Wisdom, and Greaser (2001) revealed that about 83% of adults who are blind and partially sighted also use tape recordings. Other studies with evidence supporting the high level of audio material use include Goft, Cleary, Keil, Franklin, and Cole-Hamilton (2001), and Kennel, Yu, and Greaser (2000). The majority of the users of audio materials, according to Getz (2003), are visually impaired people who generally have no other way to read unless they use Braille. For instance, about 3% of Royal National Institute for the Blind (RNIB) users use Braille. In the USA, 4% of the National Library for the Blind (NLB) users read Braille (NLB, 2002). Only 3.9% use Braille in Israel (Getz, 2003).

Schols (1995) reported that in the Netherlands a high level of use of large print was due to an ageing population who prefer large print materials. In Nigeria, a study of availability and use of alternative formats by secondary school students (Adetoro, 2011) revealed that 91.3% used Braille daily, 34.6% use audio books daily, and only 2% use large print weekly. Similar results were reported by Atinmo (2007) and Adetoro and Atinmo (2012). According to Basharu (2000), it is amazing to observe the number of users who visit the ANWAB library to borrow alternative formats for use. Basharu adds that about 95% of the users either borrow from the library or bring materials for transcription into Braille for their use.

Several studies have investigated library and information services to the visually impaired from the point of view of the provider, such as Harris and Oppenheim (2003) and Bundy (2002) to mention a few. It is important for investigations to consider the perceptions of the users themselves. User focus studies such as Creaser et al. (2002) are necessary to determine the opinions, perceptions, and activities regarding information services to the visually impaired. Williamson, Schauder, and Bow (2000) and Berry (1999) reported that users had a high level of satisfaction with services through agencies, though several public libraries were less prepared to give personal attention to their visually impaired users.

Bernardi (2004) identified two basic services that are most currently provided to the visually impaired through libraries as firstly, services based on traditional special formats; those dependent on adaptive technologies, sometimes accompanied by training activities and target services such as access to catalogues, digital texts, and special formats and inter library loans. Karen (2004) reported that Gateshead libraries in the UK provided technology training and other services to the visually impaired with their Access to Reading and Information Services (AIRS) projects.

In the US emphases were on services geared towards improving access to library resources through adaptive technologies (Goddard, 2004; Pietrala, 2004). Norwegian libraries have deployed full time information officers who assist and guide users and essentially ensure that library services are accessible to all visually impaired users (Eymard, 2002).

Users' favorable perceptions of DAISY (Digital Audio Based Information System) books as a very useful tool for information services provision, and the fact that a growing number of libraries are producing and providing Daisy books, has been widely reported (Graddock, 2003; Tylor, 2004; Goddard, 2004).

Bernardi (2004) reported the introduction of a national catalogue of electronic texts available through the Internet which allows users to search, order, and view electronic books in Braille or text format. Services of this nature are not only innovative but are well received and valued by the visually impaired. A similar initiative was carried out in the UK on an accessible catalogue for traditional and electronic texts for the visually impaired (Brophy & Craven, 1999).

Singh and Moirangthem (2010) found that Delhi libraries provided a wide range of information services to the visually impaired which includes library services, Braille production, audio book recordings, computer training, Internet service, and resource sharing. He adds that these services and other technology-based initiatives bring smiles to the faces of the visually impaired.

An ideal library and information service according to Machell (1996) is one where individuals, regardless of the degree of their visual impairment, can access information in a relevant and required format as well as in needed quantities where staff respect the needs of the users.

The provision of web based information resources by libraries providing information services to the visually impaired has in recent times been advocated in order to further widen access to information resources. These resources have moved from a simple text interface to dynamic and interactive designs. There is a need for web accessibility to be designed for all users of the library. "Design for all" in the library environment means that library information technology systems and interfaces must be designed in a way that enable them to be read and interacted with easily by all users, whether visiting or remotely accessing the library, and regardless of any disability of access preference (Brophy & Craven, 2007).

The use of alternative formats in the NGO libraries selected is a critical aspect of this study. It is therefore necessary that the theoretical assumptions for this study must essentially emphasize utilization of information resources as a consequence of users' perceptions of these services. This study was hinged on information utility theory which relates use of information with value of use and user satisfaction. This theory stresses the dynamics of information consumer behavior, which is a product of how information is perceived by its users. This assumption should help contextualize the research questions raised for the study.

4. METHODS

The descriptive survey research design was adopted for the study. Two (2) NGO libraries were purposively selected for the study because they are the two known libraries for the visually impaired in Nigeria owned by NGOs. Other NGOs providing information services to the visually impaired produce and provide alternative formats but do not own libraries. The ANWAB library and the Inlaks Library for the Visually Handicapped, both located in Lagos, have a total population of 180 visually impaired users according to the library records provided by the two libraries.

A complete enumeration approach was used to collect data from all the 180 users in the libraries using a questionnaire named "Visually Impaired Library Users Questionnaire" (VILUQ) ($\alpha = 0.77$) for a period of six weeks, and with the assistance of the library workers who knew the users well and helped in the administration of the questionnaire. The questions were read out to respondents by the researcher and the library staff and their responses were recorded on the instrument. A total of 112 out of the 180 administered copies of the questionnaire (62.2%) were successfully completed and used for the study.

The study left out some active producers and distributors of alternative formats in Nigeria because they are not libraries, though they partake in the provision of information services to the visually impaired. The study was unable to capture visually impaired persons who do not use libraries but visit transcription centers.

5. RESULTS

5.1. Respondents' Characteristics

The sample data revealed that male respondents were 78(70%) while the female respondents were 34 (30.0%). The majority of them (84, 75.5%) are between 21 and 39 years of age; 86 (77.3%) are single while 26 (22.7%) are married. The data also showed that 36 (31.8%) are totally blind, 70 (62.7%) are partially sighted, and 6 (5.4%) are low visioned. It was also found that 25 (22%) had congenital conditions while 87 (78%) had acquired vi-

sual impairment, out of which 66 (60%) became visually impaired while in school (primary / secondary) and 44 (40%) as adults.

5.2. Use of Alternative Formats

The study found that the general level of utilization of alternative formats in the libraries was high for Braille materials ($\bar{x}$ =4.46; SD=1.15) and for audio recordings/materials ($\bar{x}$ =3.32; SD=1.58), and low for large print ($\bar{x}$ =1.17; SD=0.68) and electronic resources ($\bar{x}$ =0.56; SD=1.14). The data also revealed that Braille materials were the most frequently used.

One hundred respondents (90%) used Braille daily. The frequency of use of audio materials in the libraries was less compared to Braille. A total of 51 respondents (46.3%) used audio materials either daily or two to three days a week. From this only 15 (11.8%) used audio materials daily while 38 (34.5%) used audio materials two or three days a week. However, 47 (42.7%) used audio materials once in a month. Large print editions were used daily by only 5 respondents (4.5%), and two or three days a week by 8 (7.3%). Electronic resources were used by 2 respondents daily (1.8%) and 4 (3.6%) twice or thrice weekly, while 93 (84.6) had never used electronic resources.

Table 1. Level of Use of Alternative Formats

Alternative format	Mean	Standard Deviation
Braille materials	4.46	1.15
Audio materials/recordings	3.32	1.58
Large print	1.17	1.68
Electronic resources	0.56	1.14

Table 2. Frequency of Use of Alternative Formats

Alternative format	Daily	Two / three days weekly	Weekly	Fortnightly	Monthly	Never
Braille materials	100 (90.9%)	7 (6.4%)	-	-	1 (2.7%)	-
Audio materials /recordings	13 (11.8%)	38 (34.5%)	5 (4.5%)	7 (6.4%)	41 (42.7%)	-
Large print	5 (4.5%)	8 (7.3%)	4 (3.6%)	7 (6.4%)	86 (78.2%)	-
Electronic resources	2 (1.8%)	4 (3.6%)	-	-	13 (11.8%)	93 (89.6%)

5.3. Visually Impaired Users' Perceptions of Information Services Provided by the Libraries for Leisure and Academic Purposes

The respondents were asked to indicate whether they agree or disagree with the statements testing their perceptions of information services provided to them by the libraries for leisure and academic purposes. The results showed that the respondents had positive perceptions of the libraries' information services. They were in agreement with all the items as significant percentage scores were recorded. Ninety-six (87.3%) agreed that services kept them abreast of development in their areas of interest, 92 (83.7%) viewed that the services prepared them for examinations and serve as current sources of information, respectively. Ninety (81.8%) are of the opinion that services enhance their educational pursuits, 84 (76.4%) agreed that the services provide them with enjoyment and delight, 75 (68.2%) opined that the services satisfied their leisure, 69 (62.7%) say they get satisfaction from the services provided by the libraries for leisure and academic purposes, while 66 (60%) viewed that the services provided solutions to their pressing problems and also helped them to arrive at good decisions. Sixty-five (59.1%) say they get timely information from the libraries while 45 (40.9%) disagree. Also 63 (57.3%) viewed that the services helped to reduce their uncertainties, though 47 (42.7%) had the opposite view.

5.4. Relationship between Use of Alternative Formats and Perceptions of Information Services

The hypothesis of the study is concerned with the possibility of a significant relationship between use of alternate formats and perceptions of information services by the visually impaired.

Hypothesis: There is no significant relationship between use of alternative formats and perceptions of information service in the NGO libraries by the visually impaired.

Use of alternative formats was correlated with perceptions of information services. The result showed a Pearson correlation coefficient of 0.041 with a calculated probability of 0.043, which is less than 0.05 significance level. The null hypothesis was rejected, which means there is a significant relationship between use of alternative formats and the perceptions of information services in the libraries by the visually impaired.

Table 3. Perception of Information Services by the Visually Impaired

Items	Agree / %	Disagree / %
Keep you abreast of developments in your area of interest	96 (87.3%)	14 (12.8%)
Meet your expectations	92 (83.7%)	18 (16.4%)
Prepare you for examinations	91 (82.7%)	19 (17.3%)
Serves as current source of information	91(82.7%)	19 (7.3%)
Enhance your educational pursuit	90 (81.8%)	20 (18.2%)
Provides you with enjoyment and delight	84 (76.4%)	26 (23.6%)
Satisfy your leisure	75 (68.2%)	35 (31.8%)
Gives you all round satisfaction	69 (62.7%)	41 (37.2%)
Provides solutions to your pressing problem	66 (60%)	44 (40%)
Helps you to arrive at good decisions	66 (60%)	44 (40%)
Provides you with timely information	65 (59.1%)	45 (40.9%)
Helps you to reduce your uncertainties	63 (57.3%)	47 (42.7%)

Table 4. Correlation Between Use of Alternative Formats and Perceptions of Information Services

Variables	Means $\bar{x}$	Standard Deviation
Use of alternative formats	7.95	3.41
Perceptions of information services	27.09	11.41

• Pearson correlation result: r = .041; p = 0.043; N = 112

• Correlation is significant at 0.05 level (2-tailed)

6. DISCUSSION

There were more male visually impaired respondents than females. The data also showed that a significant majority of users of these libraries are partially sighted which suggests that the blind are lagging behind in terms of use of information materials in the libraries.

There is a connection between the general level of alternative format use and the frequency of use of alternative materials in the libraries. Braille materials enjoyed a significant and high level of utilization and are also the most frequently consulted by users. As for audio materials/recordings, though they saw a high level of use and an appreciable frequency of utilization, Braille materials recorded a higher level and frequency of use. Transcription activities in Nigeria have focused on the production of more Braille materials than other formats, and this perhaps explains why Braille is the most utilized. In other words Braille is the most utilized because it is the most available (Adetoro, 2010). This contrasted with the findings of Anne (2000) and Davis et al. (2001) who reported otherwise.

It is pertinent to note that electronic resources options were seldom used by the visually impaired who visit these libraries despite the fact that the libraries indeed have Internet facilities for the visually impaired and a few other e-resources. Electronic resources provide a viable alternative for visually impaired information users, as they widen access and possibly provide the same opportunities available to the sighted to the visually impaired. These resources are hardly used though the two libraries had put in place a continuous computer, software, and Internet use training programs for their users. This perhaps is responsible for the poor utilization indices recorded for e-resources.

The users were satisfied with the services offered to them in the libraries for academic and leisure purposes. Their perceptions of the information services were positive and revealing. The NGO libraries servicing the visually impaired in Nigeria have had a positive impact on their users judging from the finding of this study. This corroborates Schroeder (1996). Though with very few outlets, it is worthy of mentioning that NGO libraries in Nigeria are the only institutions with the capacity to intervene where the government through its public libraries had failed. The NGO libraries, according to the users, have kept them abreast of information in their interest areas, have provided materials that prepared them for examinations, and have enhanced their educational pursuits. They also reveal that the libraries have not only met their expectations but they provided current information and satisfied their leisure needs, among other benefits. This is in agreement with Singh and Moirangthem (2010).

The study also showed that use of alternative format in the libraries was significantly related to users' perception of information services. This finding suggests that the level of use of alternative formats in the libraries was a function of the information services provided and vice-versa. This corroborates Adetoro (2011). The high utilization of materials was a product of the positive perceptions recorded for information services offered to the users. This of course has implications for both the government and providers of information services to the visually impaired in Nigeria. The findings of this study also have implications for public libraries in Nigeria who should borrow a leaf from these NGO libraries. African countries with similar socio-economic indices should follow the example of these libraries in providing information services to the visually impaired.

7. CONCLUSION AND RECOMMENDATIONS

The use of alternative formats in the NGO libraries studied was high for Braille and audio materials in terms of the level and frequency of use. Overall, the perceptions of the visually impaired with regard to information services were positive and encouraging while use of materials was related to users' perceptions. These are positive points for the NGO libraries for the visually impaired in Nigeria and indeed for the efforts of the private institutions who are engaged in providing information services to the visually impaired in one way or another. It is crucial to note that these libraries are better placed to adequately provide library and information services to the visually impaired positively if supported by government and other stakeholders. Though users were satisfied with the service provided by the libraries studied, the libraries need to improve service by widening their reach to a bigger community of visually impaired persons who are not library users. They need to intensify their efforts in reaching more users and pressuring the government to invest in services to persons with disabilities generally. There is still much to be done in bringing about equal access to information for the visually impaired in Nigeria. The findings of this study suggest that the attention and policy of government urgently needs to be directed to helping NGO libraries widen their reach and further improve upon information services to the visually impaired. It is clear that available equipment for transcription of materials, Internet, and e-resources to widen access to information are inadequate. These resources and availability of funds are critical to improving information services provision to the visually impaired in the libraries and in Nigeria. It is suggested that further studies should examine the information use patterns of visually impaired persons who do not use libraries but patronize other information outlets or media, and to analyze how they perceive information services via such outlets.

This study recommends that NGO libraries invest more in transcription of more materials into readable formats and in electronic resources for their users. This is because the materials available for the visually impaired in the libraries are generally inadequate compared to what is desired. Braille materials have not covered the reading interests of the users. This is also true for the other resources. They regularly bring in materials of interest in print to be transcribed for their use. The collection of the libraries in terms of subject coverage is not adequate. Audio recordings are much fewer in number than Braille, and the challenge of volunteer readers and studio equipment for transcription has kept the number of audio titles low. Large print and electronic resources are few owing to inadequate funds. NGO libraries for the visually impaired should collaborate first to widen resources and access to alternative formats and lobby government towards building libraries for the visually impaired in Nigeria. Librarians and other stakeholders should engage in advocacy to create awareness and seek funds and assistance from corporate bodies and government. They should also look out for linkages with international bodies and funders so as to improve upon what is available. With these, utilization levels can be further improved. The NGO libraries should constantly investigate how well their services meet the expectations and satisfaction of users. This is crucial for sustainability and improved services.

REFERENCES

Adetoro, A. A. (2009). *Relationship among reading interest, information materials availability and alternative format utilization by persons with visual impairment in selected libraries in southwestern, Nigeria*. Ph.D. Thesis, Department of Library, Archival and Information Studies, University of Ibadan, Nigeria.

Adetoro, N. (2010). Characteristics of visually impaired information users in Nigeria. *African Research and Documentation, Journal of SCOLMA (UK Libraries and Archives Group on Africa), 114*, 47-58.

Adetoro, N. (2011). Alternative format availability and its utilization by the visually impaired students in Nigerian secondary schools. *Indian Journal of Information Science and Services, 5*(2), 31-38.

Adetoro, N. (2012). Alternative format preferences among secondary school visually impaired students in Nigeria. *Journal of Librarianship and Information Science, 44*(2), 90-96.

Adetoro, N., & Atinmo, M. I. (2012). Reading interest and alternative format utilization by person with visual impairment in Nigeria. *African Journal of Libraries Archives and Information Science, 22*(2), 75-88.

Anne, M. (2000). Library services to Canadian students. Retrieved from

Atinmo, M. I. (2007). Setting up a computerized catalog and database of alternative format materials for blind and visually impaired persons in Nigeria. *Library Trends, 55*(4), 330-456.

Basharu, D. (2000). Equipping libraries for the blind with reading materials. *Journal of Association of Libraries for the Visually Impaired, 1*(1), 56-61.

Bernardi, F. (2004). Library services for blind and visually impaired people: Literature review. Retrieved from http://dspace-unipr.cilea.it/bitstream/1889/1147

Berry, J. (1999). Apart or a part? Access to the Internet by visually impaired and blind people with particular emphasis on assistive enabling technology and user perceptions. *Information Technology and Disabilities, 6*(3), 1-16.

Brophy P., & Craven, J. (1999). *The integrated accessible library, a model of service development for the 21ˢᵗ century: The final report of the REVIEL project*. Manchester: CERLIM.

Brophy P., & Craven, J. (2007). Web Accessibility. *Library Trends, 55*(4), 959-972.

Bundy, A. (2002). Inquiring into the roles of libraries in the online environment. Senate environment, communications, information technology and the Arts Reference Committee, Blackwood, South Australia. Retrieved from http://www.aph.gov.an/senate committee/ecta_ctte/completed_inquires/2002-04/online_libraries/submissions/sub03.doc .

Craddock, G. M. (2003). *Assistive technology shaping the future*. London: 105 Press.

Creaser, C., Davis, J. E., & Wisdom, S. (2002). Accessible, open and inclusive? How visually impaired people view library and information services and Agencies. *Journal of Librarianship and Information Science, 34*(4), 2012-214.

Croft, K., Cleary L, Keil, S., Franklin A., & Cole-Hamilton, I. (2001). *The health and well being of blind and partially sighted children and young people aged 5-25*. London: RNIB.

Davies, J. E. (2007). An overview of international research into the library and information needs of visually and information needs of visually impaired people. *Library Trends, 55*(4), 783-795.

Davis, J. Widom, S., & Creaser, C. (2001). *Out of sight but not out of mind: visually impaired people's perspectives of library and information services*. Loughborough University library information statistics unit. Available at http://www.nib.uk.org/common/research/202001/dochtml

Eymard, D. (2002). Bibliotheques at handicaps visuals. Libraries and the visually handicapped. *Bulletin des bibliotheques de France, 47*(20), 117-119.

Getz, I. (2003). *What do blind people want from talking books?* Published Proceedings of the 69ᵗʰ IFLA General Conference and Council, Berlin, August 1-9. Retrieved from http://www.archive.ifla.org/iv/ifla69/papers/074e-Getz.pdf

Goddard, M. (2004). Access through technology. *Library Journal*. Spring connected supplement, Apr. 2-6.

Harris, C., & Oppenheim, C. (2003). The provision of library for visually impaired students in UK further education libraries in response to the special educational needs and disability act (SENDA) *Journal of Librarianship and Information Science, 35*(4), 243-257.

IFLA/UNESCO (1994). UNESCO public library manifesto. The Hague: United Nations. Retrieved from www.unesco.org/webworld/librarias/manifestos/librarian.html

Karen, H. (2004). AIRS: ICT and information for the visually impaired. *Multimedia Information and Technology, 30*(4), 113-115.

Kennell, M., Yu, M., & Creaser, C. (2000). *Public library service for visually impaired people. Report to the library and information commission*. Loughborough university: Library and information unit. Retrieved from http://www.alb.uk.org/comm/research/212000dochtml

Machell, J. (1996). *Library and information services for the visually impaired people: National guidelines*. London: Library Association Publishing.

National Library for the Blind (2002). Out of sight but not out of mind. Visually impaired people's perspectives of library and information services. Research Bulletin 6. Retrieved from http://www.nib.uk.org./common/research/bulleting/202002dochtml

Pietrala, M. (2004). Serving the underserved: The vision project. *Interface, 26*(3), 5-10.

Schols, M. (1995). *Extra large: Large print on demand.* Paper presented at the 61st IFLA General Conference, Istanbul, Turkey, August 20-25. Retrieved from http://www.ifla.org/contact.html

Schroeder, F. K. (1996). Perception of Braille usage by legally blind adults. *Journal of Visual Impairment and Blindness, 90*(3). Retrieved from http://www.braille.org/papers/jvib0696/vb960310html

Singh, K. P., & Moirangthem. E. (2010). Are Indian libraries VIP-friendly? Information use and information seeking behavior of visually impaired people in Delhi libraries. *Library Philosophy and Practice.* Retrieved from http://www.webpages.uidaho.edu/-mbolin/ipp.htm

Tylor, J. M. (2004). Serving blind readers in a digital age. *American Libraries, 35*(11), 49-51.

United Nations (1993). The standard rules for the equalization of opportunities for persons with disabilities. The Hague: United Nations General Assembly, 48th Session, December, 200, Resolution 48/96. Retrieved from http://www.un.org/esa/socdev/enable/dissre04.htm

Williamson, K., Schauder, D., & Bow, A. (2000). Information seeking by blind and sight impaired citizens: An ecological study. *Information Research, 5(4)*. Retrieved from http://www.informationr.net/iv/5-4/papers79html

14

Study of US/EU National Innovation Policies Based on Nanotechnology Development, and Implications for Korea

Jung Sun Lim

Technology Innovation Analysis Center
Korea Institute of Science and Technology Information
Republic of Korea
E-mail: jsunnylim@kisti.re.kr

Jin Seon Yoon

National Nanotechnology Policy Center
Korea Institute of Science and Technology Information
Republic of Korea
E-mail: sunnyrexcom@gmail.com

Kwang Min Shin

National Nanotechnology Policy Center
Korea Institute of Science and Technology Information
Republic of Korea
E-mail: coolskm@kisti.re.kr

Seoung Hun Bae *

National Nanotechnology Policy Center
Korea Institute of Science and Technology Information
Republic of Korea
E-mail: ultratyphoon@kisti.re.kr

ABSTRACT

Recently US/EU governments are utilizing nanotechnology as a key catalyst to support national innovation policies with economic recovery goals. US/EU nano policies have been serving as a global model to various countries, including Korea. So the authors initially seek to understand US/EU national innovation policy interconnections, and then find the role of nanotechnology development within. To strengthen national policy coherence, nanotechnology development strategies are under evolution as an innovation catalyst for promoting commercialization. To strategically support nano commercialization, EHS (Environmental, Health, Safety) and informatics are invested as priority fields to strengthen social acceptance and sustainability of nano enabled products. The current study explores US/EU national innovation policies including nano commercialization, EHS, and Informatics. Then obtained results are utilized to analyze weaknesses of Korean innovation systems of connecting creative economy and nanotechnology development policies. Then ongoing improvements are summarized focusing on EHS and informatics, which are currently prominent issues in international nanotechnology development.

Keywords: nanotechnology, innovation, innovation policy, commercialization

*Corresponding Author: Seoung Hun Bae
Department of Information Analysis Director
National Nanotechnology Policy Center
Korea Institute of Science and Technology Information
Republic of Korea
E-mail: ultratyphoon@kisti.re.kr

1. INTRODUCTION

Since the global economic crisis around 2008, international policies are refocusing on innovation sources such as revitalizing manufacturing. This new trend is motivated by steady economic growth via high-tech manufacturing even under economic crisis (McKinsey Global Institute, 2012; Pisano et al., 2009; The White House, 2011; NANoFutures, 2012). The US/EU find one national innovation source from manufacturing revitalization with the support of emerging technologies. Nanotechnology is especially regarded as a key catalyst to resolve high-priority social issues including national innovation, job creation, and economic impact (President's Council of Advisors on Science and Technology [PCAST], 2011 and 2012a; High-Level Group on Key Enabling Technologies, 2011). Following this trend, the main focus of nanotechnology development policy is shifting from the promotion of fundamental exploration to innovation/commercialization (PCAST, 2012b; National Nanotechnology Initiative, 2013; Communication from the Commission to the Council, 2004, 2005), to serve as innovation engines for sustainable economic growth. After the 2008 economic crisis, the implementation of capital intensive R&D investment is becoming difficult (Roco, 2013). Thus, the US/EU are undergoing renovation of national innovation ecosystems, securing sustainable development by maximizing horizontal-vertical policy coherence so that achievements of emerging technologies are quickly materialized to resolve top priority national agendas.

Additionally, there are past analyses finding that the fast-follower approach of Asian countries has been very successful in emerging technology development (NANoFutures, 2012; PCAST, 2011, 2012a; High-Level Group on Key Enabling Technologies, 2011)), and their scientific/technological achievements positively influenced the competitiveness of high-tech manufacturing industries (McKinsey Global Institute, 2012; Pisano et al., 2009; The White House, 2011). Even though the US/EU are still international leaders of emerging fundamental research, it was not sufficient to sustain global leadership. Upgraded policy was required to maintain leadership for both economic impact and high-tech capabilities. As an implementation methodology, the US/EU have been maximizing

the coherence of national innovation strategy and emerging technology development policies. In particular, nanotechnology development implementation policy has evolved as an innovation catalyst to resolve national core issues. As a representative example, the US NNI (National Nanotechnology Initiative), which serves as one global reference model for nanotechnology development trend, now emphasizes nano based application/commercialization. The economic crisis around 2008 combined with threats by fast followers including China and Korea (National Nanotechnology Initiative, 2013; PCAST, 2010 & 2012c) accelerated the evolution of US nanotechnology development strategy as a national innovation engine. This is similar to the EU in that nanotechnology development direction has evolved to align coherence with national-level innovation policy, as well as a catalyst for innovation and commercialization (NANoFutures, 2012; High-Level Group on Key Enabling Technologies, 2011).

Throughout the current study, the authors discuss three major points as below. First, Korean nanotechnology application capabilities are suggested to be on a decreasing trend. Second, US/EU nanotechnology development policy alignment with national priority agendas has continued approximately over the decade, whereas Korea has initiated it recently compared with the US/EU. Third, the international nanotechnology development trend of supporting national commercialization is focused on key fields, including nano Environmental, Health, Safety (nanoEHS) and informatics. In the case of the US/EU, they have already initiated harvesting tangible results of nanoEHS whereas Korea is under development.

2. DEFINITIONS AND NANO-APPLICATION COMPETITIVENESS

The worldwide policy trend led by the US/EU is changing into actively exploiting emerging technologies to promote national innovation, economic growth, and job creation (The White House, 2011; NANoFutures, 2012). As a representative emerging technology, nanotechnology has attracted much attention as an innovation catalyst for national innovation. The declaration of the US nanotechnology development plan in 2000 fueled global nanotechnology development competition as a new general purpose technology to innovate existing/new industries. In the case of transforming general purpose technology into economic impact, it is important for securing sustainability in the innovation pipeline (Wiggins, 2012), which is also currently a key element in US/EU innovation policy. The importance of EHS/informatics is emphasized to secure sustainability by supporting safe/fast commercialization of nanotechnology. These trends are more easily understood along with concepts of innovation, innovation chains, and innovation systems that are summarized in the following section.

2.1. Innovation, Innovation Systems, and Innovation Chains

The OECD 'Oslo Manual' (Organization for Economic Co-operation and Development, 2005) describes innovation as the "introduction of new products, new methods of production, new markets, development of new sources, creation of new market structure in an industry." The US report of "A Strategy for American Innovation" (The White House, 2009) defines innovation as "the development of new products, services, and processes." The US report then describes recent trends of innovation in high-tech/advanced-manufacturing sectors including nanotechnology, aerospace, life sciences, and energy, leading to job creation.

The OECD/EU often utilize the concept of the innovation system, which is important for understanding recent innovation policies including science and technology fields. The OECD document (1997) explains an innovation system as a "network of institutions in the public and private sectors whose interactions initiate, import, modify and diffuse new technologies." Work by Song (2009) summarized backgrounds of how innovation systems were suggested, with a methodology overcoming drawbacks of conventional R&D policies. The focus of conventional R&D policy was nationally investing in targeted science/technology fields that have high potential of rewards. It was believed that if emerging sciences/technologies are developed, then they will easily diffuse out to societal innovation/commercialization. However, it was the reality that few emerging technologies developed by existing R&D policies materialized into social innovation/commercialization. To overcome this broken connection between R&D results and innovation/commercialization, an improved policy system was required. Within the innovation system, the R&D field is one element of innovation policy that should be aligned/interconnected with other innovation policies including economy, social, and regulation ones, and so on, so that social innovation capabilities are maximized with sustainable growth.

Under innovation systems, an innovation chain is explained as "a process of matching technical possibilities to market opportunities," as the summarized diagram in Figure 2. (Foxon, 2004; International Energy Agency, 2009).

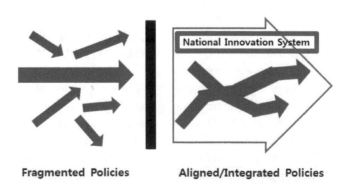

Fragmented Policies   **Aligned/Integrated Policies**

Fig. 1 Redrawing image of policy alignment/integration under a national innovation system (Song, 2009)

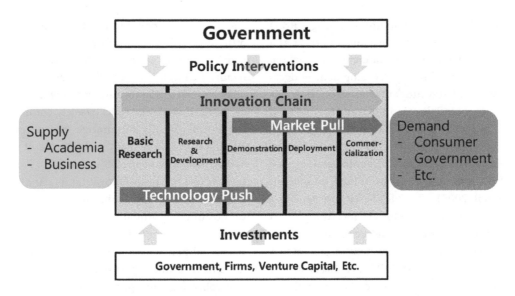

Fig. 2 Redrawing of innovation chain diagram (Foxon, 2004; International Energy Agency, 2009)

2.2. Competitiveness of Nano-Applications

Korean nanotechnology development policy has been maintaining the same framework of nanotechnology development policy over the decade, whereas global nano leaders such as the US have been significantly updating it. There would be no problem if Korea keeps its international nanotechnology capabilities well. However, several indicators show negative signs of stagnant/decreasing nanotechnology capabilities in innovation/commercialization that are central issues of the current global nano development trend. The US/EU are strengthening their nanotechnology commercialization capabilities for catalyzing national innovation with sustainability. Under these conditions, Korean nanotechnology development policy shows asymmetric achievements of fundamental and application capabilities based on the number of data. Lux research (2010) and the Korean Annual Nanotechnology Implementation Plan (National Science & Technology Council, 2013) reported that Korea is ranked in 3rd-4th position overall. However, if nanotechnology commercialization capabilities are separately considered, internationally Korea is ranked in 7th place (Científica, 2011). Recently Korean internal research reported that Korean nanotechnology competence compared to the global top (100%) decreased from 81.3% (2011) to 76.4% (2013) (Ministry of Trade Industry & Energy, 2013). Even though the number of research papers is expanding, the qualitative evaluation of nanotechnology commercialization capabilities is suggested to be on a decreasing trend.

Quantitative analysis from authors utilizing the nano product inventory of the Woodrow Wilson Center (2013) suggests that Korean nanotechnology production is undergoing a stagnant phase whereas those of the US/EU are increasing. Korea was 2nd globally in nano product production in 2011 (National Science & Technology Council, 2011). However, the updated database of the Woodrow Wilson Center in 2013 shows that Korea is ranked 3rd after the US and Germany as shown in Fig. 3. It is beyond the focus of this article, but Fig. 4's trend shows that nano production in the US/EU is on an increasing trend whereas Asian countries are in a stagnant phase.

These observations motivate the study of US/EU national policy chain ranging innovation strategy, interconnection with nanotechnology, and the importance of nanoEHS/informatics within emerging technology commercialization ecosystems. The authors then compare these findings with the current status of Korean nanotechnology development policies, including nanoEHS/informatics.

The US/EU gauge that nanotechnology R&D achievements are already mature enough to serve as a catalyst for sustainable innovation/commercialization. The focus of nanotechnology development budgets have also shifted from fundamental research development to commercialization for resolving national issues such as revitalization of advanced manufacturing (High-Level Group on Key Enabling Technologies, 2011; PCAST, 2012b; National Nanotechnology Initiative, 2013; Communication from the Commission to the Council, 2005). The US/EU felt threatened by the rapid chasing of fast followers including Korea in emerging tech capabilities and economic growth. Thus an upgraded national innovation ecosystem was required (NANoFutures, 2012; PCAST, 2011) so that emerging tech development policy is supporting a national innovation system by catalyzing sustainable commercialization and resolving social issues. Such a focus was prepared from around 2006, and now nanotechnology development aims at supporting various areas including national innovation, revitalization of advanced manufacturing, commercialization of emerging technology, and regulation for safety. Within these, nanoEHS and informatics are invested in as priority fields to support revitalization of advanced manufacturing, and to provide a scientific/institutional safety basis so that innovative nanotechnologies resolving national issues are quickly/safely commercialized. The authors briefly summarize the current US/EU national innovation chain and the role of nanotechnology, including nanoEHS/informatics. For example, the US NNI has been renovating its nanotechnology investment portfolio from 2006 to now (National Nanotechnology Initiative 2004, 2007, 2011a, 2014) to strengthen nanoEHS, commercialization, and international policy harmonization. But Korea still uses the same investment portfolio since 2001, and its first time collecting and opening the nanoEHS budget to the public was in 2013 (National Science & Technology Council, 2013). Compared to the US/EU, Korean nanotechnology plans have relatively weak alignments ranging national innovation policy, nanotechnology development strategy, coherent interagency collaboration, commercialization, and securing safe usage.

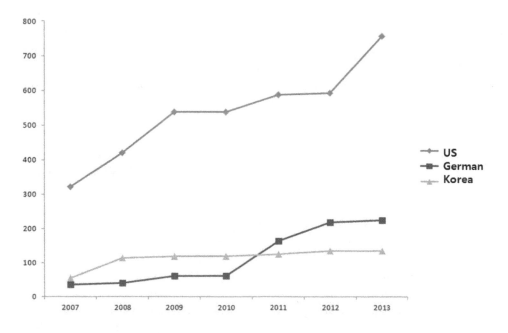

Fig. 3 Changes in numbers of products related to nanotechnology of US, Germany, and Korea

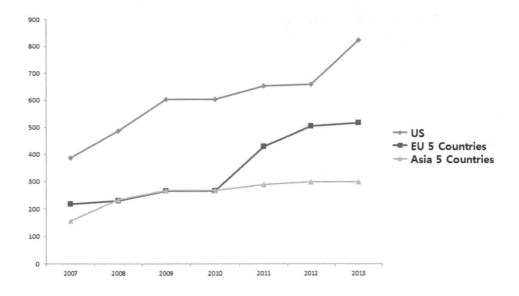

Fig. 4 Changes in numbers of products related to nanotechnology of US and EU (Germany, UK, Denmark, Switzerland, France), and Asia (Korea, China, Japan, Taiwan, Singapore)

3. US INNOVATION POLICIES INCLUDING NANOTECHNOLOGY

3.1. American Innovation

The White House announced "A Strategy for American Innovation" in 2011 to integrate national growth resources for high quality job creation and economic growth, therefore securing sustainable national prosperity. This innovation policy is implemented based on the America COMPETES Acts of 2010 (US Public Law 111-358, 2010) that was enacted to overcome the economic recession/financial crisis around 2008. Within this innovation strategy, US government is implementing advanced manufacturing partnerships (AMP) (PCAST 2011, 2012a, 2012b) and updated nanotechnology development policy (National Nanotechnology Initiative, 2014) so that emerging technologies can serve as key elements for the revival of US manufacturing that finally innovates in the US.

3.2. Advanced Manufacturing

Advanced manufacturing partnership (AMP) (PCAST, 2011, 2012a), aiming at a manufacturing revival by exploiting emerging technologies, have been implemented based on the America COMPETES Acts of 2010, as well as US innovation strategy in 2011. AMP is supported with the development of nanotechnology, especially the Nanotechnology Signature Initiative.

The US was a world manufacturing leader, and it played a key role in securing global economic leadership. Now the United States government is seriously recognizing its loss of international manufacturing competitiveness, and plans to recover it by revitalizing advanced manufacturing with the support of emerging technologies. The AMP report summarized top priority technologies required for the renaissance of US advanced manufacturing as follows: advanced sensing, nano manufacturing, IT, nano materials, and energy efficient technology (PCAST, 2012b). At the request of the Obama administration, NNI has been developing specialized nano programs to maximize policy coherence with upper strategies of national innovation and AMP. As a result, NNI developed 5 Nanotechnology Signature Initiative (NSI) programs that serve as key catalysts for creating a national innovation and advanced manufacturing renaissance. The 5 core technologies of AMP and the 5 Nanotechnology Signature

Table 1. Comparison of 5 Core Tech of AMP and 5 Nanotechnology Signature Initiative (NSI) Programs of NNI

5 Core Technologies of AMP	5 NSI Programs
Nanomanufacturing	Sustainable Nanomanufacturing
Information Technology	Nanoelectronics for 2020 and Beyond
Energy Efficient Manufacturing	Nanotechnology for Solar Energy Collection and Conversion
Nanoscale Materials	Nanotechnology Knowledge Infrastructure
Advanced Sensing and Measurement Technologies	Nanotechnology for Sensor and Sensors for Nanotechnology

Initiative programs of NNI have strong relations and it would be reasonable to see them as complementary programs as summarized in Table 1. Recently NNI announced a totally reformed NNI implementation strategy that will be summarized in the following section.

3.3. National Nanotechnology Initiative

From an early period the US government recognized the importance of nanotechnology, and announced the NNI (National Nanotechnology Initiative) in January 2000 which fueled international nanotechnology development competition. In December 2003, the Bush administration established the Nanotechnology Research and Development Promotion Act as a legal basis for the promotion of NNI. The vision of NNI is to understand and control matter at the nano scale leading to a revolution in technology and industry that benefits society. During FY 2001-2012, the US government invested $15.6 billion into NNI as a top priority national investment field in science and technology. Now, NNI is implemented as a strategic key catalyst for realizing a national innovation and manufacturing revival. The initial draft of the American COMPETES Reauthorization Act 2010, the legal basis of US innovation strategy and AMP, included the revision of the 21st Century Nanotechnology Research and Development Act (PL 108-153), but was mostly erased in the final version. Instead, administration documents including US innovation strategy, AMP, and PCAST evaluation (The White House, 2011; PCAST, 2011; PCAST, 2010, 2012c) have requested that NNI find fast-growing and promising areas so that the United States can find breakthroughs by close interagency collaboration, with joint R&D. Accelerating the growth

of these selected areas supporting nanotechnology, the US aims for economic recovery, job creation, securing national energy production, and so on. In response to these, the NNI developed 5 Nanotechnology Signature Initiative (NSI) programs between 2010 and now (three programs in 2010, and two programs in 2012). NSI's five focus areas include advanced manufacturing revival, escaping from fossil energy, new semiconductor industry development, big data, and promotion of safe commercialization. The implementation of NSI aims at resolving national critical issues, and foresees visual results within 10 years as summarized in Table 2.

The NSI budget was not classified as a 8 Program Component Area of NNI up to the FY 2014 NNI supplement report (National Nanotechnology Initiative, 2013; National Nanotechnology Initiative 2010, 2011b, 2012), but only gathered a total amount of investment. The Nanotechnology Signature Initiative investment budget in 2104 was $343 million, which is an increase of 11.4% compared to 2013. 5 NSI and investment budget information are summarized in Table 3 below. The two recently started NSI projects of "Nanotechnology for Sensor and Sensors for Nanotechnology" and "Nanotechnology Knowledge Infrastructure" directly supports AMP in two fields of nano-informatics and nanoEHS. The development of nanoEHS aims at promoting an institutionalization basis for safe commercialization. Also, the importance of information science for gathering/storage/retrieval/classification/manipulation is emphasized as emerging technologies (nano/bio/information/cognition) are converging, and their applications are promoted for high-tech manufacturing (Roco, 2013; Materials Genome Initiative, 2014).

Table 2. 5 Nanotechnology Signature Initiative (NSI) Programs and Major Goals

Starting Year	NSI Program	Goal
2010	Sustainable Nanomanufacturing	Support establishing large-scale and sustainable nano-based manufacturing system contributing to the recovery of global leadership of US manufacturing
2010	Nanoelectronics for 2020 and Beyond	Support new technologies and manufacturing systems of semiconductor industries that significantly contribute to securing US global economic leadership for decades, and continue into 21st century
2010	Nanotechnology for Solar Energy Collection and Conversion	Develop solar energy as a strong candidate for the development of alternative energy sources to overcome the dependence on conventional fossil fuel, with environmentally friendly and economically valuable results
2012	Nanotechnology Knowledge Infrastructure	Establish a national nano system supporting S&T information (big-data) and life-cycle based nano safety
2012	Nanotechnology for Sensor and Sensors for Nanotechnology	Acquire nano-based measurement and monitoring technology for the promotion of both safety and commercialization

Table 3. Summary of 2012~2014 NSI Budget (Unit: Million $)

NSI Programs	2012, Actual	2013, Estimated	2014, Proposed
Sustainable Nanomanufacturing	56	72	60
Nanoelectronics for 2020 and Beyond	92	87	80
Solar Energy Collection and Conversion	88	82	102
Nanotechnology Knowledge Infrastructure	2	2	23
Nanotechnology for Sensors	55	65	78
Total	**294**	**308**	**343**

In summary, the NNI is undergoing evolution for the support of critical national issues including the revival of advanced manufacturing that the US lost to Asian competitors including Korea. US governments have selected key nano fields including nanoEHS/informatics for advanced manufacturing revival, and the success of current US policy activities will return to Korea as an economic threat due to its heavy reliance on high-tech manufacturing industries.

3.4. NanoEHS/Informatics within National Innovation Policies

The US NSI program supports key technology fields, including nanoEHS and informatics, that have high potential for realizing national innovation/commer-cialization. The commercialization of an emerging technology such as nanotechnology has immeasurable potential in both positive and negative sides. The benefits of emerging technology could be maximized with proactive prevention of its hazards to humans and the environment. In the case of the US, nanoEHS capability is already mature and materialized as regulations of FIFRA banned the importing of Korean nano silver products to the US around 2006. Actually the US government has been growing its nanoEHS fields since the enactment of its nanotechnology promotion act (PL 108-153) up to now. The NNI has been strategically strengthening nanoEHS around 2006 by specifying the nanoEHS field as Program Component Area 7 along with a sharp increase of budget, preparing/updating nanoEHS federal strategic development plans from 2006 to 2011 (National Nanotechnology Initiative 2006, 2008, 2011c), and institutionalizing nano safety as a regulation of FIFRA/TSCA. Such regulation capabilities of nanotechnology are now supporting national innovations of manufacturing.

Informatics is an important element of supporting advanced manufacturing revival. Informatics has the potential of minimizing time periods required for new material development toward commercialization, integrating intelligent manufacturing processes, and exploiting existing information for various purposes. The NNI launched its NKI program under NSI as of 2012 for stimulating nano informatics, for multiple reasons.

4. EU INNOVATION POLICIES INCLUDING NANOTECHNOLOGY

Similar to the US, the European Commission (EC) also realized the value of nanotechnology from early on and incubated nanotechnology as a key catalyst for resolving national economic and social issues. The importance of nanotechnology in EU policy can be found from past European Commission reports (Commission of European Communities, 2004), and in the recent trend of utilizing nanotechnology for realizing European innovation that is included in the European 2020 Strategy as Key Enabling Technology (KET) (High-Level Group on Key Enabling Technologies, 2011).

The document "concerning nanotechnology opinion on the strategy of the European Union (12/05/2004)" (Commission of European Communities, 2004) proposed safe, integrated, and responsible development of nanotechnology. This trend is one setting the pace of European innovation policy so that the EU dominates global nano science/technology and responds to future needs regarding environment, health, and possible social issues.

The European Action Plan 2005-2009 (24/09/2004) (Communication from the Commission to the Council, 2005) regarding nano science/technology development states 8 core areas as listed below to promote safe and responsible development of nanotechnology. The European Commission monitors the progress of this investment portfolio and the collaboration/participation of member countries from the early stages of nanotechnology development.

- Research, Development and Innovation
- Infrastructure
- Interdisciplinary Human Resources
- Industrial Innovation
- Integrating the Societal Dimension
- Public EHS and Consumer Protection
- International Cooperation
- Implementing a Coherent/Visible Strategy at European-Level

4.1. EC Framework Program (FP) 7

The EU has been developing nanotechnology in its Framework Program (FP) as Nanoscience, Nanotechnology, Materials, and New Production Technologies (NMP). Horizon 202 (2014-2020) is under implementation as post FP7. The FP7 Cooperation program, budget, and related configuration are summarized in Fig. 5.

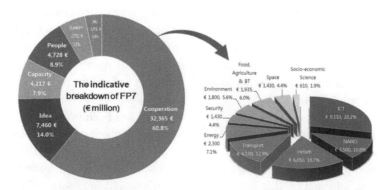

Fig. 5 FP7 Cooperation program, part of the budget and related configuration

The FP program is composed of four parts, 1) Cooperation, 2) Idea, 3) Capacity, and 4) Human Resources (People). The nanotechnology development program is involved under the cooperation part that has the largest investment budget under FP. Under the cooperation part, Nanoscience, Nanotechnology, Materials, and New Production technology (NMP) research and development support integrated development of nanotechnology. The implementation of NMP aims at strengthening the competitiveness of the EU industry and leading existing resource-intensive industries toward a knowledge-based economy. Nanotechnology is regarded as a key technology supporting high value-added production and knowledge-based industries (including the development of new technologies bringing SME competitiveness). NMP budgets through FP7 (2007-2013) and main four investment areas are summarized as below in Table 4.

1) Nanoscience and Nanotechnology (NanoScience and Nanotechnology): Nano-scale research and development of nanotechnology in development

2) Advanced Materials (Materials): NT and BT materials for new products

3) New Production (New Production): Conditions for continuous innovation and technical/institutional/human resource utilization, nanotechnology, and safety (EHS)

4) Industrial production technology integration (Integration of technologies for industrial Production): Through the use of new technologies and new materials promoting industrial development in Europe

The European Union regards advanced technology, especially nanotechnology, as a key R&D area for exploring 1) fundamentals, 2) application/commercialization, and 3) innovation. A more detailed diagram for these 3 major contribution areas of nanotechnology is summarized as below in Table 5.

Table 4. 2007~2013 NMP Budget Summary (Unit: Million Euro)

Year (FP7)	2007	2008	2009	2010	2011	2012	2013
NMP	372	390	421	413	461	511	615
NMP/ Total R&D	6.8%	6.4%	6.2%	5.5%	5.4%	5.0%	5.7%
NMP budget increase rate		4.8%	7.9%	-1.9%	11.6%	10.8%	20.4%

Table 5. Nanotechnology Contribution to Fundamentals / Visualization / Application

NT: the 3 Main Axis			Remark
Nanotechnology	Enabling Program Components	Next Gen. nanomaterials -devices & systems	Non application specific Research (TRL 1-4), Fundamental
		Safe development & application	
		Societal dimension	
		Synthesis and manufacturing	
		Capacity enhancing Techniques	
	Cross KET application focus areas	Nano enabled surfaces	Application specific R&D&I with NT support (TRL 5-8), Application
		Nanostructures and Composites	
	Nanotechnology Innovation Showcase	Nanomedicine	Application uniquely enabled by NT (TRL 5-8), Innovation
		Environmental technologies	

4.2. Horizon 2020

Horizon 2020 is an integrated program of the existing Framework Program (FP), the Competitiveness & Innovation Programme (CIP), and the European Institute for Technology (EIT) to simplify the program operation and accessibility of participating institutes/researchers. The EU plans to invest approximately 40% of its entire R&D budgets through the Horizon 2020 program. Horizon 2020 is the new European growth and job creation program aiming for the recovery of Europe from economic crisis. Europe stresses that investing in R&D is a solution to overcome the current economic crisis, and plans to allocate an R&D budget up to 3% of GDP by 2020. Horizon 2020 is investing in 3 main component areas of "Excellent Science," "Industrial Leadership," and "Societal Challenges."

In particular, Horizon 2020 research and development was established by analyzing existing economic/social changes, therefore enables promoting innovation in broad areas including environment, climate change, aging society, and so on. These major goals are achieved by collaboration of industry-academia-public institutions and integrated/coherent policies covering R&D-education-innovation system. The Nanotechnology (NMP) in Horizon 2020 acts in the 'leadership in Enabling and Industrial Technology (LEIT)' section. Nanotechnology is a key enabling technology (KET) to recover the competitiveness of European industries, and focuses on crossing the valley of death for societal challenges. Nanotechnology serves as a key catalyst technology supporting these major goals by developing five major components as follows: 1) the next generation nano-materials, nano-devices and nano-systems, 2) safe development and applications of Nanotechnologies, 3) the social dimension of Nanotechnology, 4) Efficient synthesis and Manufacturing of Nanomaterials, Components, and Systems, and 5) Capacity enhancing techniques, measuring methods and Equipment.

In order to provide the solutions for societal challenges, European Commission started European Economic Recovery Plan (Commission of European Communities, 2008) that includes 3 PPP(public-private partnership) programs of Factories of the Future(FoF), Energy efficient Building(EeB), and Green Car(GC).

4.3. NanoEHS/Informatics within National Innovation Policies

Similar to the US, the EC also regards nanotechnology as a national innovation catalyst. Therefore the nano enabled commercialization promotion policy is paired with the development of nanoEHS throughout the European Action Plan 2005-2009, FP 7, and Horizon 2020. For example, the FP7 program covers activities from fundamental research to commercialization of technologies (innovation) of nanotechnologies in DG Research and development (RTD). NanoEHS was one of the key parts in 3) New production as well as The NanoSafety Cluster (NSC) initiative that was organized in 2009 to maximize synergies between the FP6 and FP7 projects, addressing all aspects of Nanosafety. Horizon 2020 (Post-FP7) was started in 2014 and set to run until 2020, and Nanotechnology as NMP is located under 'Industrial Leadership' and 'Leadership in Enabling and Industrial technologies (LEIT),' and focuses on the level of technological readiness (TRL) 3/4 - 8. Nanotechnolgy is one of the 6 key enabling technologies (KETs) driving competitiveness and growth opportunities, contributing to solving societal challenges with safe development/applications. Like the US regulation of FIFRA/TSCA, the EC also established REACH regulation that proactively monitors potential hazards of nanomaterials. In both the US/EU cases, their recent nanotechnology development direction is highly aligned with national innovation strategies of promoting nano enabled commercialization paired with nanoEHS. The EC has been collecting ongoing nanoEHS programs and budgets that are spread out over FP6-7 under the program of the nanosafety cluster since 2009. The EC supported 13 nanoEHS programs with a budget of 31 million euro under FP6, and 34 programs with 106 million euro under FP7. Their annual reports summarizing nanoEHS programs each year are available from the project home page (http://www.nanosafetycluster.eu/).

Nano policy elements of EU are not clearly separate such as in the US NNI program, but are integrated in the national program of Horizon 2020. The importance/interconnection of advanced manufacturing, nanotechnology, informatics for smart/fast production, and nanoEHS for safe commercialization are already fused in plans such as Factory of the Future (http://ec.europa.eu/research/participants/portal/desktop/en/

opportunities/fp7/calls/fp7-2013-nmp-ict-fof.html) in FP7 and Horizon 2020 (http://ec.europa.eu/research/participants/portal/desktop/en/opportunities/h2020/calls/h2020-fof-2014.html#tab2).

5. KOREAN INNOVATION POLICIES IN-CLUDING NANOTECHNOLOGY

The mainstream of US/EU nanotechnology development policies are focused on application/commercialization goals that finally support national innovation policy. But Korean nanotechnological achievements are still weighted on fundamental/basic areas (Bae et al., 2013), and application/commercialization capacities show negative signs as described in Fig. 3. Below, the authors summarize limitations of Korean nano policies, and contrast the progress of US/EU policies to suggest possible future improvements for Korean nano policies.

5.1. Presidential Election Pledge

As a reminder, the main focus of global nanotechnology development trends is shifting from fundamental exploration to innovation/commercialization. Also, US/EU nanotechnology development policies are horizontally and vertically interconnected with neighboring policies to catalyze national innovation and commercialization. The Korean government also understands the importance of nanotechnology, and President Park Geun-Hye highlighted nanotechnology as an important supporter for creative economic policy (Park, 2012).

5.2. National Comprehensive Development Plan for Nanotechnology (NCDPN)

Since 2001, the South Korea government has been implementing the National Comprehensive Development Plan for Nanotechnology (NCDPN), revising it every five years. The first NCDPN (2001-2005) was planned to complete constructing major infrastructures within 5 years, and to achieve 10 world-top class technologies within 10 years. The second phase of NCDPN (2006-2010) was aimed at 3 major goals of becoming one of the top 3 nano competitive countries, preempting emerging markets by fusing with existing IT·BT·ET, and realizing the goal of a safe/prosperous

country by 2015. The 3rd phase of NCDPN (2010-2020) was established to realize 4 major goals of achieving 30 top world-level practical skills, building infrastructure for research/education, creating nanotechnology based industries, and strengthening social/ethical responsibilities (National Nanotechnology Policy Center, 2012).

Through phases 1-2 of NCDPN, South Korea achieved building bases for nano R&D and industrialization. The implementation of the 3rd NCDPN achieved a significant increase of nano R&D budgets responding to social/market demand, and challenged making 30 core technologies for promoting nano commercialization. In particular, interagency collaboration was emphasized to respond to nanotechnology pre-occupation by the US/EC/Japan, support green growth, and create a new growth engine for society.

Up to now the Korean government has successfully incubated the competitiveness of nanotechnology by implementing NCDPN. Recently the Korean government is beginning to reconsider the importance of promoting nano/convergence technologies as a breakthrough for innovation and economic growth. Superficially, Korea has been following global nanotechnology development trends well, but related data and indicators show negative signs of stagnation/decrease in Korean nanotechnology competitiveness and commercialization capabilities. Recently there have been discussions for the necessity of reforming the nanotechnology development policy framework to support nano/convergence based industries in a seminar held by the National Party (Kim, E.-D., 2013) and in research (Bae, 2013).

5.3. NanoEHS/Informatics within National Innovation Policies

The US/EU have been strengthening their national innovation chains of utilizing nanotechnology by renovating nanotechnology development for the realization of national innovation strategies, executing them by manipulating R&D budgets, and preparing a legal basis for sustainable application. Compared to the US/EU, Korean nanotechnology development is argued to have weak points as described below.

Korean nanotechnology policy has maintained the same investment portfolio since 2001 by fixing it as 3 components (R&D, infra, and education), but has been adopting international core issues of nanotechnology development including innovation and nanoEHS. However, investment budgets for key issues including nanoEHS were rarely monitored, and therefore it is difficult to evaluate progress (National Nanotechnology Policy Center, 2012). The US has been collecting nanoEHS budgets from 2006, and the EU has been managing nanoEHS budgets and programs under the name of the nanosafety cluster since 2009. In the case of Korea, the importance of nanoEHS has been emphasized from the 3rd phase NCDPN by planning for raising nanoEHS budgets up to 7% over all. However, it is very recent that the nano EHS investment amount was officially monitored, only since the 2013 Korean Nanotechnology Annual Implementation Report (National Science & Technology Council, 2013). Even still, national nano related budget assessment had showed approximately 2x differences depending on the source (collection from agencies participating in NCDPN, and the National Science & Technology Information Service under National Science & Technology Council), and this issue is improved since the 2014 Korean Nanotechnology Annual Implementation Report (National Science & Technology Council, 2014). In the case of the '1st national comprehensive nano safety plan (2012-2016)' (National Science & Technology Council (2011) led by the Ministry of Environment, this interagency collaboration plan is encountering difficulties in finding clear connections with the Korean Nanotechnology Promotion Act or NCDPN, meaning a weak national level of policy alignment. Also, Korea still does not have a developed legal tool supporting sustainable usage of nano e-material/products such as FIFRA, TSCA, and REACH in the US/EU cases.

Compared to the US/EU situations, Korean development of nanoEHS in R&D and legal tools is not clearly aligned for contributing nano based commercialization that finally supports a national innovation chain. Now the Korean government is putting prime importance on creative economy policy, but the nanotechnology policy design contributing to national innovation with economic growth is still questionable in various aspects such as controlling nano investment portfolios, supporting targeted technology fields including nano commercialization/nanoEHS, and synchronizing them with national innovation through interagency collaboration. In the case of informatics,

it is too early to discuss whether national innovation policy clearly covers nano informatics for advanced manufacturing. Overall, Korean interpolicy connections of utilizing nano for national innovation need further development when compared with the US/EU.

Recently the Korean national assembly held a single forum sharing the issues of Korean nano policies described above, and discussed the necessity of revising its nanotechnology development promotion act (Kim, E.-D., 2013), including strengthening national nanosafety fields that support national innovation. The current nanotechnology promotion act and NCDPN require strengthening nanoEHS more systematically. On the continuation of this forum, a nanotechnology development promotion act revision bill was proposed (Kim E.-D. et al., 2014b) for first including nanoEHS elements.

6. CONCLUSION

Stimulated by the rapid chasing of Asian followers including Korea, the US/EU changed the focus of their nanotechnology development policies from fundamental exploration to application/commercialization. US/EU nanotechnology policies and legislative/administrative activities have been aligned with national visions over the last decade to maximize national capabilities for national innovation and societal challenges. These US/EU trends are reflected in 2014 NNI strategy and EU KET policy goals that support advanced manufacturing revival.

Compared to the US/EU, Korean nano policies show limitations for supporting nanotechnology commercialization and national innovation. The authors have investigated these weaknesses throughout previous original research (Bae S.-H. et al., 2013) and the support seminar held in the National Party (Kim E.-D., 2013) with the policy report of nanotechnology promotion act amendment direction (Kim, E.-D., 2014). These works discuss the necessity of promoting interagency collaboration with the required amendment direction of the Nanotechnology Development Promotion Act. Based on these activities, National Party member Kim Eul-Dong currently a proposed nanotechnology promotion act amendment bill (Kim, E.-D., 2014b). The main purpose of the amendment bill is strengthening nano commercialization and EHS/ informatics to further support the Korean policy of creative economy. Initiated by this law revision, additional national efforts should be continued to reinforce a national innovation ecosystem by promoting nano commercialization with EHS/informatics.

US/EU policies have been focusing on advanced manufacturing revival with the support of nanotechnology commercialization capabilities as a counterattack against fast-followers, and Korea currently shows negative signs of decreasing commercialization capabilities and social acceptance of nano applications. If Korea does not react to US/EU nano policies of strengthening advanced manufacturing, then its consequences might return to us as an economic threat due to the heavy reliance of high-tech manufacturing industries.

REFERENCES

Bae, S.-H., Lim, J.-S., Shin, K.-M., Kim, C.-W., Kang, S.-K., & Shin., M. (2013). The innovation policy of nanotechnology development and convergence for the new Korean government. *Journal of Nanoparticles Research, 15*, 2072.

Cientifica (2011). Global funding of Nanotechnologies and its impact. Wales: Cientifica.

Commission of European Communities (2004). Communication from the Commission - Towards a European strategy for nanotechnology. Brussels: European Commission.

Communication from the Commission to the Council (2005). The European Parliament and the Economic and Social Committee - Nanosciences and nanotechnologies: An action plan for Europe 2005-2009. Brussels: European Commission.

Commission of European Communities (2008). Communication from the Commission to the European Council: A European Economic Recovery Plan, Brussels: European Commission.

Foxon T., Makuch Z., Mata, M., & Pearson, P. (2004). Innovation systems and policy-making processes for the transition to sustainability. *Proceedings of the 2003 Berlin Conference on the Human Dimensions of Global Environmental Change, Environmental Policy Research Centre*, Berlin (pp. 96-112).

High-Level Group on Key Enabling Technologies (2011). Final report: High-level expert groups on KETs. Brussels: European Commission.

International Energy Agency (2009). Ensuring green growth in a time of economic crisis: The role of energy technology. IEA Publishing.

Kim, E.-D. (2013). Seminar on amendment of Nanotechnology Development Promotion Act for the realization of creative economy. Seoul: National Assembly of Korea.

Kim, E.-D. (2014a). Amendment direction for Nanotechnology Development Promotion Act. Seoul: National Assembly of Korea.

Kim, E.-D., & 22 National Party Members (2014b). Revision bill of Nanotechnology Development Promotion Act. Seoul: National Assembly of Korea.

LUX Research (2010). National competitiveness ranking by nanotechnology. Boston: LUX Research.

Materials Genome Initiative (2014). Materials Genome Initiative strategic plan. Washington DC: National Science and Technology Council.

McKinsey Global Institute (2012). Manufacturing the future: The next era of global growth and innovation. New York: McKinsey & Company.

Ministry of Trade Industry & Energy (2013). 2013 Technology level evaluation. Seoul: Ministry of Trade Industry & Energy

NANoFutures (2012). Integrated research and industrial roadmap for European NT. Brussels: European Commission.

National Nanotechnology Initiative (2000). National Nanotechnology Initiative: The initiative and its implementation plan. Washington, DC: National Science and Technology Council.

National Nanotechnology Initiative (2004). National Nanotechnology Initiative Strategic Report. Washington, DC: National Science and Technology Council.

National Nanotechnology Initiative (2006). Environmental, health, and safety research needs for engineered nanoscale materials. (September, 2006). Washington, DC: National Science and Technology Council.

National Nanotechnology Initiative (2007). The National Nanotechnology Initiative strategic report. Washington, DC: National Science and Technology Council.

National Nanotechnology Initiative (2008). Strategy for nanotechnology-related environmental, health, and safety research. Washington, DC: National Science and Technology Council.

National Nanotechnology Initiative (2010). NNI supplement to the president's 2011 budget. Washington, DC: National Science and Technology Council.

National Nanotechnology Initiative (2011a). National Nanotechnology Initiative strategic report. Washington, DC: National Science and Technology Council.

National Nanotechnology Initiative (2011b). NNI supplement to the president's 2012 budget. Washington, DC: National Science and Technology Council.

National Nanotechnology Initiative (2011c). Environmental, Health, and Safety (EHS) research strategy. Washington, DC: National Science and Technology Council.

National Nanotechnology Initiative (2012). NNI supplement to the president's 2013 budget. Washington, DC: National Science and Technology Council.

National Nanotechnology Initiative (2013). NNI supplement to the president's 2014 budget. Washington, DC: National Science and Technology Council.

National Nanotechnology Initiative (2014). National Nanotechnology Initiative strategic report. Washington, DC: National Science and Technology Council.

National Nanotechnology Policy Center (2012). National nanotechnology policy direction for global competitiveness of Korea Economy. Seoul: Korea Institute of Science and Technology Information

National Science & Technology Council (2011). Nano safety management master plan (2012-2016). Seoul: National Science & Technology Council.

National Science & Technology Council (2013). 2013 annual implementation plan of nanotechnology. Seoul: National Science & Technology Council.

National Science & Technology Council (2014). 2014 annual implementation plan of nanotechnology. Seoul: National Science & Technology Council.

Organization for Economic Co-operation and Development (1997). National innovation systems. Paris: OECD Publications.

Organization for Economic Co-operation and Development (2005). The measurement of scientific and technological activities. Paris: OECD Publications.

Park G.-H. (2012). Presidential election pledge for 18th presidential election. Seoul: Saenuri National Party.

Pisano, G. P., & Willy, C. S. (2009). Restoring American competitiveness. *Harvard Business Review*, Boston: Harvard Business Publishing.

President's Council of Advisors on Science and Technology (2010). Report to the president and congress on the third assessment of the National Nanotechnology Initiative. Washington, DC: National Science and Technology Council.

President's Council of Advisors on Science and Technology (2011). Report to the president on ensuring American leadership in advanced manufacturing. Washington, DC: National Science and Technology Council.

President's Council of Advisors on Science and Technology (2012a). Report to the president capturing a domestic competitive advantage in advanced manufacturing. Washington, DC: National Science and Technology Council.

President's Council of Advisors on Science and Technology (2012b). Report of the advanced manufacturing partnership steering committee, annex 1: Technology development workstream report. Washington, DC: National Science and Technology Council.

President's Council of Advisors on Science and Technology (2012c). Report to the president and congress on the fourth assessment of the National Nanotechnology Initiative. Washington, DC: National Science and Technology Council.

Roco, M. C., Bainbridge, W. S., Tonn B., & Whitesides G. (2013). Convergence of knowledge, technology, and society: Beyond convergence of nano-bio-info-cognitive technologies. Lancaster, PA: World Technology Evaluation Center.

Song W.-J. (2009). Policy theory of national innovation system. Seoul: Science and Technology Policy Institute, STEPI Working Paper Series, WP 2009-01.

The White House (2013). The president's plan to make America a magnet for jobs by investing in manufacturing. Washington, DC: The White House.

The White House (2014). Remarks by the president on the National Network for Manufacturing Innovation. Washington, DC: The White House.

The White House (January, 2013). Blueprint for an America built to last. Washington, DC: The White House.

The White House. (February, 2011). A strategy for American innovation, securing our economic growth and prosperity. Washington, DC: The White House.

The White House. (September, 2009). A strategy for American innovation: Driving towards sustainable growth and quality jobs. Washington, DC: The White House.

US Public Law 111-358 (January, 2010). America COMPETES Reauthorization Act of 2010. Washington, DC: US Congress.

Wiggins, R., & Ruefli T. W. (2012). Schumpeter's ghost: Is hypercompetition making the best of times shorter? *Strategic Management J, 26*, 887–911.

Woodrow Wilson Center (2013). Nanotechnology consumer product inventory. 2013.10 update. Retrieved from http://www.nanotechproject.org/inventories/consumer/

15

Facebook: Hate it or Love it, But Can You Ignore it?
A Comparative Study of US and India

Shivani Arora

SBS College, Delhi University
Delhi, India
E-mail: dr.shivani.research@gmail.com

Daniel Okunbor *

College of Arts and Sciences
Fayetteville State University
Fayetteville, North Carolina, USA
E-mail: diokunbor@uncfsu.edu

ABSTRACT

Facebook has been a part of our lives for the last decade. For a company started in 2004 to have penetrated the lives of people across the globe is commendable. The perpetuation of Facebook has led to a phenomena called Facebook Addiction Disorder. Companies are using Facebook to promote their business and people are using it to promote themselves, in addition to staying connected. In this paper, an effort is made to study respondents from India and the United States of America in order to gauge their dependence on Facebook, and a comparative view of it is presented.

Keywords: Facebook, FAD, Facebook Addiction Disorder, Social Networking

1. INTRODUCTION

Facebook has been gaining ground since its inception in 2004. In less than a decade, it has become synonymous with the term Social Networking. The buzz around it has increased in the recent past in India, which has the potential to provide Facebook with a stronger user base. India has huge untapped potential for Facebook. The initiatives by the government of India, including the Digital India drive has further strengthened Facebook's interest in India, with its CEO Mark Zuckerberg visiting India twice in around a year.

*Corresponding Author: Daniel Okunbor
Professor
College of Arts and Sciences
Fayetteville State University
Fayetteville, North Carolina, USA
E-mail: diokunbor@uncfsu.edu

Indian Prime Minister Narendra Modi's visit to Facebook headquarters has further strengthened the already sturdy growth of Facebook. The prime minister's visit implies that being on social media isn't a matter of choice; the sooner you start taking benefit from it, the better the advantage you will have.

With a strong hold in the US and building up in India, there is a consensus on its advantages, especially the ease with which users can "connect," irrespective of the geographical boundaries.

The team at Facebook has been working incessantly on changing and improving the experience of its customers. Zuckerberg's Facebook has been anything but static since its inception, and the competitors that were complacent like Orkut and Google+ have lost ground. They are either abandoned or are not able to compete. Facebook studies its customers to offer them features, similarly introducing its "like" button, its click to "buy," emojis, and so on. The customized offers it makes raises the question of privacy in the minds of users, again with Facebook making all its efforts to issue statements and figure out ways to address privacy issues.

Is there a perpetual need to study everything that Facebook does, or isn't there? This question can best be answered through this paper.

Social networking, especially Facebook, has become an imminent part of life and discussions around it have grown, the flipside being that the dependence of people on Facebook has grown, at a fast pace. There's a thin line between dependence and addiction, and this line is very easy to cross. Various psychologists and researchers in the field have established the symptoms and effects excessive usage can have on users once they become addicted. The symptoms have been defined for research based on the studies by the psychologists. This paper tries to study various aspects of its usage, by studying the respondents through a questionnaire and then comparing respondents from India and the United States, in order to decipher the usage along with the differences, if any, and then comparing them to yield results for us to further investigate.

2. REVIEW OF LITERATURE

In this section a review of articles and studies related to Facebook's focus on India, and on Facebook Addiction Disorder and various aspects related to it, has been considered. The articles have been quoted and studied to analyze trends, and a review of empirical studies has been undertaken to observe which areas have been explored, and which need further investigation. This was done in order to formulate objectives and undertake productive research. The review has also been undertaken to earmark problem areas related to excess Facebook usage. Besides, these studies will provide insight into the various efforts directed towards better understanding of the complexities involved.

Facebook has been very positive about its Indian presence and has been focusing on India since the Digital India initiative was launched. Mark Zuckerberg visited India in 2014 and met Prime Minister Modi to discuss various aspects of collaboration between the two. In the article "Facebook's Mark Zuckerberg latest tech CEO to visit India" by Guynn (2014), she shares all that had been planned for the Indian focus. She also discusses Facebook's Chief Operating Officer Sheryl Sandberg visit to India, Facebook's second largest market. She also met with Modi, who used social media during his election campaign and also is using it in governance.

In the article "Facebook in India: Can Mark Zuckerberg's plan really help the poor?" by Suhay (2015), the controversial internet.org site is discussed in detail. Zuckerberg emphasized that free Internet should be a basic right, whereas some sections of people see an underlying marketing gimmick for Facebook rather than a philanthropic one.

As a result of the opposition Facebook is facing from many sections including e-commerce giants, in their study "Facebook addiction - New psychological scale," Andreassen et al. (2012) show that

- Younger people are more at risk of developing Facebook addiction as compared to older ones
- Anxious and socially insecure people use Facebook more that those who are not, since they find it convenient to communicate via social media as compared to face-to-face
- Organized and ambitious people tend to stay away from addictive use; rather, they tend to use it for work
- Women are more at risk of developing Facebook Addiction Disorder (FAD) due to its social nature.

The study "Facebook addiction: Factors influencing an individual's addiction," by Sherman (2011) suggests that although Internet addiction has been studied, social networking addiction has not been researched. The study investigates how factors such as personality, gender, procrastination, boredom, and one's values may affect amount of time spent on Facebook. It further concludes that users are either overly possessive about their usage thereof or not. The research conducted was a combination of qualitative and quantitative techniques, using scholarly articles that focused on personality types and Internet addiction. Based on the results from the qualitative study, a quantitative survey instrument was devised, which includes Likert-style statements that test personality type, values, boredom, and procrastination.

Psychologist Dr. Michael Fenichel (2010) describes Facebook Addiction Disorder (FAD) as a situation in which Facebook usage "overtakes" daily activities like waking up, getting dressed, using a telephone, or email checking. According to Joanna Lipari (as cited in Fenichel, 2010), a clinical psychologist at UCLA, some signs of Facebook addiction are:

i)   Losing sleep over Facebook; staying logged in throughout the night and eventually becoming too tired for the next day;

ii) As a bench mark, spending one hour or more on Facebook is too much;

iii) Being obsessed with exes who reconnect on Facebook;

iv) Ignoring work for Facebook;

v)   The thought of getting off Facebook leaving the user in cold sweat.

Shaw (2013), in the article "Status update: Facebook Addiction Disorder," opines that a user is suffering from Facebook Addiction Disorder (FAD), a disease referred to by psychologists, if he/she has more online friends than real life friendships; also, if users check Facebook more than five times a day (spending hours updating their status), or if checking their Facebook account is the first thing that they do in the morning.

The excuses cited by Facebook addicts have included:

i)   The urge of human interaction and the ease of it through Facebook/Twitter;

ii) Getting a message on Facebook/Twitter is exciting since it feels like someone is interested in "me."

To check this urge to be on Facebook pages, a web application can be used which shuts off the computer after the user has spent a pre-determined amount of time.

Ellison, Steinfield, and Lampe (2007), in their study "The Benefits of Facebook 'friends': Social capital and college students' use of online social network sites," provide scale items to judge addiction of social networks, viz.,

i.   Facebook is a part of my everyday activities

ii.   I am proud to tell people, I am on Facebook

iii. Facebook has become a part of my daily routine

iv.   I feel out of touch when I haven't logged onto Facebook for a while

v.   I feel I am a part of the Facebook community

vi.   I would be sorry if Facebook shut down

vii. Approximately how many Facebook friends do you have?

viii. In the past week, on average, how much time per day have you spent actively using Facebook?

Also, Agyemang (2009), in his article, "Infected with Facebook Addiction Disorder?," refers to a study by Cambridge University suggesting an argument contrary to the belief that Facebook disrupts social life. It was asserted that it aids people to be more sociable, giving people more choice as to how and with whom they conduct their relationships.

Haisha (2011), in her article "Is your Facebook addiction a sign of loneliness?", discusses a unique aspect of Facebook addiction which differentiates it from other types of addictions. Unlike addictions to drugs, alcohol, and sex, where guilt is a major factor, Facebook addicts feel that they have reasons to be addicted, since they claim to be doing business. Some are self-employed professionals looking for clients, some are job seekers trying to network for a new job, and some are corporate employees trying to extending their company's message. Their time on Facebook is actually escapism disguised as working. Also, most of these people are addicted to their past—reconnecting with their friends, old classmates, former lovers, and so on.

In other research on social networks, Yang and Tang (2003) focused on students' performance in an online course offered at the National Cheng-Chi University in Taiwan. They found that social networks that serve advising roles have a positive impact on students' performance and that networks that are adversarial have a negative impact.

The review of the available literature reveals that studies have included various aspects of Social Networking Addiction (with special reference to Facebook) including its symptoms; positives of usage (as well as negatives); and the implications and impact of Social Networking Addiction. Among the studies listed here are also included the professional opinions of those psychiatrists and psychologists regarding the influx of Facebook Addiction Disorder (FAD) cases.

3. PURPOSES AND METHODOLOGY OF THE STUDY

This research study will investigate the Facebook usage of respondents. The focus will be on how often people use this tool to converse with or keep current with their friends' social or personal lives. The significance of the study is to examine the impact of social networking on its users and the merits and demerits of Facebook usage, particularly the aspects that pertain to dysfunctional behaviors.

Facebook is growing bigger and worldwide, and there's a need to study its impact. Research questions include:

- What is the threshold for Facebook usage to be classified as dysfunctional, such as causing addiction disorder?
- What are the differences in Facebook usage perception in a geographical context? In this case, usage in Western Asia (India) and North America (United States) will be compared.

The research design that will be used in this study is based on the mixed research model. This model is chosen in order to achieve full potential, including the benefits of mixed methodology, and to provide a comprehensive investigation of the research questions. These benefits include: 1) the ability to engage in both inductive and deductive reasoning, 2) allowing of a qualitative approach to complement the results of the quantitative approach and vice-versa, 3) maximizing of the advantages of quantitative and qualitative methodologies and minimizing of demerits, 4) application of both objective and subjective points of view, 5) allowing of researchers to choose explanations that best produce desired outcomes, 6) researchers' values play a large role in the interpretation of results, and 7) a mixed model is pragmatic and more realistic and serves as the middle ground for positivist and constructivist theories (Tashakkori & Teddlie, 1998). These benefits of a mixed model are of great importance to this study. The open-ended questions are intended to complement the closed-ended questions and vice-versa to help produce stronger analyses and desired outcomes.

The qualitative approach of this research study will utilize content analysis based on open-ended questions of the survey questionnaire. Content analysis is chosen for this research because it is well suited to the study of the methodical and to the description of the content of recorded human communication. Babbie (2002) defines content analysis as "any technique for making inferences by objectively and systematically identifying specified characteristics of messages."

Judgment sampling was used to study 151 undergraduate students from Delhi University and 120 from Fayetteville State University, Fayetteville, North Carolina, USA. The questionnaire was sent to 1,000 respondents but as a limitation, only 151 and 120 respondents, respectively, filled it up. The quantitative portion of this research study will involve a cross-sectional approach for data collection. This data analysis will utilize a statistical package provided by Google Docs. The percentage of the total agreement has been taken by adding the strongly agree and agree percentages, and the same for disagreement levels. The simplicity of the method, combined with the qualitative discussions, will give us the real crux of the comparison. To keep it simple, the agreement levels of the two sets of respondents are compared and conclusions drawn accordingly. For this study, we will be using Google Forms' spreadsheet that keeps the responses.

4. FINDINGS

The purview of the paper is to study the various aspects of Facebook usage affecting the respondents from the United States (prefixed with the code U) and India (prefixed with I). The coding for various aspects is

1. RwF: Restless without Facebook
2. FGa: Prefer Facebook over family gathering
3. IPl: Facebook is an integral part of life

4. FRe: Accepting friends' requests
5. WT: Facebook is a waste of time

The responses are studied and analyzed; the findings are interesting, and in this area:

Symptom 1: RwF (Restless without Facebook): I feel restless if I cannot connect whenever I want

34% of Indian respondents agree that they feel restless, as compared to only 11% of US respondents. Now, the agreement of one-third of Indian respondents with the statement is an indication of dependency on Facebook.

47% and 72% of respondents from India and the United States, respectively, disagreeing with the statement is a positive finding. That the feeling of restlessness

is not there if they are not able to log on is certainly a positive sign. US respondents seem stronger as compared to Indian respondents in their dependency. The informal discussions reveal that the possibility of not getting connected in the US is remote, so they do not know how that will make them feel.

To comprehend the same, very few (only 10%) from the US feel dependent on Facebook as compared to 33%, which makes a clear statement that US respondents are less addicted than Indian respondents in the case of Symptom 1.

Symptom 2: FGa (Prefer Facebook over Family gathering): I prefer to be on Facebook rather than going to a family gathering.

There's a general belief that Facebook keeps its users

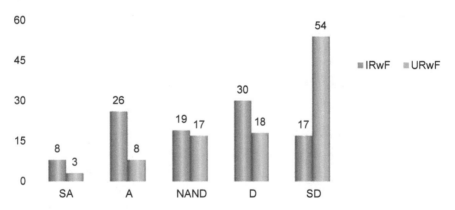

Fig. 1 Facebook unavailability leaves me restless

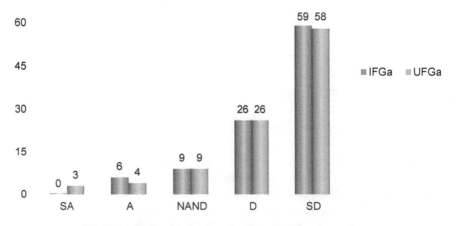

Fig. 2 I prefer Facebook over a family gathering

away from their families, but the response to the statement clearly negates this. Similar response patterns to this statement reveal that the respondents do not prefer the pseudo-life of Facebook as opposed to family gatherings. Therefore, it is concluded that both sets of respondents are completely in sync as to their response to this statement. Both categorically reveal that they don't prefer Facebook to family gatherings.

Symptom 3: IPl (Integral Part of Life): Facebook is an integral part of my life

Established in 2004, within 12 years Facebook has attained a status which the other social networking sites can only dream of. Most of its competitors, such as Orkut and Google+, have not been able to keep pace with it. Hence the statement about Facebook being an integral part of their lives.

79% of US respondents disagree that Facebook is an integral part of their lives as compared to only 41% of Indian respondents. 31% of the Indian respondents agree that Facebook is an inseparable part of their lives as compared to only 9% from the US, thereby implying that respondents from India seem to be more dependent on Facebook than their counterparts.

Again, Symptom 3 is more pronounced in Indian respondents as compared to their US counterparts. Very few (only 11%) from the US consider Facebook an integral part of their life as compared to 33% from India. Here again, the dependency and hence the chances of addiction are greater in respondents from India as

compared to the US.

Symptom 4: FRe (Friends Request): I accept all friend requests

This is an extremely pertinent statement to ensure safety and security online. The competition of having the maximum number of online friends was spotted, and the more the number of online friends, the more problems are associated with the same (Walton, 2013). Some experts advise that it is important to be conservative while accepting friend requests.

A very positive and uniform finding is that both set of respondents do not accept all the "friend requests" that come their way, implying that they try and evaluate before accepting requests from strangers.

The two sets of respondents are completely in sync and respondents do not accept all the friend requests that come their way.

Symptom 5: WT (Waste of Time): Facebook is a waste of time

26% of respondents from India and 25% of respondents from the US agree that Facebook is a waste of time, whereas 32% from India and 38% from US disagree. In this particular case, 41% (Indian respondents) and 38% (US respondents) are indecisive regarding the same. What does that mean?

Informal discussions revealed that the response has a very interesting interpretation. The respondents sometimes find it useful and at other times a complete

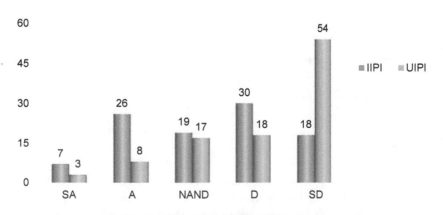

Fig. 3 Facebook is an integral part of life

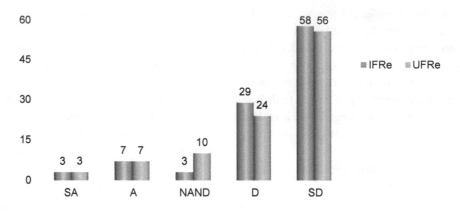

Fig. 4 I accept all friend requests

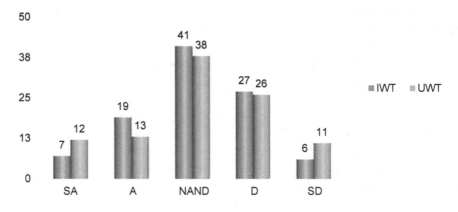

Fig. 5 Facebook is a waste of time

waste of time. There's unanimity in responses which implies something very close to our belief that neither its usefulness can be denied nor its flip/addictive side. Facebook is very useful and successful in spreading information, messages, causes, and so on, and at the same time it leads to a wasting of time, highlighting the addictive and useless angle of usage.

5. CONCLUSIONS

The comparison amongst the young respondents from India and the US has yielded some interesting expected results and at the same time, some unexpect-

ed results. Out of five symptoms, responses on the two are different and the other three show similar opinions. The respondents from India are more dependent on Facebook as compared to respondents from the US in the following two categories, i.e. feeling restless without Facebook and considering it an integral part of their lives. The two symptoms point out that the addictive streak is conspicuous in Indian respondents as compared to their counterparts in the US.

Unanimous and positive results have been revealed in the following cases, which convey that the respondents from both categories prefer to be at family gatherings as compared to preferring to spend time online. This is a very positive outcome and supports the positives given by Facebook.

The "friend requests" are not accepted blindly by either set of respondents. The flip side of accepting "friend requests" from all, whether known or unknown has put many people in trouble, so the respondents are mature enough to be selective. Both set of respondents agree that there are positives and negatives associated with Facebook, which cannot be denied, so they consider it both a waste of time and at the same time, useful.

Based on the statements studied, the respondents from the US are not as much affected by the Facebook phenomena in an addictive way as compared to Indian respondents, who seem to be more dependent on Facebook and hence have a higher chance of addiction.

This research might come in handy when dealing with youths bordering on or suffering from Facebook Addiction Disorder. The differences in usage in the two sets of respondents would aid those concerned people in the two continents in dealing with them differently. It helps to deepen the understanding of the phenomena called Facebook, which has changed the way people interact, socialize, and live their lives.

6. FURTHER RESEARCH/ LIMITATIONS OF THE STUDY

The research in this field is imperative, and it mainly advocates against the raucous use of an important networking tool. Social networking websites are a boon when used judiciously. There are certain limitations of the study. The respondents have been chosen from Western Asia (India) and North America (United States) only, since the researchers belonged to these areas. That made data collection and discussion easier. The researchers feel that the geographical area can be expanded and so can the sample size. Both were restricted due to the restrictions of funds and time.

Another limitation is that Facebook is only a part of social networking, and so further research can be expanded to other social networking websites like Instagram, Twitter, and so on.

Innumerable stories exist of people growing in their careers through LinkedIn, missing people being found with the aid of Facebook posts, and a never ending list. But when looked at on its flipside, it is the mental

health issues caused by excessive use, cyber bullying, terrorism, narcissism, and many problems which crop up. The use of any good thing is justified, but when it becomes an addiction or serious symptoms start showing up, it's time to think and to start creating awareness and providing solutions.

REFERENCES

Agyemang, F. (2009). Infected with Facebook Addiction Disorder? *GhanaWeb*. Retrieved from http://www.ghanaweb.com/GhanaHomePage/features/Infected-with-Facebook-Addiction-Disorder-FAD-171018.

Andreassen, C., Andreassen, S., Torsheim, T., Brunborg, S., & Pallesen, S. (2012). Development of a Facebook addiction scale. *Psychological Reports, 110*(2), 501-517.

Babbie, E. (2002). *The basics of social research*. Belmont, CA: Wardsworth Group.

Black, T. R. (1999). *Doing quantitative research in the social sciences*. London, UK: Sage Publications.

Calderon, J. (2012, February 21). Facebook Addiction Disorder in Malaysia. *Newsweek* (Japan). Retrieved from http://justincalderon.wordpress.com/2012/02/21/facebook-addiction-disorder-in-malaysia-newsweek-japan/

EDUCAUSE Center for Applied Research (ECAR). (2008). *Research study on social networking sites*. ECAR Research Study 8. Boulder, CO.

Ellison, N.B., Steinfield, C., & Lampe, C. (2007, July). The benefits of Facebook "friends:" Social capital and college students' use of online social network sites. *Journal of Computer-Mediated Communication, 12*(4), 1143-1168.

Fenichel, M. (2010). Are you a Facebook addict? Retrieved from http://www.addiction-intervention.com/addiction/process-addictions/are-you-a-facebook-addict/.

Guynn, J. (2014, October 1). Facebook's Mark Zuckerberg latest tech CEO to visit India. *USA Today*. Retrieved from http://www.usatoday.com/story/tech/2014/10/01/facebook-mark-zuckerberg-india-internetorg/16533515/.

Gadgets 360. (2016). Facebook spent Rs. 300 Crores on free basics ads in India: Report. Retrieved from http://gadgets.ndtv.com/internet/news/facebook-spent-rs-300-crores-on-free-basics-ads-in-india-report-788348?site=classic.

Haisha, L. (2011). Is your Facebook addiction a sign of loneliness? *SelfGrowth*. Retrieved from http://www.selfgrowth.com/articles/is-your-facebook-addiction-a-sign-of-loneliness

Henderson, J. M. (2012). 3 reasons you should quit social media in 2013. *Forbes*. Retrieved from http://www.forbes.com/sites/jmaureenhenderson/2012/12/29/3.

Hopkins, W. G. (2000). Quantitative research design. *Sportscience, 4*(1). Retrieved from www.sportsci.org/jour/0001/wghdesign.html.

Indo-Asian News Service. (2015). Social media addiction affecting sex life of young Indians, claim experts. *NDTV*. Retrieved from http://gadgets.ndtv.com/social-networking/news/social-media-addiction-affecting-sex-life-of-young-indians-claim-experts-699371.

Meikle, J. (2012, February 3). Twitter is harder to resist than cigarettes and alcohol. *The Guardian*. Retrieved from http://www.guardian.co.uk

OFCOM. (2008, April 2). Social networking: A quantitative and qualitative research report. Retrieved from http://stakeholders.ofcom.org.uk/binaries/research/media-literacy/report1.pdf.

Paddock, C. (2012, April). Facebook addiction - New psychological scale. *Medical News Today*. Retrieved from http://www.medicalnewstoday.com/articles/245251.php.

Tashakkori, A., & Teddlie, C. (1998). *Mixed methodology: Combining qualitative and quantitative approaches*. Thousand Oaks, CA: SAGE Publications.

Sherman, E. (2011). *Facebook addiction: Factors influencing an individual's addiction*. Boston: Erica Sherman.

Shaw, E. (2013, January 29). Status update: Facebook Addiction Disorder. *The Glen Echo*. Retrieved from http://theglenecho.com/2013/01/29/status-update facebook-addiction-disorder

Suhay, L. (2015, December 28). Facebook in India: Can Mark Zuckerberg's plan really help the poor? *Christian Science Monitor*. Retrieved from http://www.csmonitor.com/Technology/2015/1228/Facebook-in-India-Can-Mark-Zuckerberg-s-plan-really-help-the-poor.

Walton, A. (2013). Jealous of your Facebook friends? Why social media makes us bitter. *Forbes*. Retrieved from http://www.forbes.com/sites/alicegwalton/2013/01/22/jealous-of-your-facebook-friends-why-social-media-makes-us-bitter/#48f0866d4c0dc37b2654c0d8.

Yang, H., & Tang, J. H. (2003). Effects of social network on students' performance: A web-based forum study in Taiwan. *Journal of Asynchronous Learning Networks, 7*(3), 93-107.

Yuan, K., et al. (2011). *Microstructure abnormalities in adolescents with Internet Addiction Disorder*. *Plos One*. Retrieved from http://www.plosone.org/article/info:doi/10.1371/journal.pone.0020708.

16

Principles for Helpful Sequence and Deduction of Knowledge Organization Systems - An Exploratory Study

A.Y. Asundi*

Department of Library and Information Science
& Officer-in-Charge, IT Centre
Bangalore University, India
E-mail: ashokasundi@rediffmail.com

ABSTRACT

Dr. Ranganathan's "Principles for Helpful Sequence" among the set of normative principles play an exclusive role in the arrangement of subject isolates. Each subject in the universe of subjects is regulated by a guiding principle of its own which analogously determines the sequence of Arrays in ordering the subject surrogates or isolates. For example, the "Principle of Later-in-Evolution" is applied for sequencing isolates of Animal and Plant Species; this concept can be applied to one of the tools of KOS viz. *Taxonomies*. The application of Principles for Helpful Sequence is summarily presented and in the process the paper highlights the inherent elements of knowledge organization in each one of these principles in a manner that might map the future course of research in this area with the potentiality to bring about a relation between principles for helpful sequence and KOS.

Keywords: Library Classification, Principles for Helpful Sequence, Knowledge Organization Systems

1. INTRODUCTION

Among the numerous contributions of Dr. Ranganathan's to conform to scientific method in Library Science, two contributions are unique and notable. They are "Five Laws of Library Science," published in 1931, and the "Dynamic Theory of Library Classification," begun in 1935. There are two classificationists of the modern era, Dr. S.R. Ranganathan and Henry Evelyn Bliss, in addition to E.C. Richardson and

***Corresponding Author:** A.Y. Asundi
Former Professor and Chairman
Department of Library and Information Science
& Officer-in-Charge, IT Centre
Bangalore University, India
E-mail: ashokasundi@rediffmail.com

W.C. Berwick Sayers, who attempted to develop a theory for library classification (Parkhi, 1972). The theory developed by Bliss was a descriptive and static theory. The theory developed by Bliss remained quiescent, as further research in this context lacked organizational and professional support. Ranganathan's theory was based on a set of normative principles which served as theory for the design of a scheme for Library Classification and also for a set of Scheme of Classes. From this initiation he proposed a postulate of faceted classification and developed his theory accordingly, envisaging autonomy to classifier to develop the theory without expecting the classificationist's approval, as the latter has given exclusive basis for the developmental process. The purpose of this exercise is to identify KOS in an attempt to correlate them with the principles for helpful sequence. In this context the Postulates for Modes of Formation of Subjects can be quoted as an example. It is stated that this knowledge is a dynamic continuum and new disciplines and subjects will be deduced from this spiral of growth of knowledge. The new subjects are to be suitably accommodated in a Scheme of Classes to keep the Classification system up-to-date, and at the levels of Idea and Notational Planes, which can automatically be carried out by the classifier based on the 'typology of relations' characterized by the modes of formation of subjects. The case of Biochemistry might be exemplified here. Biochemistry is designated as a **Fused Basic Subject** and it would be assigned an exclusive notation of GX and its place is assigned between Biological Sciences (G) and Earth Sciences (H) (Ranganathan, 1987). A complete case study on the formation of Biochemistry is made by Gopinath and Seetharama (1975). A Scheme for Library Classification provides several guidelines for recognizing new and emerging subjects, for example Literary Warrant, and also for deciding on their location in the sequence of innate subjects.

A classification in general involves three processes:

1. Division and Grouping
2. Arranging the members of the group and the groups themselves in a helpful sequence
3. Representing the ranked members of a group by a suitable notation.

The theoretical basis of designing a classification system can be studied from the descriptive account of three planes of work viz. Idea Plane, Verbal Plane, and Notational Plane, the basic foundations of a dynamic theory of library classification. The guidance of work in the first stage of Classification, that is *Division and Grouping*, is the work of the Idea Plane and regulated by Canons (rules of division) and Postulates (rules for logical assumption). The work *of arranging the members of a group and the groups* as above is an exclusive task carried out with the help of "Principles for Helpful Sequence", which is the core discussion of this paper. The entire work of both developing a dynamic theory for library classification, and a set of normative principles was enunciated and evolved by Ranganathan (1967).

2. NORMATIVE PRINCIPLES

The definition of Normative Principle as given in Prolegomena is as follows:

> Normative Principles can be postulated for work in different levels from the level of the basic process of thinking, through the level of library science (or for any other discipline) as a discipline, to the level of each of its various sub-disciplines — such as classification and cataloguing and even still to the deeper levels (Ranganathan, 1967).

The word 'Normative' is derived from the root term 'norm', meaning rules or an authoritative standard. Normative means 'establishing a standard'. So the phrase Normative Principles refers to the principles of establishing standards for designing various tools, methods, and techniques of Library Science. So the basis of normative principles deals with establishing standards for developing a dynamic theory of library classification.

The entire work of the theoretical basis of designing a Classification can be visualized from the set of Normative Principles as shown in the following table.

As per the above table the Level "Classification" refers to division and grouping which is carried out with the use of Canons. The work on the Level classification dealt with by Canons from the core of the Idea Plane, in conjunction with contributions to this area, has also come from Richardson, Sayers, and Bliss. But the contribution to the Level Helpful Sequence in Array dealing with "Principles for

Table 1. Normative Principles

S. No.	Level	Name of Normative Principle
1.	Basic Process of thinking	Basic Laws
2.	Library Science	Fundamental Laws
3.	Classification	Canons
4.	**Helpful Sequence in array**	**Principles for Helpful Sequence**
5.	Work of Classifying	Postulates and Principles for Facet Sequence

Source: Ranganathan's Prolegomena to library classification, 1967. Part-D. P.113

Helpful Sequence" is work exclusive of dynamic theory. The application of these two levels would overcome the bottlenecks in the division and arrangement of the universe of subjects. This pronounced hypothesis can be demonstrated with examples from a discipline like Astronomy.

The discipline Astronomy was part of Mathematics till the sixth Edition of Colon Classification and has been assigned the status of an independent Basic Subject in the seventh Edition of the scheme with Class Number BX (Ranganathan, 1987). The Sub-disciplines of Astronomy are some "Known" and some "Unknown" cosmic bodies. Accordingly the subdisciplines of Astronomy comprise "Known" and "Unknown" entities. Then the known entities have to be arranged in some sequence, such as Alphabetical, Epoch of Origin, and so on. Which of these characterizations gives a helpful sequence for the present or for the future representations of Astronomical knowledge? The known astronomical bodies in this context are the Sun and the Nine Planets orbiting around the Sun. So here comes the problem of arranging these bodies. The Principles for Spatial Contiguity endorse the arrangement of isolates (bodies) in space along a unidirectional linear sequence and the "Principle of Away from Position" as one of the guiding principles applied in this context. The Principle of Away from Position is defined as:

> If the subjects in an array of subjects or the isolates in an array of isolates can be conveniently taken to start from a certain point and diverge away from it roughly along a line, they may be arranged from the starting point along the diverging line.

Here in the Astronomy subject all the planets in the orbit would be arranged beginning with the Sun at the Centre and the other Planets in the divergent line of their sequence of orbital paths. This is one of the simple examples that can be comprehended by everyone and has a majority agreement to this sequence of planetary bodies. Thus the set of Principles for Helpful Sequence (with their corollaries) regulating the sequence of sub-divisions of a discipline and to deeper finite levels.

3. PRINCIPLES FOR HELPFUL SEQUENCE

The Principles for Helpful Sequence are shown in the third level of the Normative Principles that deal with the details of the arrangement of the isolates in the schedules to be created by the division of subjects into sub-disciplines. These principles suggest that there should be some guiding principle to implement the "Canon of Helpful Sequence."

The 12 main Principles for Helpful Sequence with their manifestations as described by Ranganathan (1967) and Parkhi (1972) are given in Table 2. One and more Principles can be applied to a Discipline or to Sub-disciplines. For example, in Botany the Principle of Later-in- Evolution is applied for deriving the species of plant kingdom (Taxonomy) and then taking a Plant as an entity; to arrange parts of a Plant, the Principle of Bottom-Upwards is applied. A parallel example is also found for the Agriculture Subject Schedule (J- Agriculture) in Colon Classification for the arrangement of parts of a Plant as a parallel to Utility Array. Similarly in Medicine, for the parts of the

Human Body the Principle of Top-Downwards is used and for the Organs the Principle of Centre to Periphery is used.

Principles go in consonance with domain specific and logical ideas, which has facilitated the arrangement of groups of entities in a discipline and helped in bringing chaos to order along a natural and logical thinking process as part of "Basic Laws of Thinking"

from the first level of Normative Principles (See Table 1). It would also be presumed that without the guidance from the Principles for Helpful Sequence the arrangement of sub-disciplines in disciplines would have been too complex and tedious. Table 2 gives a set of such principles pronounced by Ranganathan in his theory with subject examples.

Table 2. Principles for Helpful Sequence with some examples

S. No.	Name of the Principle	Subject Example
1.	**Principles for Chronology and Evolution**	
	a) Principle of Later in Time	Religion
	b) Principle of Later-in-Evolution	Botany
2.	**Principles of Spatial Contiguity**	
	a) Principle of Spatial Contiguity	Geography
	b) Principle of Away from Position	Astronomy - Planets
3.	**Principles for Entities along a Vertical Line**	
	a) Principle of Bottom-Upwards	Botany - Parts of a Plant (From Root to Fruit)
	b) Principle of Top-Downwards	Medicin e- Parts of Human body (Starting from Head)
4.	**Principles for Entities along a Horizontal Line**	
	a) Principle of Left-to-Right	Transportation - Highway
	b) Principle of Right-to-Left	Transportation - Highway
5.	**Principles Involving "Front" and "Back"**	
	a) Principle of Front-to-Back	Railway Train
	b) Principle of Back-to-Front	Time isolates - earliest to recent
6.	**Principles along the Circular Line**	
	a) Principle of Clockwise Direction	Zodiacal Signs
	b) Principle of Counter-Clockwise	No. specific example at present. If warranted the Principle will be used.
7.	**Principles for Entities along a Radial Line**	
	a) Principle of Periphery-to-Centre	Layers of Earth
	b) Principle of Centre-to-Periphery	Medicine - Organs (Bone to Hair)
8.	**Principles Involving Quantity**	
	a) Principle of Increasing Quantity	Mathematics - Geometry
	b) Principle of Decreasing Quantity	Library Science - Libraries
9.	**Principle of Increasing Complexity**	Linguistics - Alphabet to Sentence
10.	**Principle of Canonical Sequence**	Mathematics - Basic divisions of Mathematics
11.	**Principle of Literary Warrant**	Agriculture: Arrangement of Crops
12.	**Principle of Alphabetical Sequence**	Automobiles- Car Brands

4. KNOWLEDGE ORGANIZATION

4.1 Analogy of an Indian Tradition

When we talk of knowledge and its organization, social and cultural realities serve as useful analogies to explain the former precisely. Incidentally it would be desirable to understand what is knowledge and the related aspects of knowledge organization. Let us take an example from an Indian traditional practice:

It is a common practice and a tradition in India in all functions and celebrations, to light a lamp. The basic philosophy of this practice as per vedic saying is *"Tamaso ma jyotirgamaya"* (From darkness lead me to light) and it means from ignorance to knowledge. A lit lamp as per Indian tradition signifies "Knowledge". (Raghavan, 2012).

As per the general theory of order outlined by Diemer (1974 as cited in Dahlberg, 1978) there are three aspects to everything:

a) The point of view of a totality
b) The point of view of an element or elements
c) The point of view of relations between the elements

If a lamp is conceived of as a totality, its parts as its elements and each element are ordered according to the elemental relationship between the elements and/or parts of the lamp. The application of one of the Principles for Helpful Sequence viz., the "Principle of Bottom Upwards" can be applied to arrange the parts or elements of the lamp. This is precisely what can be conceived of as an analogy to exemplify knowledge organization and how knowledge organization can be conceptualized where all components of the lamp are assembled systematically to construct a lamp post. In furtherance of this analogy other tools of knowledge organization like ontologies are also inherent in the form of the "wick" and "oil" essential to characterize a lighted lamp. A "Lit Lamp" would thus be taken as an analogy to exemplify the relationship between Knowledge and Knowledge Organization.

The significance correlating *Lamp* with KO is to identify the elements of knowledge and the lit lamp in order to consider a holistic approach to understand knowledge and its organization with the following attributes:

· The characterization of Knowledge

· The elements of Knowledge (the Lit Lamp and its parts, the oil/ghee, the wick)
· The purpose of Knowledge (the Lit Lamp dispels darkness, knowledge does away with ignorance)
· The properties of Knowledge (light) (the upward direction of the flame conceived as vices (Vasanas) and ego, imparting knowledge, increasing clarity, conviction)
· The organization of Knowledge (Lamp) has significance to know a wealth of intellectual and spiritual perceptions from it.
· The oil or the ghee represent the vices (vasanas) and wick the ego.

4.2. Knowledge Organization: Conceptual Basis

In the presentation of the ideas in this discourse, a bottom-up (inductive reasoning) approach is adopted to expound the complexities of knowledge and knowledge organization (KO). Both concepts are hard to explain and no precise definition could be articulated. Some simple and descriptive account of KO is given here, extracting from various sources.

In simple terms KO as a discipline is defined as the organization of information in bibliographic records. On the other hand, Dahlberg (2006) states that:

"Knowledge organization is the science of structuring and systematically arranging knowledge units (concepts) according to their inherent knowledge elements (characteristics) and the application of concepts and classes of concepts ordered by this way for the assignment of the worthwhile contents of referents (objects/subjects) of all kinds".

The lit lamp illustrated above would be an explanatory example for this definition. More precisely Dahlberg (1998 as cited in Ohly, 2007) defines "knowledge organization as a subject area comprising the organization of a) units of knowledge concepts and b) all types of objects related to particular terms or categories, so as to capture what is known about the world in some orderly form allowing it to be further shared with others". The two definitions stated in two different periods of time themselves show contrastingly different intents of knowledge and its organization.

The descriptive account of knowledge organization

given by Hjørland (2008) is much more distinct from the above two definitions. He considered KO on two levels to define and deliberate its scope and application. The narrower sense of KO is applied to mostly LIS activities such as classification, indexing and cataloguing, and so on. In the broader sense of the term, he states that it is applied to organization of knowledge in educational institutions, social organizations, and he describes how it is organized in the reality of sciences, like in Chemistry, Biological Sciences, Linguistics and Geography, and so on. It is further explained that in chemistry the periodical table is the taxonomic visualization of chemical elements and the family of languages would be another taxonomic presentation in the context of linguistics. These, according to him, are the realities in sense of their organization.

It is further emphasized by Hjørland (2008) and Miska (1964 as cited in Hjørland, 2008) that KO has been a practical activity, as the classification schemes devised in the late nineteenth century are continued to be used. It is remarked by Hjørland (2008) that "genuine theoretical bases to KO are very rare but seem mandatory in relation to the challenges with which this field is confronted." This paper is a pursuance attempt to characterize the Dynamic Theory of Library Classification formulated by Ranganathan has qualities to make it a "genuine theoretical base" both for the practical library classification activity and to the KO, as Classification schemes are also one of the Knowledge Organization Systems. It is important that theoretical assumptions based on different practices have to be used to formulate these assumptions as clearly as possible in order to make comparison possible. As a matter of fact, the "educational consensus" approach adopted by Henry Evelyn Bliss has some good elemental issues relating to modern KOS as much as the postulatonal approach adopted by Ranganathan. Thus a consolidation exercise of integrating some good theoretical bases from the classic to modern periods has to be done to formulate a KO theory.

Ranganthan did do an exercise to develop the dynamic theory independent of a single practical classification scheme, and used Colon Classification only to affirm his assumptions. There is a base for considering the dynamic theory that can be applied to KO both

in its narrower and broader sense and meaning. For example, the use of the "Principle of Literary Warrant" of Wilhelm Hulme (1911 as cited in Hjørland, 2008) is evidence of its application to KO in broader meaning. Another argument in favoring this argument is taken from Hjørland (2008) again, where he has identified six approaches to study KO and has enlisted the "faceted analytical approach" as one of them. The faceted approach has provided a methodology of "modes of formation of subjects" and it is how new knowledge is formed or formulated by combination of a priori existing knowledge/disciplines.

4.3. Knowledge Organization Systems

The practical Library Classification schemes are the traditional and also most durable systems of KO. Bliss, in the titles of his two books, probably was the first to use the phrase "Knowledge Organisation" in relation to bibliographic classification. The lists of Knowledge Organization Systems (KOS) vary to some extent from author to author. The paper by Lei Zeng (2008) is used here as a basis for the enumeration of KOS. The types of KOS according to the complexity of their structures and major functions can be grouped and listed below:

* **Term Lists**
  · Lists (pick lists)
  · Dictionaries
  · Glossaries
  · Synonym Rings
  · WordNet

* **Metadata-like Models**
  · Authority Files
  · Directories
  · Gazetteers

* **Classification and Categorization**
  · Subject Headings
  · Classification and Categorization Schemes
  · Taxonomies

* **Relationship Models**
  · Thesauri
  · Semantic Networks/Maps
  · Ontologies

4.4. Deducing KOS from Principles

The application of the dynamic theory of library classification evolved by Ranganathan has been reflected in the study of Faceted Classification models and categories. This paper has ventured to use another normative principle of the theory "Principles for Helpful Sequence" to demonstrate their applications in the tools and components of KO viz. KOS.

The core object of this paper therefore is to demonstrate how the Principles for Helpful Sequence can be employed to derive a helpful order in the tools for KOS such as Ontologies, Gazetteers, Taxonomies, Term Lists, and so on. This is probably a first attempt in this direction and has provided a superficial indication of their applications for further exploration.

a) On Ontologies

Among the above KOS tools the LIS is quite familiar with the majority of them and has been applying them effectively in the traditional and web-based knowledge organization of bibliographic records in libraries (Catalogue, OPAC) and in bibliographic databases (Bibliographies), Online databases, and in other sources of bibliographic records such as Abstracting and Indexing Services, and today even in the databases of electronic information resources. So the term Ontologies is somewhat unfamiliar and un-comprehended in its application in KOS. Therefore the term is explained in its nouveau context:

> "In philosophy ontology is a theory about the nature of (things) existence; of what type of things exist; Ontology as a discipline studies such theories. Artificial Intelligence (AI) and Web researchers have co-opted the term for their own jargon and for them Ontology is a document or a file that formally defines the relation among the terms. The most typical kind of ontology for the web has taxonomy (Web-pages) and a set of inference rules (In Expert Systems/AI)".

For instance, Expert Systems which are by-products of AI consist of an inference engine which is built on a set of ontologies (inferring relationship among terms).

It is obvious that most of the Principles for Helpful Sequence are built on relationships among different terms and concepts. A body of knowledge is based on conceptualization and the object concepts and other entities that are assumed to exist together inherently are in relationships among them that hold them together.

Two examples in this context would illustrate the above intricate summations on the role of ontology in KOS. In the subject Medicine (in CC) the human body is divided into its component parts and is arranged on the **"Principle of Top - Downwards"** from head to toe. Here the terms and concepts are arranged according to their inherent relations and to hold them together to conceive a body (Physical Appearance).

Another example in the same subjects where the diseases are ordered follows as per the schema shown below:

Illustration - 1:

Disease> Organ (affected) Facet> Incident of Disease (Kind) > *General/ Infection /Parasite / Poison/ Functional disorder/ Nutrition/ Structural/ Foreign Matter/ Other*

Here the body of knowledge of "Diseases" is presumably categorised based on the *"Principle of Increasing Complexity"* and also the *"Principle of Literary Warrant."* In other words, these principles would be under consideration for the future incidence of organizing diseases. The relationships between the Organ (Affected) and the kind of incidence of disease are nothing but ontologies. This can be illustrated by the example of a Disease like "Typhoid":

Illustration - II

TYPHOID>Intestine (organ affected) >(Incidence-1) Infection>Bacterial (Incidence-2> Number of cases (Literary Warrant)

b) Taxonomies

Genealogy is a part of Taxonomies, and Genealogy is of ideas and objects. The best example in this context is the use of the *"Principle of Later in Time."* The first vacuum tube, the predecessor of the microprocessor, was invented by John Ambrose Fleming in 1904 and later it proceeded to the development of the Microprocessor. The genealogy of Vacuum Tube to Microprocessor with dates is presented in the follow-

Table 3. Genealogy of Microprocessor (Intel - 4004)

Idea	Product	Person(s)	Year
Photoelectric Effect	Electric/Vacuum Tube	John Fleming	1904
Solid State or Semi-conductor device or / Silicon Chips	Triodes and Diodes	Bardeen, Brattain and Shockley	1947
Integrated Circuit	IC Chip	Kilby and Noyce	1958
Microprocessor (Intel- 4004)	Single Micro Chip	Intel (Faggin, Hoff and Mazor)	1971

ing table (Table 3).[6,7,10,18]

c) Gazetteers

Gazetteers as the formal sources of geographic information have been in the list form and in a form giving a descriptive account of place names, their locations, latitudes and longitudes, and other related features. They also provide information on rivers, mountains, oceans, and other geophysical entities and concepts. Every Library Classification scheme since the time of DDC has a separate and exclusive scheme of classes for Geographical Isolates (as in CC) and Areas (as in DDC). So they have been an integral part of KOS and in particular of Library Classification Schemes. The maps, atlases, and encyclopedias have been sources of Gazetteers apart from the independent Gazetteers of nations, like the Gazetteer of India. The scope of gazetteers ranges from the smallest geographical areas to international levels.

In recent years Gazetteers have been regarded as indispensable tools with the advent of Geographical Information Systems (GIS) and the Global Positional System (GPS). There are new courses instituted under and designated as Geoinformatics. This shows the importance of Gazetteers as KOS. The utility of Gazetteers in Georeferencing is well documented and substantially highlighted by Buchel and Hill (2010).

The *"Principle of Spatial Contiguity"* specifies the mode of developing a helpful order for Geographical entities and concepts. The Principle states "If the isolates (Subdivisions) in a schedule occur continuously in space—roughly along a unidirectional (North-South, East-West) line or radial line or a circle they should be arranged in a parallel spatial sequence, except for when any other overwhelming consideration rules it out.

d) Lists, Authority Files, Subject Headings

This category of KOS consists of quite a large number of tools which are mainly the vocabulary tools of languages. In this group the authority files need some special attention as building authority files is a continuous and never ending process. The authority files may be for terms, concepts, names of places, or names of persons, and they are the tools used both in KO and in KM in particular in Content Management Systems. The metadata is one of the authority files which are used in KM and CMS.

Two Principles, *"Principle of Literary Warrant and Principle of Alphabetical Sequence"* are the ones which provide guidance for the compilation and consolidation of term lists by gathering new terms to update tools like glossaries and dictionaries. It is stated that the alphabetical sequence eliminates all ambiguities in ordering the concepts and terms.

The Authority Files are associated with the vocabu-

---

[6] Integrated circuit. In About.com Retrieved May 18,2013, at
  http://inventors.about.com/od/istartinventions/integrated_circuit.htm
[7] John_Bardeen. In Wikipedia. Retrived May 18,2013, at http://en.wikipedia.org/wiki/John_Bardeen?
[10] Microprocessor. In About.com. Retrieved May, 18,2013, at
  http://inventors.about.com/od/mstartinventions/a/microprocessor.htm
[18] Vacuum Tube. . In About.com. Retrieved May, 18, 2013, at
  http://inventors.about.com/od/mstartinventions/a/Vaccuum_tube.htm?

laries to update them. When new terms are identified, old terms are replaced with new terms giving more comprehensive scope and coverage. For example, Ecology and Environment, Genetics — Microbiology and Biotechnology are terms with inclusive meaning and definitions of old concepts. So the principle of literary warrant governs the socialization of such new terms. Normally the arrangement of Authority files follows the alphabetical sequence and the Principle of Alphabetical Sequence is applied here for the arrangement of terms, particularly in Subject Headings.

e) Other KOS Tools and Principles

Among the given Principles the utility of the majority of them is presented with suitable examples from KOS and some illustrations too. The other KOS systems like Thesaurus, Subject Headings, Semantic networks, and Classification and Categorization schemes have been formally well articulated with their long term use in the organization, representation, and search and retrieval process. In fact the Classification schemes have a very basic foundation of knowledge organization and have demonstrated their predominance in them too.

A Thesaurus for example shows some very concrete relations among terms — equivalent, associative, and hierarchical. These relationships have been part of organizing vocabularies in the Vocabulary Control Devices per se the Thesaurus, which is one of the predominantly researched areas in Semantic Web. A beginning is made to venture on a new application of a dynamic theory of library classification and attempts by researchers may be made to carry out further explorations in this direction.

5. CONCLUSION

The discipline of knowledge organization, though well discussed now in the web environment, has its roots in the times of Aristotle, Comte, and Kant, who created philosophical systems of knowledge then extant. Based on their contributions later classificationists tried to develop a theory for Knowledge Organization, in the limited sense of Library or Document Classification, for facilitating shelf arrange-

ment. In the subsequent decades these also served as a basis for subject cataloguing, indexing, and thesaurus construction, from Cutter to Ranganathan. Hence the traditions of Library Classification also conceived as KOS have potentialities to augment their basis for the development of a theory for KO and in this paper a small beginning is made. It can also be repeated here that KOS have also considered Facet Analysis as one of the techniques suitable not only for the classification of documents but has been proved suitable for structuring Website construction as demonstrated by La Barre (2006). So it could be concluded that there is enough ground for the development of a systematic and stable theory for knowledge organization from the traditional and classic library classification discourses of years past.

ACKNOWLEDGEMENTS

The author is very much grateful to Profs. Gary Marchionini and Dong-Geun Oh, the Co-Editors-in-Chief of the Research Journal "*Journal of Information Science Theory and Practice*" published by the Korea Institute of Science and Technology Information, Daejeon, Republic of Korea.

The author also gratefully acknowledges contributors for their valuable published material and statements he has drawn from the special issue on "What is Knowledge Organization," in *Knowledge Organization — International Journal, 35(2-3), 2008*. Ergon-Verlag.

REFERENCES

Buchel, O., & Hill, L. L. (2010). Treatment of Georeferencing in knowledge organization systems: North American contributions to integrated Georeferencing. *Knowledge Organization-International Journal, 37*(1), 72-78.

Dahlberg, I. (1978). *Ontical structures and universal classification* (Sarada Ranganathan Endowment for Library Science Series, No. 11). Bangalore: Sarada Ranganathan Endowment for Library Science.

Gopinath, M.A. & Seetharama, S. (1975). Interdisciplinary subjects and their classification. In A.

Neelameghan (Ed.), *Ordering systems for global information networks: Proceedings of the Third International Study Conference on Classification Research* (pp. 121-135). Bangalore: DRTC, SRELS and FID/CR.

Hjørland, B. B. (2008). What is knowledge organization. *Knowledge Organization - International Journal, 35*(2-3), 86-101.

La Barre, K. (2006). *The use of faceted analytico-synthetic theory as revealed in the practice of website construction and design* (Doctoral dissertation). Indiana University, Bloomington, IN.

Lei Zeng, M. (2008). *Knowledge organization systems (KOS). Knowledge Organization - International Journal, 35*(2-3), 160-182.

Ohly, H. P. (2007). Past and future of knowledge organization. In K.S. Raghavan (Ed.), *International Conference on Future of Knowledge Organization in the Networked Environment* (pp. 1-6). Bangalore: DRTC, Indian Statistical Institute.

Parkhi, R. S. (1972). *Library classification: Evolution of a dynamic theory.* Delhi: Vikas Pub. House.

Raghavan, L. (2012). Why do we light a lamp before the deity. *Visvaayudha - A Monthly Magazine of All India. Vishnusahasranama Cultural Federation, 15* (180), 8.

Ranganathan, S. R. (1967). *Prolegomena to library classification* (3rd ed.). Assisted by M.A. Gopinath. Reprinted 1989. New Delhi: Ess Ess Publishers for Sarada Ranganathan Endowment for Library Science.

Ranganathan, S. R. (1987). *Colon Classification* (7th ed.). Revised and Edited by M.A. Gopinath. Bangalore: Sarada Ranganathan Endowment for Library Science.

17

Deriving the Properties of Object Types for Research Data Relation Model

Suntae Kim*

Korea Institute of Science and Technology Information
245 Daehak-ro, Yuseong-gu, Daejeon, Korea
E-mail: stkim@kisti.re.kr

ABSTRACT

In this study, the properties of the object types required to describe the relationship among research data resources, which may be generated during the life cycle of the research, are derived. The properties of Fedora Commons and DSpace, which are open source software used for resource management, and schema properties published in DataCite were analyzed. Based on relation names of Fedora Commons, nine new relation names were derived. Thirty-eight object type properties consolidating the target properties of the analysis were derived. The result of this study can be used as basic material for crosswalk research studies of object type relation terms to ensure interoperability among the systems.

Keywords: Object type relation, Fedora Commons, DSspace, DataCite, Research Data, Scientific Data

1. INTRODUCTION

High-performance observation, measurement, and laboratory equipment are utilized in various domains. The development of high-speed networks and the related research environment has resulted in the generation of various types of data in large quantities. Thus it has become a responsibility for organizations which manage and service research data to build an environment for systematic data management and

*Corresponding Author: Suntae Kim
Senior Researcher
Korea Institute of Science and Technology Information
245 Daehak-ro, Yuseong-gu, Daejeon, Korea
E-mail: stkim@kisti.re.kr

data reuse. This is so because locating a desired data set and searching for relevant data among an enormous amount of data accurately and quickly will guarantee high productivity of their research projects.

This problem requires related ontology research. Soldatova and King (2006) emphasized early on that formal description of experiments for efficient analysis, annotation, and sharing of the results is a fundamental part of the practice of science and that ontology is required to achieve this objective. The properties required for describing resources may vary with the domain, but there may be a number of common properties that describe the relationship among the resources.

In this study, the object type properties that may be used for describing the relationship among the resources are examined and analyzed. In this process, integrated object type properties are derived and the related properties are categorized into groups.

2. RELATED WORK AND GOALS

Research and experimental scenarios include capturing data with the equipment, creating data through simulations, transferring data to the computer, performing computation, and storing the resulting data. Research involves various work steps. Building up the relationships among the data at each work step is necessary for searching and discovering research data and for reproducing the research later. Therefore, research studies on ontology that describe the relationship among data, i.e., the relationship among the resources, are required. However, so far, the ontology has focused on studying data type properties. Soldatova and King (2006) proposed the ontology EXPO and linked the SUMO (the Suggested Upper Merged Ontology) with a subject-specific ontology for experiments. Washington and Lewis (2008) claimed that ontology has made it easy to share scientific data. They conducted research on ontology usability for genetic studies. Especially, they emphasized that fast search and comparison of various data sources using the ontology would be useful. They claimed that there

would be no shortage of genetic data and pointed out that it would be rather a matter of how quickly one could obtain and analyze the desired data from a large amount of genetic data.

Goranova et al. (2011) suggested an ontology to acquire the meaning of general scientific data produced through observations and measurements. The proposed ontology can be used to describe the meaning of the scientific data generated through simulations and experiments in the field of physics. Shotton (2011) suggested an ontology by mapping the DataCite elements to the global ontology terms.

The above studies tend to focus on the data type properties used for describing the properties of resources in certain domains, but the studies focusing on describing the relationship among resources are still scanty.

3. RESEARCH METHODOLOGY

The Korea Institute of Science and Technology Information (KISTI) is developing the research data platform named P-CUBE.[1] The P-CUBE's major modules use open source software platforms such as Fedora Commons, DSpace, and MySql. They are well known as robust open source software. KISTI is developing functions by using these open source software platforms which are recognized as powerful repository tools. Fedora Commons is used for a storage layer and DSpace is used for an application layer. Thus object type properties which are used in these systems need to be analyzed. DataCite announced a metadata schema to publish the data. In this schema, there are object type properties. The P-CUBE has the function to publish data by using the DataCite metadata. So the DataCite metadata Schema should be analyzed also.

As data properties vary with data types and research areas, property analysis was conducted, limited to the object type properties that describe relationships among the resources. Ontology terms declared in Fedora Commons (hereinafter referred to as "FCO"), Dublin Core - Library Application Profile[2] terms used in Dspace (hereinafter referred to as "DSO"), and the

---

[1] The P-CUBE (Platform for Convergence and Unification of Big E-resources) is a platform providing easy access for safe storage and reuse of scientific data. (See http://www.datacite.kr)
[2] DC-Lib Application Profile (2013, April 3). DC-Lib Application Profile. Retrieved from http://www.dublincore.org/documents/library-application-profile/

terms defined in DataCite metadata schema[3] standard (hereinafter referred to as "DCO") were analyzed. The terms were grouped according to their uses. DSO and DCO terms were analyzed based on group names suggested by the Fedora Commons. The relation group level in the FCO was expanded to include properties declared in DCO and the DSO.

In addition to FCO, DSO, and DCO, a variety of ontology properties may exist to describe relationships among the resources. However, in this study, only the properties of Fedora Commons and DSpace, the resource management open source software used worldwide, were analyzed. Also, resource-relation properties of DataCite, an international community to provide a permanent approach to resources by allocating Digital Object Identifiers (DOI) to resources, were analyzed as well. Accordingly, this study is considered as a meaningful work of research analysis.

4. DSPACE RESOURCE RELATION MODEL ANALYSIS

The Resources managed in DSpace are used for the DSpace data management model. Community, the highest concept in DSpace, may include one or more sub-communities or collections. The collection that binds logically related items may also include one or more items. An item includes metadata and bitstreams. A bitstream means files collected in DSpace, and one may have relationships with other items, collections, and communities. It may have relationships with other bitstreams as well. In order to describe these resource relations, DSpace provides the following object type properties.

DSpace provides qualified Dublin Core (DC) as a default option. However, it is possible to set multiple schemas and to select metadata fields from the combination of these schemas. The item can have different types of descriptive metadata as bitstreams. Simple descriptive metadata for the communities and collections are stored in DBMS.

DSpace, which provides qualified DC as the default

schema, can use resource relation elements declared in DC.

<relation> elements declared in the DC metadata element set are used to describe the related resources, and the qualified DC declares the following 10 elements as their sub-elements:

· isVersionOf: This means a substantial change in the content, rather than a change of the format.
· isFormatOf: A resource with the same content as the related resource but expressed in a different format.
· hasFormat: A resource with another format related to it.
· isReplacedBy: Resource used, replaced, or discarded by the related resource.
· Replaces: Uses, replaces, or discards the current resource, instead of the related resource.
· isPartOf: A resource which is a physical or logical part of the related resource.
· hasPart: A resource which physically or logically includes the related resource.
· Requires: The current resource requires the related resource to support its function, delivery, or integrity.
· isReferencedBy: A resource physically or logically referenced by the related resource
· References: The current resource may refer to or cite the related resource, or point it out in a different way.

It also has the following two unique aspects:

First, it does not declare the <hasVersion> element. With regards to this, 'DCMI-Libraries Working Group' states that DSpace does not include <hasVersion> as the <isVersionOf> element can deliver the meaning more clearly than <hasVersion> does. In other words, the declaration 'A isVersionOf B' more clearly expresses that Version B was created before Version A,' than the declaration 'A hasVersion B' does.

Second, it does not declare the <isRequiredBy> element. This element is declared in the qualified DC to describe the resource information physically or logically required by the related resources, but is not used in the DC-Lib Application Profile.

---

[3] DataCite Metadata Schema Repository.(2013, May 1). DataCite Metadata Schema RepositoryRetrieved from http://schema.datacite.org/

5. FEDORA COMMONS RESOURCE RELATION MODEL ANALYSIS

The resource relation model ontology provided by Fedora Commons consists of 22 object type properties, which can be divided into nine relation groups. It declares <fedoraRelationship> as the highest property. The relationship among the properties declared in the FCO is illustrated in Fig. 1. The FCO declares the properties to describe such relationships as Derivation, Equivalence, Dependency, Descriptive, Commentary, Metadata, Part/Whole, Membership, and Set Membership. The properties of 'Descriptive' relationship are declared as higher properties of 'Commentary' and 'Metadata' relationships, and the properties of 'Part/Whole' relationship as higher than 'Membership' and 'Set Membership' relationships.

6. DATACITE RESOURCE RELATION MODEL ANALYSIS

As of March 2013, DataCite version 2.2[4], published in July 2011, is the latest version registered, and the metadata work group operated by DataCite is working on version 2.3.

A <relationType> property provided by DataCite schema is used to describe the relationships between the resources registered and maintained and the related resources. The schema document provides a list of control terms that can be used as values in the <relationType> property. The following is the list of allowable object type properties. When it is assumed that each property is described as ['Resource A' - Property - 'Resource B'], DataCite's ontology terms mean the following:

- IsCitedBy (A is cited by B)
- Cites (A cites B)
- IsSupplementTo (A is supplemented to B)
- IsSupplementedBy (A is supplemented by B)
- IsContinuedBy (A is continued by B)
- Continues (A continues B)
- IsNewVersionOf (A is a new version of B)
- IsPreviousVersionOf (A is a previous version of B)
- IsPartOf (A is part of B; it may be used as a property of a series element)
- HasPart (A includes B)
- IsReferencedBy (A is used as an information source of B)
- References (A uses B as its information source)
- IsDocumentedBy (B is a document describing A)

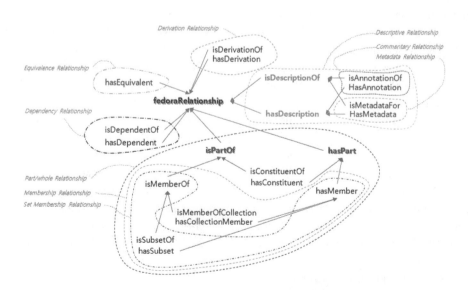

Fig. 1 Fedora Commons Object Relation Properties

[4] Starr, J., Ashton, J., Brase, J., Bracke, P., Gastl, A., Gillet, J., ... Ziedorn, F. (2011). DataCite Metadata Schema for the Publication and Citation of Research Data. Retrieved from http://schema.datacite.org/meta/kernel-2.2/doc/DataCite-MetadataKernel_v2.2.pdf

· Documents (A is a documents describing B)
· isCompiledBy (A is created through compilation by B)
· Compiles(B is created through compilation by A)
· IsVariantFormOf (A is another form of B)
· IsOriginalFormOf (A is the original form of B)

7. SCIENTIFIC DATA RESOURCE RELATION MODEL ANALYSIS

The ontology map used for Fedora Commons, DSpace, and DataCite data modeling, which is limited to the object type properties only, is illustrated in Fig. 2. There are 43 object type properties in total. Among 18 properties declared in DataCite, five properties of <isNewVersionOf>, <isReferencedBy>, <references>, <isVariantFormOf> and <isOriginalFormOf> have equivalents in the DSpace ontology.

Fig. 2 illustrates FCO, DCO, and DSO to define object type properties to describe relationship among the resources. Area (A) indicates object type properties

declared in FCO, and those written in italics mean the name of each property group. Area (B) indicates object type properties declared in DCO. Area (C) indicates object type properties declared in DSO.

In order to conduct an integrated consolidated analysis of FCO, DCO, and DSO, the relation groups and properties were studied based on five questions: 1) Do the same property names have the same meaning? 2) Are there any other property names that have the same meaning? 3) Are the relation groups of FCO applicable to DCO and DSO? 4) Is a new relation group needed? 5) Is there a need to include a property that is not used in DSO? The following is the answer to these five questions.

First, for question one, <isPartOf> and <hasPart> relations included in the Part/Whole relation group of FCO exist as the same property names with the same meanings in DCO and DSO. DCO and DSO declare <isReferencedBy> and <references> properties with the same property names and same meanings. Second, for question two, <isNewVersionOf>, <isVariant FormOf>, and <isOriginalFormOf> properties of

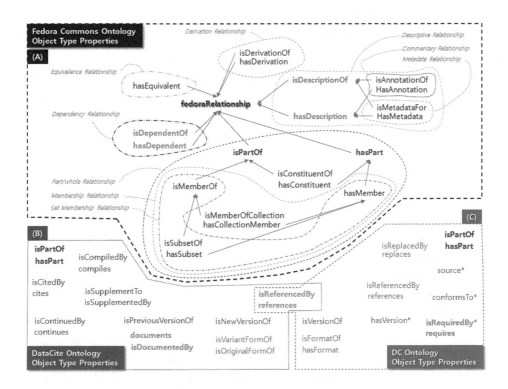

Fig. 2 The ontology map used for Fedora Commons, DSpace, and DataCite data modeling, which is limited to the object type properties only

DCO are completely equivalent to <isVersionOf>, <isFormatOf>, and <hasFormat> properties of DSO. <isDescriptionOf> and <hasDescription> properties of FCO are equivalent to the <Documents> and <isDocumentedBy> properties of DCO. Third, for question three, among object type properties declared in DCO, "isCompiledBy, compiles, isCitedBy, cites, isNewVersionOf, isPreviousVersionOf, isVariant FormOf, isOriginalFormOf, isContinuedBy, continues, isReferencedBy, references, and isSupplementTo, isSupplementedBy" relationship properties cannot be included at their current levels in the relation groups of FCO and require a separate group.

Also, among object type properties declared in DSO, "isVersionOf, hasVersion, isReplacedBy, replaces, isFormatOf, hasFormat, isReferencedBy, references, and conformsTo" relationship properties cannot be included at their current levels in the relation groups of FCO and require a separate group. "isDocumentedBy, documents, isPartOf, and hasPart" properties of DCO and "source, isRequiredBy, requires, isPartOf, hasPart"

properties of DSO, which are equivalent to those of FCO, can be included in the existing groups of the equivalent groups of FCO. Fourth, for question four, properties that do not have any equivalent property group in FCO require a separate group, but need to maintain the highest level group of the existing FCO and can be grouped through expansion of "Relation Level II." Fifth, for the last question, "source, hasVersion, and isRequiredBy" properties of DSO are semantically interchangeable with the corresponding properties of FCO and DCO, and thus can be included. On the other hand, the <conformsTo> property does not have an equivalent property in FCO and DCO but is considered to be necessary for integration with the DSO application ontology created in various systems.

8. DISCUSSION

Table 1 shows object type properties finally derived

Table 1. Object type properties and source from FCO, DSO, and DCO

Relation level I	Relation level II	Relation level III	Object type property	Source
Derivation[1]			isDerivationOf, hasDerivation	FCO
	Compilation		*isCompiledBy, compiles*	DCO
	Citation		*isCitedBy, cites*	DCO
	Version		*isNewVersionOf, isPreviousVersionOf*	DCO
	Replacement		*isReplacedBy, replaces*	DSO
Equivalence[1]			hasEquivalent	FCO
	Format		*isVariantFormOf, isOriginalFormOf*	DCO
Dependency[1]			isDependentOf, hasDependent	FCO
Descriptive[1]			IsDocumentedBy, documents	DCO
	Commentary[1]		isAnnotationOf, HasAnnotation	FCO
	Metadata[1]		isMetadataFor, hasMetadata	FCO
	Continuation		*isContinuedBy, continues*	DCO
	Reference		*isReferencedBy, references*	DCO
	Conformity		*conformsTo***	DSO
Part/Whole[1]			isPartOf, hasPart	FCO
	Membership[1]		isMemberOfCollection, hasCollectionMember	FCO
		Set Membership[1]	isSubsetOf, hasSubset	DCO
	Supplement		*isSupplementTo, isSupplementedBy*	DCO

to describe resource relations and their sources. Integration of the derived properties complies with DataCite property standards.

Key points of the analysis results are: 1) Compilation, Citation, Version, and Replacement relation groups are added to the Derivation relation group. As the Derivation group may include properties that include source relationship between resources, "isCompiledBy" and "compiles" properties of DCO are included in the Compilation group; "isCitedBy" and "cites" properties of DCO in the Citation group; "isNewVersionOf" and "isPreviousVersionOf" properties of DCO in the Version group; and "isReplacedBy" and "replaces" of DSO in the Replacement group. 2) The Equivalence relation group includes the Format relation group. As the Equivalence group may include properties that describe the relationship among resources with the same meaning but different formats, "isFormatOf" and "hasFormat" properties of DSO and "isVariantFormOf" and "isOriginalFormOf" properties of DCO are included in the Format group. 3) To the Descriptive relation group, Continuation, Reference, and Conformity relation groups are added.

The properties included in the Descriptive group describe additional information about resources. For example, they may include metadata that describes raw data rather than relationships among raw data, and properties that describe annotations. Therefore, "isContinuedBy" and "continues" properties of DCO are included in the Continuation group, and "isReferencedBy" and "references" properties declared both in DSO and DCO are included in the Reference group. <conformsTo> of DSO, the property describing the relation with the standards or guidelines that the resources conform to, is included in the Conformity group. 4) To the Part/Whole relation group, the Supplement relation group is added. As "isSupplementTo" and "isSupplementedBy" properties of DCO can be included in the Part/Whole group, the Supplement relation group is included as a sub-group of the Part/Whole relation group and is also included in the Supplement relation group.

In this paper, the suggested object type properties are composed of five terms in Relation level I, twelve terms in relation level II, one term in relation level III, and thirty-four terms in object type properties. Not all object type properties in FCO, DSO, and DCO are omitted because the object type properties are examined by the meaning of the terms and the representative terms are deducted.

KISTI is planning to disseminate the P-CUBE to the KOPRI (Korea Polar Research Institute). The data which are created and assimilated in this discipline may have specific object type properties. As mentioned already in the RESEARCH METHODOLOGY section, the property analysis was conducted limited to the object type properties that describe relationships among the resources. The data type properties for ontology are not analyzed because each disciplinary area has their own properties to describe their data in their fields. So additional studies for domain specific data type properties and object type properties are needed.

9. CONCLUSIONS

Along with the development of hardware and software and evolution of the network environment, various forms of data have been produced in large quantities. As people have become more aware that the research data produced with the nation's investments in research and development are national assets, there have been active movements in developed countries to collect, manage, conserve, and service raw data to validate the literature-based research results. In this regard, research efforts about metadata to describe resources have been constantly carried out. In this study, the object type properties required to describe the relationship among research data resources were derived.

In this study, the object type properties declared in FCO, DSO, and DCO were analyzed, and then integrated. The systems which use the Fedora Commons or DSpace can be expanded by using this ontology to describe relations among the managed data. The properties of Fedora Commons and DSpace, which are open source software platforms for resource management, and the schema properties published in the DataCite community were analyzed. Based on the relation group names of Fedora Commons, nine new relation group names including Format were derived.

Through integration of the properties, 38 object type properties including <isDerivationOf> were derived.

The groups and the object type properties derived in this study can be used to describe the relationships among resources for resource management in various fields, without being limited to certain domains.

REFERENCES

Goranova, M., Shishedjiev, B., & Georgieva, J. (2011). Research on Building Scientific Data Ontology. *2011 Developments in E-systems Engineering* (pp. 541-546). Dubai: IEEE Press.

Soldatova, L. N., & King, R. D. (2006). An ontology of scientific experiments. *Journal of the Royal Society Interface 3*, 795-803.

Shotton, D. (2011). DataCite2RDF—Mapping Data Cite Metadata Scheme Terms to ontologies. Retrieved from http://opencitations.wordpress.com/2011/06/30/datacite2rdf-mapping-datacite-metadata-scheme-terms-to-ontologies-2/

Washington, N., & Lewis, S. (2008). *Ontologies: Scientific Data Sharing Made Easy*. Retrieved from http://www.nature.com/scitable/topicpage/ontologies-scientific-data-sharing-made-easy-77972.

APPENDIX

The table below shows object type properties to describe resource relations and the group of each property. For expression of the relation name, the relationships noted with the superscript '1)' comply with the relation group expression of FCO. The properties noted with '*' mean the properties declared in the Dublin Core-Library Application Profile, though not declared in DSO. Each relation level has a hierarchical structure. Property names defined in FCO, DSO, and DCO have no hierarchical structure. Relations shown in the same column indicate that these properties have the same meanings. Newly included property names and the corresponding object type properties are noted in italics.

Crosswalk for FCO (Fedora Commons Ontology), DSO (Dspace Ontology), DCO (DataCite Ontology). Relations I, II, III show the relation depth.

Relation level I	Relation level II	Relation level III	FCO	DSO	DCO
Derivation[1)			isDerivationOf	source*	
			hasDerivation		
	Compilation				*isCompiledBy*
					Compiles
	Citation				*isCitedBy*
					cites
	Version			*isVersionOf*	*isNewVersionOf*
				*hasVersion**	*isPreviousVersionOf*
	Replacement			*isRequiredBy*	
				replaces	
Equivalence[1)			hasEquivalent		
	Format			*isFormatOf*	*isVariantFormOf*
				hasFormat	*isOriginalFormOf*
Dependency[1)			isDependentOf	isRequiredBy*	

Relation level I	Relation level II	Relation level III	FCO	DSO	DCO
Descriptive[1]			hasDependent	requires	
			hasDescription		IsDocumentedBy
			isDescriptionOf		Documents
	Commentary[1]		isAnnotationOf		
			HasAnnotation		
	Metadata[1]		isMetadataFor		
			hasMetadata		
	Continuation				*isContinuedBy*
					Continues
	Reference			*isReferencedBy*	*isReferencedBy*
				references	*References*
	Conformity			*conformsTo**	
Part/Whole[1]			isPartOf	isPartOf	isPartOf
			hasPart	hasPart	hasPart
			isConstituentOf		
			hasConstituent		
	Membership[1]		isMemberOfCollection		
			hasCollectionMember		
		Set Membership[1]	isSubsetOf		
			hasSubset		
			isMemberOf		
			hasMember		
	Supplement				*isSupplementTo*
					isSupplementedBy

18

A Critical Study on Attitudes and Awareness of Institutional Repositories and Open Access Publishing

S. Dhanavandan*

Library
Gandhigram Rural Institute-Deemed University, India
E-mail: dhanavandan@gmail.com

M. Tamizhchelvan

Library
Gandhigram Rural Institute-Deemed University, India
E-mail: tamizhchelvan@gmail.com

ABSTRACT

This paper discusses awareness of institutional repositories and open access publishing among faculty members in Annamalai University, Tamil Nadu, India. The authors distributed 200 questionnaires among the faculty members in Annamalai University. Out of 200 questionnaires, 160 responses (80.00%) were received from faculty members. The respondents mentioned the motivating factors while using an institutional repository and indicated the benefits, constraints and strategies to develop open access in publications. It is evident from the table that more than 95% among the average of the faculty members confirm the benefits of open access in publications. 150 (93.75%) of faculty members have awareness, 6 (3.75%) have no idea and 4 (2.50%) state no opinion about awareness of institutional repository and open access publishing.

Keywords: Institutional repositories, open access publishing, benefits and constraints, user feedback

1. INTRODUCTION

There is a rapidly expanding stock of scientific knowledge. Open Access has become an increasingly strong movement in recent years. The aim is to make research literature, especially peer-reviewed academic articles, free for anyone in the world to access. Yet access to this pool of knowledge is often difficult

*Corresponding Author: S. Dhanavandan
Assistant Librarian
Gandhigram Rural Institute-Deemed University, India
E-mail: dhanavandan@gmail.com

because of the relatively high cost of journals in their printed and web–based versions. Many of the Open-access journals are scholarly journals that are available online to the reader. According to *Wikipedia,* Open Access journals are "without financial, legal, or technical barriers other than those inseparable from gaining access to the internet itself". Some are subsidized, and some require payment on behalf of the author. Priti Jain (2012) commented, "A commitment to scholarly work carries with it a responsibility to circulate that work as widely as possible: this is the access principle. The right to know and the right to be known are inextricably mixed". Another vital issue is that removing access barriers will accelerate research, enrich education and share learning. There is therefore a critical need to make research results available to as many academics and elite classes as possible free of charge. Because of this need, concerned institutions and organizations have felt challenged. One such initiative, which has been undertaken to demonstrate that scientific knowledge need not be published in forms that make access expensive, is the Budapest Open Access Initiative.

2. INSTITUTIONAL REPOSITORIES

Institutional repositories have been established in academic and research libraries. University based institutional repositories manage, disseminate, and preserve where appropriate, digital materials created by the institution and its community members. They also organize and access these materials, (Lynch, 2003). A survey conducted by the Coalition for Networked Information (CNI) found that research libraries have taken on a leadership role in both policy formulation and operational deployment roles for institutional repositories at research universities (United States Higher Education Institutions, 2005).

The libraries' role towards build up in institutional repositories is articulated as follows (Crow, 2002):

1. Academic libraries have the responsibility for managing and archiving all printed materials in IRs.
2. Library program and budgets will have to support faculty open access publishing activities.
3. To the organizational imperatives to invest in the future, institutional repositories offer a compelling response.
4. Libraries are to provide the document preparation expertise to help authors contribute their research to IRs.

3. OPEN ACCESS - CONCEPT AND DEFINITION

Repositories are increasingly being made more 'open' to make content accessible to wider user groups, sometimes at a global level. Not all repositories are open: some are designed to support sharing within a specific group and are sometimes described as 'closed'. These repositories often require authentication and some have varying levels of access and 'degrees of openness'. "Open Access" is a term that is used in a specific sense and most often used in relation to collections of research papers.

According to the Budapest Open Access Initiative (BOAI), the concept of Open Access refers to "[the] free availability on the public internet, permitting any users to read, download, copy, distribute, print, search, or link to the full texts of these articles, crawl them for indexing, pass them as data to software, or use them for any other lawful purpose, without financial, legal, or technical barriers other than those inseparable from gaining access to the internet itself" (BOAI, 2003).

4. LITERATURE REVIEW

Manjunatha (2001) found in his studies, research scholars made awareness of Institutional Repositories and keen interest in access to IRs in their university. It shows that institutional level IRs have scope to build repositories. Barwick (2007) made efforts in setting up an institutional repository at Loughborough University and made available to the institutional access. Erickson et al. (2008) have applied the basic techniques to build an institutional repository for external resources like blogs, wikis, and other web resources. Managing the publication and sharing of research artifacts is within the individual's scholarly network. There is steady increase in the usage of the repository model for archiving and sharing digital resources and in an item-tagging scheme that suggests user preference of the resource as a platform for enhancing professional rather than personal interests. User interactivity by way of textual scholarly discussions on the repository platform is however almost nonexistent (Asunka et al., 2011).

5. NEED FOR THE STUDY

The main aim of this study is to make an attempt to find out awareness of open access in publications and institutional repositories by the faculty members. The problem of this study is to find out the extent of benefits, constraints, and strategies to develop and improve the institutional repository and open access in publications among faulty members in Annamalai University.

6. OBJECTIVES OF THE STUDY

Based on the need of the study the following objectives are framed:-

1. To determine awareness about IR and open access publishing
2. To determine awareness about IR software and open access publishing
3. To know the sources from where users are aware about IR and open access publishing
4. To identify the motivating factors for using IR and open access publishing
5. To find out strategies to develop and improve the IR and open access in publications

6. To assess user's satisfaction towards IR and open access publishing

7. METHODOLOGY

This study is to find out the awareness of institutional repositories and open access in publishing among faculty members in Annamalai University. The questionnaires were personally distributed to 200 faculty members among faculty members. Out of 200 questionnaires, 160 responses (80.00%) were received from faculty members. The collected data were analyzed and tabulated through statistical tools like simple percentages.

8. ANALYSIS AND INTERPRETATION

The frequency of 200 questionnaires was distributed to faculty members, including Assistant Professors, Associate Professors and Professors in Annamalai University to determine awareness of institutional repositories and open access in publishing in Table 1.

Table 1 shows the distribution of questionnaires to the faculty members in Annamalai University, Annamalai Nagar. Out of 200, 160 questionnaires were received from the faculty members and the response rate is 80%.

Table 2 shows the gender wise distribution of faculty members in Annamalai University based on this study.

Table 1. Distribution of Questionnaires

Faculties	Distributed Questionnaires	%	Received Questionnaires	%	Not Replied	%
Assistant Professor	130	65.00	105	52.5	25	12.50
Associate Professor	50	25.00	42	21.00	8	4.00
Professor	20	10.00	13	6.50	7	3.50
Total	**200**	**100.00**	**160**	**80.00**	**40**	**20.00**

Table 2. Gender Wise Distribution of Faculty Members

Faculties	Male	%	Female	%	Total	%
Assistant Professor	80	50.00	25	15.62	105	65.62
Associate Professor	30	18.75	12	7.50	42	26.25
Professor	8	5.00	5	3.12	13	8.12
Total	**118**	**73.75**	**42**	**26.25**	**160**	**100**

Among the total number of 105 Assistant Professors 80 (50.00%) are male and 25 (15.62%) are female. Out of 42 Associate Professors 30 (18.755) are male and 12 (7.50%) are female. In the Professor category, 8 (5.00%) are male and 5 (3.12%) are female out of 13 (8.12%). From the above discussion it is inferred that out of 160 faculty members, 118 (73.75%) respondents are male and the remaining 42 (26.25%) respondents are female.

The data presented in Table 3 shows the Awareness of Institutional Repository and Open Access Publishing stated by the faculty members in Annamalai University. Out of 105, 99 (61.88%) Assistant Professors have awareness of Institutional Repository and Open Access Publishing and 4 (2.50) Assistant Professors mention no awareness and 2 (1.25%) have no opinion about institutional repository and open access publishing. Out of 42 Associate Professors, 39 (24.38%) have the awareness of institutional repository and open access publishing, 2 (1.25%) of Associate professors

have no knowledge about IR and one Associate Professor states no opinion about awareness. It is concluded from the table, that out of 160 faculty members, 150 (93.75%) have awareness, 6 (3.75%) have no idea, and 4 (2.50%) state no opinion about awareness of institutional repository and open access publishing.

Table 4 indicates the sources for users' institutional repository and open access publishing awareness by the respondents from Annamalai University. Out of 160, 52 (32.50%) faculty members mention Workshop, Seminars and Orientation Program for getting sources for institutional repository and open access publishing; this number includes 35 (21.88%) Assistant Professors, 13 (8.13%) Associate Professors and 4 (2.50%) Professors. 30 (18.75%) faculty members mention library professionals and their assistants for getting sources for institutional repository and open access publishing; this number includes 19 (11.88%) Assistant Professors, 9 (5.63%) Associate Professors and 2 (1.25%) Professors.

Table 3. Awareness of Institutional Repositories and Open Access Publishing

Awareness of Institutional Repository & Open Access Publishing	Assistant Professor	Associate Professor	Professor	Total
Yes	99 (61.88)	39 (24.38)	12 (7.50)	150 (93.75)
No	4 (2.50)	2 (2.50)	0	6 (3.75)
No Opinion	2 (1.25)	1 (0.63)	1 (0.63)	4 (2.50)
Total	**105 (65.63)**	**42 (26.25)**	**13 (8.13)**	**160 (100)**

Note. Figures in parentheses denote percentage.

Table 4. Sources for Users' IR and Open Access Publishing Awareness

Sources For Users' IR Awareness	Assistant Professor	Associate Professor	Professor	Total	Rank
From Library Professionals and their assistants	19 (11.88)	9 (5.63)	2 (1.25)	30 (18.75)	2
Through Library Website & Manual	17 (10.63)	6 (3.75)	3 (1.88)	26 (16.25)	3
From Bulletin Board & Periodicals	13 (8.13)	5 (3.13)	1 (0.63)	19 (11.88)	4
Through Internet & Online resources	9 (5.63)	5 (3.13)	2 (1.25)	16 (10.00)	6
Workshop, Seminars and Orientation Programs	35 (21.88)	13 (8.13)	4 (2.50)	52 (32.50)	1
With Colleague/Friends	12 (7.50)	4 (2.50)	1 (0.63)	17 (10.63)	5
Total	**105 (65.63)**	**42 (26.25)**	**13 (8.13)**	**160 (100)**	

Note. Figures in parentheses denote percentage.

Table 5 indicates reasons for developing institutional repository and open access publishing awareness by the respondents from Annamalai University. Out of 160, 22 (13.75%) faculty members mention two reasons equally such as, To increase the visibility of the institution as well as individuals and To digitize and preserve scholarly material on campus. In the same case 21(13.13%) equally mention two reasons, such as Response to administrative interest, and To participate in the scholarly communication process.

Table 6 shows the motivating factors stated for using institutional repositories in Annamalai University by faculty members. Among the total number of 160, 142 (88.75%) faculty members state that my work is deposited and quickly disseminated to all, and 151 (94.38%) faculty members choose the repository is well

indexed and archived. And, 149 (93.13%) state the public opinion of the university is increased, 133 (83.13) express depositing my work in the repository protects it from plagiarism and creates publicity, and 139 (86.88%) state my work is published alongside other high quality research and attracts the user.

As per Table 7 the data results indicate the support and coordination by the library staff members while using the institutional repository in the library. Out of 160, 101 (6.13%) Assistant Professors, 37 (23.13%) Associate Professors and 11 (6.88%) Professors state that librarians promote awareness through orientation to utilize the institutional repository. And, 99 (61.88%) Assistant Professors, 35 (21.88%) Associate Professors, and 9 (5.63%) Professors state Library staff are familiar with developing IRs and all content is appreciated.

Table 5. Reasons for Developing a Repository and Open Access

Reasons for developing institutional repository & Open Access	Assistant Professor	Associate Professor	Professor	Total
Response to administrative interest	12 (7.50)	7 (4.38)	2 (1.25)	21 (13.13)
To provide open access to materials to the user community	11 (6.88)	4 (2.50)	1 (0.63)	16 (10.00)
To digitize and preserve scholarly material on campus	13 (8.13)	6 (3.75)	3 (1.88)	22 (13.75)
To participate in the scholarly communication process	15 (9.38)	5 (3.13)	1 (0.63)	21 (13.13)
Response to requests from faculty and students	10 (6.25)	5 (3.13)	2 (1.25)	17 (10.63)
To create the awareness of research and development activities.	9 (5.63)	3 (1.88)	0	12 (7.50)
To develop collaborative workspace/file sharing space for resource sharing	6 (3.75)	5 (3.13)	1 (0.63)	12 (7.50)
To increase the visibility of the institution as well as individuals	16 (10.00)	4 (2.50)	2 (1.25)	22 (13.75)
To support the Archives for Teaching and learning process	13 (8.13)	3 (1.88)	1 (0.63)	17 (10.63)
Total	**105 (65.63)**	**42 (26.25)**	**13 (8.13)**	**160 (100)**

Note. Figures in parentheses denote percentage.

Table 6. Motivating Factors for Using Institutional Repositories

Sl. No.	Motivating Factors	Yes	%	No	%	Total
1	My work is deposited and quickly disseminate to all	142	88.75	18	11.25	160
2	The repository is well indexed and archived based on end user	151	94.38	9	5.63	160
3	The public opinion of the University is increased	149	93.13	11	6.88	160
4	Depositing my work in the repository protects it from plagiarism and creates publicity	133	83.13	27	16.88	160
5	My work is published alongside other high quality research and attracts the user	139	86.88	21	13.13	160

Further among 160, 102 (63.75%) Assistant Professors, 39 (24.38%) Associate Professors and 13 (8.13%) Professors, it is stated that the librarian is recommend for implementation to deposit in IRs.

The data presented in Table 8 shows the benefits in open access in publication indicated by faculty members in Annamalai University. Out of 160 faculty members, 102 (63.75%) Assistant Professors, 39 (24.38%) Associate Professors, and 13 (8.13%) Professors confirm that self archiving is possible round the clock in open access in publication and 101 (63.13%) Assistant Professors, 37 (23.13%) Associate Professors, and 9(5.63%) Professors state that open access makes for easy accessibility to the research work and create further research. And a further 96 (60.00%) Assistant Professors, 34 (21.25%) Associate Professors,

Table 7. LIS Professionals Support While Using Institutional Repositories

LIS Professionals Support and Cooperation Using IR	Assistant Professor		Associate Professor		Professor		Total
	Yes	No	Yes	No	Yes	No	
Librarians promote awareness through orientation to utilize IR	101 (63.13)	4 (2.50)	37 (23.13)	5 (3.13)	11 (6.88)	2 (1.25)	160 (100)
Library staff are familiar with developing IR and all content is appreciated	99 (61.88)	6 (3.75)	35 (21.88)	7 (4.38)	9 (5.63)	4 (2.50)	160 (100)
Library staffs give general information about the repository	102 (63.75)	3 (1.88)	39 (24.38)	3 (1.88)	13 (8.13)	0	160 (100)
Recommend the implementation to deposit in IR	97 (60.33)	8 (5.00)	36 (22.50)	6 (3.75)	13 (8.13)	0	160 (100)

Note. Figures in parentheses denote percentage.

Table 8. Benefits of Open Access in Publishing

Benefits	Assistant Professor		Associate Professor		Professor		Total
	Yes	No	Yes	No	Yes	No	
Articles can be accessed online with free of charge	88 (55.00)	17 (10.63)	40 (25.00)	2 (1.25)	11 (6.88)	2 (1.25)	160 (100)
Open access provides larger potential evidence and audience	92 (57.50)	13 (8.13)	38 (23.75)	4 (2.50)	11 (6.88)	2 (1.25)	160 (100)
It increases impact of researcher's work	97 (60.33)	8 (5.00)	36 (22.50)	6 (3.75)	13 (8.13)	0	160 (100)
It makes for easy accessibility to the research work and creates further research	101 (63.13)	4 (2.50)	37 (23.13)	5 (3.13)	9 (5.63)	4 (2.50)	160 (100)
It provides free online access to the literature necessary for ones research	94 (58.75)	11 (6.88)	41 (25.63)	1 (0.63)	10 (6.25)	3 (1.88)	160 (100)
Publications are made free for authors	99 (61.88)	6 (3.75)	35 (21.88)	7 (4.38)	9 (5.63)	4 (2.50)	160 (100)
It provides opportunity for increased citation to published scholarly work	96 (60.00)	9 (5.63)	34 (21.25)	8 (5.00)	10 (6.25)	3 (1.88)	160 (100)
It helps in career development and world-wide attraction	98 (61.25)	7 (4.38)	40 (25.00)	2 (1.25)	11 (6.88)	2 (1.25)	160 (100)
Self archiving is possible round the clock	102 (63.75)	3 (1.88)	39 (24.38)	3 (1.88)	13 (8.13)	0	160 (100)

Note. Figures in parentheses denote percentage.

Table 9. Barriers and Constraints Using Open Access in Publishing

Sl. No. 1	Barriers and Constraints	Assistant Professor		Associate Professor		Professor		Total
		Yes	No	Yes	No	Yes	No	
1	Inadequate skills to navigate the internet and web technology	90 (56.25)	15 (9.38)	40 (25.00)	2 (1.25)	12 (7.50)	1 (0.63)	160 (100)
2	Lack of knowledge of the existence of open access journals on the internet	85 (53.13)	20 (12.50)	39 (24.38)	3 (1.88)	11 (6.88)	2 (1.25)	160 (100)
3	Unstable power supply	97 (60.63)	8 (5.00)	37 (23.13)	5 (3.13)	13 (8.13)	0	160 (100)
4	Slow speed while accessing of internet facilities	100 (62.50)	5 (3.13)	38 (23.75)	4 (2.50)	12 (7.50)	1 (0.63)	160 (100)
5	Unpredictable permanence of open access movement due to unstable financial support	92 (57.50)	13 (8.13)	41 (25.63)	1 (0.63)	10 (6.25)	3 (1.88)	160 (100)
6	Being hesitant to leave established publishers	98 (61.25)	7 (4.38)	36 (22.50)	6 (3.75)	9 (5.63)	4 (2.50)	160 (100)
7	Full texts of some open access journals are not easily down loadable	94 (58.75)	11 (6.88)	33 (20.63)	9 (5.63)	11 (6.88)	2 (1.25)	160 (100)
8	Some journals are published with water mark or symbols	85 (53.13)	20 (12.50)	39 (24.38)	3 (1.88)	11 (6.88)	2 (1.25)	160 (100)

Note. Figures in parentheses denote percentage.

and 10 (6.25%) Professors agree that open access helps in career development and world-wide attraction and audience. It is evident from the table that more than 95% among the average of the faculty members confirm the benefits to open access in publications.

Table 9 reveals the barriers or constraints while using open access publications. Out of 160 faculty members, 96 (56.25%) Assistant Professors, 40 (25.00%) Associate Professors, and 12 (7.50%) Professors mention inadequate skills to navigate the internet and web technology and 97 (60.63%) Assistant Professors, 37 (23.13%) Associate Professors, and 13 (8.13%) Professors also state unstable power supply is a main barrier while using open access in publications. And, following 98 (61.25%) Assistant Professors, 36 (22.50%) Associate Professors, and 9 (5.63%) Professors state being hesitant to leave established publishers and 94 (58.75%) Assistant Professors, 33 (20.63%) Associate Professors, and 11 (6.88%) Professors mention full texts of some open access journals are not easily down loadable as one barrier to using open access. So, it is revealed from the table that above 65% of the faculty members mention constraints while using open access in scholarly communications.

Table 10 indicates the Strategies to Develop and

Improve Open Access for Publications mentioned by the faculty members in Annamalai University. Out of 160, 101 (63.33%) Assistant Professors, 37 (23.13%) Associate Professors and 11 (6.88%) Professors mention the establishment of institutional repositories and 99 (61.88%) Assistant Professors, 35 (21.88%) Associate Professors and 9 (5.63%) Professors indicate the strategies to develop open access in publications. And also the majority of faculty members mention as strategies the provision of funds for open access movement by Government and that organizations should propose more open access journals for the user community.

Table 11 displays the user feedback about institutional repository and open access publishing from faculty members in Annamalai University. Out of 160, 137 (85.63%) faculty members are satisfied with the institutional repository and open access publishing, which includes 92 (57.50%) Assistant Professors, 35 (21.88%) Associate Professors, and 10 (6.25%) Professors. And also, 13 (8.12%) faculty members are not satisfied with the institutional repository and open access publishing; this includes 6 (3.75%) Assistant Professors, 5 (3.12%) Associate Professors, and 2 (1.25%) Professors.

Table 10. Strategies to Develop and Improve Open Access in Publications

Strategies	Assistant Professor		Associate Professor		Professor		Total
	Yes	No	Yes	No	Yes	No	
Provision of appropriate mechanisms and infrastructure for training and exploration of knowledge	88 (55.00)	17 (10.63)	40 (25.00)	2 (1.25)	9 (5.63)	4 (2.50)	160 (100)
Acquisition of knowledgeable skill in information technology usage by researchers	92 (57.50)	13 (8.13)	38 (23.75)	4 (2.50)	11 (6.88)	2 (1.25)	160 (100)
Provision of funds for open access movement by Government	97 (60.33)	8 (5.00)	36 (22.50)	6 (3.75)	3 (8.13)	0	160 (100)
Establishment of institutional repositories	101 (63.13)	4 (2.50)	37 (23.13)	5 (3.13)	11 (6.88)	2 (1.25)	160 (100)
Provision of constant power supply	94 (58.75)	11 (6.88)	41 (25.63)	1 (0.63)	10 (6.25)	3 (1.88)	160 (100)
High Internet connectivity needs to be improved	99 (61.88)	6 (3.75)	35 (21.88)	7 (4.38)	9 (5.63)	4 (2.50)	160 (100)
Organizations should propose more open access journals	96 (60.00)	9 (5.63)	34 (21.25)	8 (5.00)	10 (6.25)	3 (1.88)	160 (100)

Note. Figures in parentheses denote percentage.

Table 11. User's Feedback about Institutional Repository and Open Access Publishing

User's feedback	Assistant Professor	Associate Professor	Professor	Total
Satisfied	92 (57.50)	35 (21.88)	10 (6.25)	137 (85.63)
Not Satisfied	6 (3.75)	5 (3.12)	2 (1.25)	13 (8.12)
No Opinion	7 (4.38)	2 (1.25)	1 (0.63)	10 (6.25)
Total	**105 (65.63)**	**42 (26.25)**	**13 (8.13)**	**160 (100)**

Note. Figures in parentheses denote percentage.

9. FINDINGS AND REMARKS

- The questionnaires were distributed to the 200 faculty members in Annamalai University : 160 (80.00%) questionnaires were received and 40 (20.00%) questionnaires were not replied to.
- It is inferred that out of 160 faculty members, 118 (73.75%) respondents are male and the remaining 42 (26.25%) respondents are female.
- It is concluded that 133 (83.13%) express that depositing their work in the repository protects it from plagiarism and 139 (86.88%) state their work is published alongside other high quality research.
- It also shows that 102 (63.75%) Assistant Professors, 39 (24.38%) Associate Professors, and 13 (8.13%) Professors agree that the librarian is recommended for implementation to deposit in the IR.

- More than 95% among the average of the faculty members confirm the benefits of open access in publications.
- It is stated that 99 (61.88%) Assistant Professors, 35 (21.88%) Associate Professors, and 9 (5.63%) Professors encourage the more strategies to develop open access in publications.

10. CONCLUSION

Institutional Repositories have a vital role in that removing access barriers will accelerate research, enrich education, and share learning. Open Access to research journals and literature accelerates research and enriches education and knowledge sharing between more developed countries and less developed countries. Open Access provides larger potential evidence and audience; it makes for easy accessibility to research work and enables further research. It is also shown that more than 95% among the average of the faculty members confirm the benefits, constraints, and new strategies to develop open access in publications. From the responses, faculty members appreciated the roles of library professionals for their support and coordination in design and archival activities of institutional repositories. The recommendation of the faculty members is to ensure that the mandatory submission policies and the benefits of repositories and the purpose and benefits of archiving open access in publishing are communicated to all academics.

REFERENCES

Asunka, S., Chae, H. S., & Natriello, G.(2011). Towards an understanding of the use of an institutional repository with integrated social networking tools: A case study of pocketknowledge. *Library Information Science Research,* 3(1): 80-88.

Barwick, J. (2007). Building an institutional repository at Loughborough University: Some experiences. *Program Electronic Library and Information Systems,* 41(2): 113-123.

Bethesda Statement (2003). Bethesda statement on open access publishing. http://www.earlham.edu/~peters/fos/bethesda.htm (Retrieved on 19-10-2013).

Crow, J. (2008). Open access and scholarly communication SPARC/ Science commons. http://ar.org/ Sparc. (Retrieved on 19-10-2009).

Erickson, J., Rutherford, J., & Elliott, D. (2008). *The future of the institutional repository: Making it personal"* in. In: Third International Conference on Open Repositories Southampton, United Kingdom.

Jain, P. (2012). Promoting Open Access to Research in Academic Libraries, Library Philosophy and Practice, January-June, 2012. http://www.webpages.uidaho.edu/~mbolin/jain.pdf

Manjunatha, K. & Thandavamoorthy, K. (2001). A study on researchers' attitude towards depositing in institutional repositories of universities in karnataka (India). *International Journal of Library and Information Science,* 3(6): 107-115.

Open Access Journals (n.d). *Wikipedia.* http://en.wikipedia.org/wiki/Open_access_journal

Suber, P. (2006). An introduction to open access. http//www.blurtit.com/q72848.html.

Permissions

List of Contributors

Muzammil Tahira, Arayti Bakri and Rose Alinda Alias
Department of Information Systems Faculty of Computing Universiti Teknologi Malaysia (UTM), Malaysia

Ani Shabri
Department of Mathematical Sciences Faculty of Science Universiti Teknologi Malaysia (UTM), Malaysia

Shailendra Kumae and Gareema Sanaman
Department of Library & Information Science University of Delhi, India

A.O. Issa
Department of Library and Information Science University of Ilorin, Nigeria

B.R. Akangbe
The Polytechnic Library Kwara State Polytechnic Ilorin, Nigeria

K.N. Igwe
Department of Library and Information Science Akanu Ibiam Federal Polytechnic Unwana, Nigeria

M.B. Aliyu
Department of Library and Information Science Federal Polytechnic Offa, Nigeria

Tae-Sul Seo, Hwanmin Kim and Eun-Gyeong Jung
Information Service Center, Korea Institute of Science and Technology Information, Daejeon, Korea

C. P. Uzuegbu and C. O. Nnadozie
Department of Library and Information Science Michael Okpara University of Agriculture Nigeria

Soo Young Rieh
School of Information University of Michigan, U.S.A.

S. Craig Finlay
Franklin D. Schurz Library Indiana University South Bend, U.S.A.

Seungmin Lee
Department of Library and Information Science Sookmyung Women's University, Requblic of Korea

Jacob Dankasa
University of North Texas Denton, USA

Sk. Mamun Mostofa and Muhammad Mezbah-ul-Islam
Department of Information Science and Library Management, Faculty of Arts, University of Dhaka Bangladesh

Abdulmumin Isah, Athulang Mutshewa, Batlang Comma Serema and Lekoko Kenosi
Department of Library and Information Studies University of Botswana, Gaborone

Abdolreza Noroozi Chakoli
Department of Knowledge and Information Science and Scientometrics Shahed University, Tehran, Iran

Roghayeh Ghazavi
Scientometrics Department Isfahan University of Medical Sciences, Isfahan Knowledge and Information Science Shahid Chamran University of Ahvaz, Ahvaz, Iran

Niran Adetoro
Department of Library and Information Science Tai Solarin University of Education, Ijagun, Ijebu-Ode

Jung Sun Lim
Technology Innovation Analysis Center Korea Institute of Science and Technology Information
Republic of Korea

Jin Seon Yoon, Kwang Min Shin and Seoung Hun Bae
National Nanotechnology Policy Center
Korea Institute of Science and Technology Information
Republic of Korea

Shivani Arora
SBS College, Delhi University Delhi, India

Daniel Okunbor
College of Arts and Sciences Fayetteville State University Fayetteville, North Carolina, USA

A.Y. Asundi
Department of Library and Information Science & Officer-in-Charge, IT Centre Bangalore University, India

Suntae Kim
Korea Institute of Science and Technology Information 245 Daehak-ro, Yuseong-gu, Daejeon, Korea

S. Dhanavanda and M.Tamizhchelvan
Library Gandhigram Rural Institute-Deemed University, India

Index

A

Academic Research, 101-103, 105, 107-109, 111
Activity Indicator (ai), 2
Advanced Manufacturing, 158-162, 164, 167
Advanced Manufacturing Partnership (amp), 159
Applied Sciences and Technology, 29, 32
Artificial Intelligence (ai), 185

C

Commercialization., 154-156, 158, 160, 165-166
Computer Mediated Discourse Analysis (cmda), 76, 78
Computer-mediated Communication (cmc), 77
Corrected Quality Ratio (cq), 3
Credibility Assessment, 64-67, 69, 71-75

D

Dhaka University Library (dul), 112-113
Digital Libraries (dl), 125
Digital Library Initiative (dli), 128
Digital Library Management System (dlms), 130
Digital Object Identifiers (dois), 38
Digital Preservation, 87-99
DI Initiatives, 125, 132

E

Educational Developmental Periods, 80
Ehs (environmental, Health, Safety), 154
Electronic Content, 19
Electronic Resources, 12-13, 15-16, 22-26, 37, 145, 148, 150-151
Esprit De Corps, 60
European Conference on Research and Advanced Technology for Digital Libraries (ecdl), 128

F

Facebook Addiction Disorder (fad), 172-173
Fedora Commons, 189-193, 195-196
Framework Program (fp), 162, 164

G

Gazetteers, 184-186

General And Industrial Administration, 50
Global Environment, 128

H

Hellen Keller Unit (hku), 14
Heterogeneous Metadata, 91, 98
Higher National Diploma (hnd), 29
Hirsch Core (h-core), 2
Human Resource Utilization, 163

I

Information Behavior Research, 66
Information Environment, 27-30, 37, 55, 88, 115, 123
Information Package, 87, 89, 91-97
Information Resources, 12, 21, 24, 26-28, 35, 48, 58, 89, 91-92, 94, 98, 126-127, 147, 185
Information Services, 13-14, 21, 24, 38-39, 50, 54, 121, 124, 127, 134, 144-145, 147-152
Innovation Chains, 156, 165
Innovation Policy, 154, 156, 158-159, 162, 167
Innovation Systems, 154, 156, 168
Institutional Repositories, 99, 198-199, 201-202, 204-206
International Conference on Theory and Practice of Digital Libraries (tpdl), 128

K

Key Enabling Technology (ket), 162, 164
Knowledge Management (km), 112-113
Knowledge Organization Systems (kos), 188
Knowledge Retention, 118, 122
Korea Institute of Science and Technology Information (kisti), 38, 190
Korea Science Citation Database (kscd), 42

L

Leisure and Academic Purposes, 149
Libraries of The Future, 126, 134
Library and Information Science (lis), 115
Library Management, 49, 55, 60, 62, 112, 116, 123-124, 130

Library Services, 12, 16, 20, 25-26, 114, 119, 122, 124, 126, 134, 145, 147, 152

Liquidation, 60

M

Machine Readable Catalogue (marc), 113

Management Principles, 49-50

Materials Genome Initiative, 160, 167

Mean Absolute Error (mae), 10

Mean Square Error (mse), 7

Multi-layered Element Relationships, 92

N

Nano-application, 155

Nanosafety Cluster (nsc), 164

Nanoscience, 162-163

Nanotechnology Signature Initiative (nsi), 160-161

Nanotechnology., 156, 162-163, 167-168

National Capital Region (ncr), 12-13

National Library of Malaysia (nlm), 115

Natural Sciences, 137, 142

Nni (national Nanotechnology Initiative), 155, 160

Non-governmental Organizations, 144

O

Object Type Relation, 189

Ontologies, 183-185, 196

Open Access Initiative, 27, 29, 31, 33, 35, 37, 199

Open Access Initiatives (oai), 30

Open Access Publishing, 31, 198-202, 204-206

P

Patronization, 122

Polytechnic Library, 27, 33-36

Principle of Canonical Sequence, 182

Principles for Helpful Sequence, 179, 181-183, 185, 187

Principles of Spatial Contiguity, 182

Publication Indicators, 135

R

Repository and Open Access, 198, 200-202, 204-205

Research and Development (rtd), 164

Research Evaluation Indicators, 135, 137, 143

Research Hypothesis, 146

Resource Description, 87-92, 95, 98

Resource Description Framework (rdf), 95

Revitalization, 155, 158

Royal National Institute for The Blind (rnib), 146

Rwf (restless without Facebook), 174

S

Scalar Chain, 56-57

Scientific Production, 135-137, 142

Scientometric, 1-2, 11, 143

Semantics, 87, 98

Shannon Entropy Method, 135, 137

T

Taxonomies, 131, 179, 184-185

Technological Infrastructure, 118, 121

Technological Readiness (trl), 164

Theory Development, 101-103, 105-106, 108-111

Topicality, 64, 67, 69, 73, 85

Traditional Media Content (tmc), 64, 66

U

Unity of Command, 53

User-generated Content, 64-66, 69, 77

Printed in the USA
CPSIA information can be obtained
at www.ICGtesting.com
JSHW051325221024
72173JS00006B/1293